On Being in the Middle

On Being in the Middle

Doing Theology in the Face of Uncertainty

W. J. de Kock

WIPF & STOCK · Eugene, Oregon

ON BEING IN THE MIDDLE
Doing Theology in the Face of Uncertainty

Copyright © 2024 W. J. de Kock. All rights reserved. Except for brief quotations in critical publications or reviews, no part of this book may be reproduced in any manner without prior written permission from the publisher. Write: Permissions, Wipf and Stock Publishers, 199 W. 8th Ave., Suite 3, Eugene, OR 97401.

Wipf & Stock
An Imprint of Wipf and Stock Publishers
199 W. 8th Ave., Suite 3
Eugene, OR 97401

www.wipfandstock.com

PAPERBACK ISBN: 978-1-6667-0616-1
HARDCOVER ISBN: 978-1-6667-0617-8
EBOOK ISBN: 978-1-6667-0618-5

03/25/24

Scripture quotations marked (NIV) are taken from the Holy Bible, New International Version®, NIV®. Copyright © 1973, 1978, 1984, 2011 by Biblica, Inc.™ Used by permission of Zondervan. All rights reserved worldwide. www.zondervan.com The "NIV" and "New International Version" are trademarks registered in the United States Patent and Trademark Office by Biblica, Inc.™

Scripture quotations marked (MSG) are taken from *The Message*. Copyright © 1993, 1994, 1995, 1996, 2000, 2001, 2002. Used by permission of NavPress Publishing Group.

Scripture quotations marked (NLT) are taken from the Holy Bible, New Living Translation, copyright © 1996, 2004, 2007, 2013 by Tyndale House Foundation. Used by permission of Tyndale House Publishers, Inc., Carol Stream, Illinois 60188. All rights reserved.

To Marian, Carmen, and Jonny, Zoé and Casey,
and our canine friends

Contents

Preface ix

Introduction 1

PART A | ALONE IN THE MIDDLE

1. Afrikaner 15
2. Head 29
3. Hand 54
4. Heart 67
5. Being 84
6. Human 95
7. Anxiety 106

PART B | WITH GOD IN THE MIDDLE

8. Trinity 121
9. Indwelling 130
10. Belonging 144
11. Conversing 159
12. Loving 174
13. Serving 185
14. Growing 199

Methodological Postscript 220

Bibliography 229

Preface

Growing up as a middle child in a family of boys, I often found myself in the middle of everything. I was perpetually searching for my place, not knowing where I fit in. This book explores how that experience, and other experiences of being in the middle, have shaped my perspective and influenced how I navigate the world around me.

The concept of "being in the middle" took on a new layer of complexity when I considered it from the perspective of my cultural identity. As an Afrikaner, I was acutely aware of our historical positioning, navigating the space between the wider world and the insular sense of purpose that was ingrained in our Afrikaner community. This sense of being in the middle was rooted in a misguided belief of being God's chosen race, a notion that shaped our history and collective identity.

I have lived through a time when "being in the middle" between the world and Africa, Afrikaner theologians used it as an excuse to justify white supremacy, justifying oppressive systems and policies that perpetuated inequality and suffering. This historical context deeply influenced my theological journey, compelling me to challenge and redefine traditional theological constructs in order to dismantle the discriminatory ideologies that had been woven into the fabric of my community.

I have been teaching theology on three continents for more than three decades. Over this time, I have realized that my understanding of the task of theology is deeply influenced by my experiences of being in the middle. It has given me a unique vantage point to critically engage with traditional theological frameworks and advocate for a more inclusive and expansive understanding of faith. Throughout this book, I hope to share not only my journey of navigating the complexities of "being in the middle," but also use that experience to explore what it means to do theology in the uncertainties of life.

This book is written from the perspective of a child of apartheid, the middle son of loving Christian parents, who encountered a radical bishop in his young adulthood, whose life trajectory was forever changed as I discovered through an encounter with a little black boy with fetal alcohol syndrome that the ideology and theology of my motherland were as a drug that caused a spiritual deformity in me, racism. Theology can be used for evil, there is no doubt, but this book explores how theology can also be a catalyst for liberation, healing, and radical transformation that leads to practical wisdom.

On Being in the Middle adopts a methodology that not only seeks to understand the divine from the perspective of those who navigate the uncertainties of life's "in-between" spaces but also proposes that theology is fundamentally a Christian practice. This practice aims to integrate our love and knowledge of God with the intent to live wisely and in union with God. This approach rejects simplistic answers and embraces a complex, narrative-driven exploration of faith, encouraging believers to embody their theology as they seek justice, love mercy, and walk humbly with their God amid the challenges of the modern world. The book's structure is a pilgrimage through the terrain of doubt and ambiguity to a place of deeper appreciation of what it means to live in union with God, even when we face tyrannical answers and uncertainties.

My heart is full of gratitude for my students from South Africa, Australia, and the USA, whose rich diversity of experiences has deeply informed the perspectives within this book. I am also immensely thankful for my dedicated readers, whose keen insights and constructive criticisms have significantly shaped the final manuscript. A special mention is reserved for Wade Matthews, my seminary friend, who not only was the first reader but also provided extensive and detailed feedback that was instrumental in refining the content and enhancing the depth of the theological discussions. To my editor, Roger McDonald, I owe my thanks for his meticulous attention to detail and the profound empathy he holds for my ideas and experiences, which has brought clarity and coherence to this work. And of course, Archie, my canine friend, who faithfully got up early in the morning and was my constant companion as I did this labor of love.

Lastly, to Marian Bosch, Sweetie, my partner for life and the mother of our beautiful girls Carmen and Zoe. Your unwavering love, and understanding for my quirks, that would send most people packing, inspire and encourage me.

In this book, I invite thinkers, believers, and seekers traversing life's grey areas but also to those who have endured the tyrannical aspects of theology. This book offers a personal vantage point—standing in the middle, where the heart resides, it invites readers to bring forth their sacrosanct questions. In its pages, you're encouraged to hold your uncertainties and questions up in the light of God's presence, without fear or anxiety, embracing the assurance that God is in the middle with us.

August 2024
Melbourne, Australia

Introduction

My first wristwatch from my father was a treasured possession for most of my childhood. Its beauty, elegance, and, especially, accuracy fascinated me. The sweep hand captivated me, gliding smoothly and gracefully as it counted each second. I would stare, mesmerized by the vanishing intervals, pondering the mysteries of time and what lay within it. These intermediate moments represented the intertwining of past and present; a threshold between the previous second and the next in an as yet unknown and perhaps unknowable sequence. You may find it strange that a boy in his first decade would find this fascinating, but it may not be that strange if you know I am the middle child. Growing up in the middle, sandwiched between an older and younger brother, I often found myself in these in-between moments. I was neither the firstborn, with all the privileges and responsibilities that came with it, nor the youngest, who received the most attention and indulgence from our parents. Instead, I existed in this liminality, navigating the space between two others. A boy in the middle. In this state of being betwixt and between, I acquired a perspective on life from the middle. This book will explore the journey of being in the middle and how we do theology from this perspective.

Growing into adulthood, I have developed a keen interest in the concept of liminality—a fascinating in-between space marked by ambiguity and uncertainty. It's a state where individuals, events, or objects linger, not fully shaped or dissolved. It is a locus in which individuals are neither entirely present but are in a state of transition—a condition of becoming. For Arnold van Gennep and later Victor Turner, liminality refers to the transitional or threshold state that occurs during rituals and other significant social events.[1]

---

1. Van Gennep, *Rites of Passage* (1960); and Victor Turner describes liminality as the in-between state of being in *Forest of Symbols* (1967), *Ritual Process* (1969), and *Dramas, Fields, and Metaphors* (1974). I am more familiar with the work of Turner and

Turner's concept of liminality specifically refers to the stage in a rite of passage when an individual is in a state of "betwixt and between"—no longer in their previous status or role, but not yet fully initiated into the new one. In this state, traditional social hierarchies and norms are often suspended, and the individual is in a state of heightened openness and receptivity. Theorists often describe our presence in liminal space as a time of confusion, uncertainty, and ambiguity, but also as a time of potential for change and transformation. The idea of liminality is often associated with the concept of "twilight," as it refers to a threshold or transitional state.[2]

In most ancient cultures, mothers essentially raise their sons to a point when the men of the tribe take the boys into the wilderness to initiate them in "men's business." The pain and exhaustion of the ordeal drive the boys together. Their survival depends on their ability to form community in this space between boyhood and manhood. No longer children but not yet adults, at this stage and in this time they dwell in liminality.

This state of being in-between is a ubiquitous mark of human existence that encompasses all major transitions and changes throughout life. It marks the threshold between what has been and what is yet to come, from the moment of birth to the end of life. During liminal moments, we face heightened awareness and sensitivity to our surroundings, forcing us to use all our senses to navigate new environments and situations and establish new connections with others. Whether it is migration to a new country, starting a new job, or experiencing a significant life change, liminality is a fundamental feature of the human experience, shaping our lives and influencing our interactions with the world.

Significantly, in the creation narrative we see humans physically located between two rivers, the Tigris and Euphrates Rivers, and Eden is the "land of two rivers." Humans are in-betweeners. Perhaps more notable is the knowledge that humans are God's image bearers who stand between God and his creation. According to the psalmist, King David of Israel, humans are:

"You have made them a little lower than the angels and crowned them with glory and honor."[3]

---

will follow his description of liminality.

2. The term liminal is derived from the Latin word *limen* meaning "threshold," so the idea of liminality is related to the idea of a threshold or transitional state. Hence there is a similarity with the concept of twilight, as it also refers to a transitional state, in this case between day and night

3. Ps 8:5 (NIV).

The psalmist cherishes the idea that humans are both creatures created by God and the image bearers of God in creation. In one sense, we are limited and finite beings, dependent upon God for our existence. However, as beings made in God's image, we also have dignity and worth, reflecting some of God's qualities in our lives. We exist in the middle, where we are both created and creators, finite and eternal. Despite this, there is a mystery in this relationship, since God gave us the freedom to choose, to hold him dear, or to trust someone else.

The third chapter of the Bible tells us that Adam and Eve saw that the tree provided nutritious fruit and appealed to the eye. It was also a valuable source of wisdom. Despite God's warning to desist, they ate some of the fruit.[4] We will return to this narrative later in the book, but for now, it is sufficient to say that this action separated humans from God. After the relational rupture with God, life has become more difficult. Serpents strike, crops fail without back-breaking labor, children are born in pain, and human relationships suffer unmet desires. As God tells Eve, "You will desire your husband, and he will rule over you."[5] From this point, God seems distant and difficult to behold. As life's meaning evaporates, the human heart breaks. But all is not lost, since God promises from Eve's offspring, somewhere in the distant future, a redeemer will appear who will "bruise the serpent's head."[6] So, from here on, humans live between what has been and what might be, or at the threshold of what might be.

BEING IN-BETWEEN IS A BIBLICAL IDEA

The imagery of the wilderness and the journey of the Israelites from Egypt to the promised land in the Old Testament illustrates the concept of living at a threshold, in a space between what was and what will be. The wilderness is a place of transition. It is a space between the known and the unknown, the familiar and the unfamiliar, the secure and the insecure. The author of Ecclesiastes gives us a sobering perspective that all of our efforts, no matter how successful, will eventually be forgotten—"all is vanity."[7] He is not alone in this sentiment. The Old Testament prophets

---

4. See Gen 3:6.
5. Gen 3:14 (NIV).
6. Gen 3:15 (NIV).
7. Eccl 1:2 (NIV).

recognized the difficulties of the world and longed for a messiah who would be the light to lead them out of the "deep shadows."[8]

Even though the word *liminality* is not found in the New Testament, we find the concept of being in a state of transition or threshold there. Jesus describes the in-between state of human existence. He often spoke of both the present and the future kingdom of God. He announced that the kingdom of God was near[9] and that it was already present in his person and work.[10] However, he also referred to the kingdom as something that would come in its fullness in the future.[11] The New Testament describes the period between death and final resurrection as a time of waiting for the full realization of God's promises.[12] Paul also describes our present existence as a "light and momentary affliction,"[13] and that even creation "groans" in anticipation of redemption.[14] Here, we have a present experience of God's kingdom, but it is not yet the full realization of his promises. This is like a seed planted in the ground. The seed has the potential to grow and blossom into a magnificent plant, but it must first go through a period of waiting and transformation. In the same way, we are waiting for the full realization of God's kingdom.

Oscar Cullmann, a French theologian, asserts that the teachings of the New Testament and Paul reflect both elements—the age to come as already present and as future. Drawing on his own experience of World War II, he illustrates his point by delineating between a decisive day and victory in war. He explains that, "The decisive battle in a war may already have occurred in a relatively early stage of the war, and yet the war still continues. Although the decisive effect of that battle is perhaps not recognized by all, it nevertheless already means victory. But the war must still be carried on for an undefined time, until 'Victory Day.'"[15] According to this influential view, the age to come has already begun in the first

---

8. Isa 9:2 (NIV).
9. See Mark 1:15.
10. See Matt 12:28.
11. See Matt 25:34.
12. Phil 1:6 and 23; 2 Cor 5:8.
13. 2 Cor 4:17 (NIV).
14. Rom 8:22–23 (NIV).
15. Cullmann, *Christ and Time*, 84. Many interpreters of Paul, including notable scholars such as W. Kümmel, E. Kasemann, H. Ridderbos, and C. Beker, have followed Cullmann's lead in understanding the "already/not-yet" eschatological tension as a central aspect of Paul's message.

coming of Christ, particularly in his death and resurrection, signifying the inauguration of a new era. However, this "already" aspect of the eschatological reality is not fully realized or completed; rather, it remains in a state of anticipation and expectation. Similarly, Christ's death and resurrection initiated the fulfillment of eschatological promises, bringing about the age to come. Nevertheless, the "not-yet" aspect corresponds to V-Day, symbolizing the final culmination of God's redemptive plan—the second coming of Christ.

This theological perspective has profound implications for believers' understanding of the world and their place in it. The Christian life is thus characterized by an existence on the threshold between these two epochs—an overlap between the present age and the age to come. If we were to draw two circles, a simple Venn diagram to illustrate the New Testament view of the human experience, where the two circles that represent the "already and the not-yet" overlap, we would see that we live in the merged space of the already and the not-yet. The in-between space is where we live, in liminality. The space between what is and what is not-yet, the space between ontological union with Christ and physical separation. Paul can confidently say of Christians that they died, and their lives are now "hidden with Christ in God."[16] He also calls on these believers in the same passage to put to death, therefore, whatever belongs to their earthly nature.[17] We live "human life in this world in union with God."[18] As Christians, we live between Christ's already-established kingdom and his yet-to-arrive kingdom. As a result, we do not explore theology in the focused glare of an operating theater. Rather, we try to be faithful to revelations and discern what it means to live out our faith in the present. We walk in the twilight, between knowledge and ignorance, trusting in the promises of God. We approach theology "through a glass darkly."[19]

BETWEEN BIRTH AND ATTACHMENT

Newborns occupy a state of transition as they enter the world and experience new sensations, relationships, and social norms. They no longer belong to their mother's body but nonetheless lack independence and

16. See Col 3:3.
17. See Col 3:4.
18. Richards, *Practical Theology of Spirituality*, 50.
19. 1 Cor 13:12 (NIV).

self-sufficiency. This period of transition is a liminal or threshold experience where they hover between two distinct stages of development and must navigate uncertainty as they grow and develop into their own personas. From neuroscience, we learn that babies rely on their senses to grope through this liminal experience. Making sense[20] comes later. Their sensory experiences and perceptions shape their understanding of the world before they can consciously process and interpret that information. They automatically process sensory information, allowing them to react to their environment before they learn to consciously interpret it.

As they experience sensations, emotions, or physiological changes, their brains alert them to pre-propositional, non-conceptual phenomena. These "pre-propositional affective mentalities"[21] form the initial foundation on which they consciously but non-conceptually learn to understand their bodies. The platform gives them an evolving sense of well- or ill-being, helping them navigate their enlarging environment and respond to challenges and opportunities in a timely manner. Rational consideration can help modulate these "pre-propositional affective mentalities." Nevertheless, they are a way in which the brain neurologically assesses the internal and external environment to make affective judgments and take action in the world. This ability to sense, to follow our hearts, is an early skill that we rely on to survive and thrive in liminality. When we interact with others, we constantly pick up cues about their trustworthiness through various sensory channels. The human brain's amygdala processes this information, along with interpreting emotions and social signals. At the same time, the brain's neocortex, responsible for conscious thought and decision-making, is involved in interpreting the sensory information related to trust and distrust.

In this liminal experience of birth, every one of us longed for a physical and emotional bond with someone we could trust in this time of neonatal uncertainty. According to John Bowlby in *Attachment and Loss* we develop internal working models of attachment during these early childhood experiences with our primary caregivers.[22] These inner blueprints are mental representations or frameworks of ourselves, others, and relationships. They help to organize and make sense of experiences, and can influence how an individual perceives and reacts to later relationships. We develop these models based on the consistency, availability, and

---

20. I am guided here by Thompson and Fujimura, *Soul of Desire*.
21. See Panksepp, "On the Embodied Neural Nature," 158–84.
22. Bowlby, *Attachment and Loss*, 1:91.

emotional responsiveness of our caregivers. Caregivers who are attuned to the needs of infants will sense their emotional condition and respond in a manner that helps them regulate their feelings. This might include offering comfort, a calming presence, and providing reassurance in liminality, as well as helping them to recognize and express their feelings.

As a psychiatrist, Curt Thompson has observed that being "soothed, seen, safe and secure" are essential signs of a secure attachment relationship.[23] These elements reflect the basic needs and desires that we have for connection and are thought to be crucial for the development of a healthy sense of self. We are "soothed" through the comfort and support we receive from our caregivers in response to distress. Being "seen" is the recognition and validation of one's emotions, thoughts, and experiences. Being "safe" refers to the physical and emotional absence of threat we feel in our relationships, and being "secure" is the sense of stability and predictability that comes from having dependable attachments. According to Thompson, these elements also contribute to a sense of security and stability in people's spiritual lives, both in human relationships and in their relationship with God.

Juvenile male initiates cling to each other through their ordeal on the way to manhood. Mothers cradle their newborn babies close in the long sleepless hours of the night. So humans after the break with God live with the threat of non-being and meaninglessness. Perhaps this is the pivotal point of faith and doubt. We cannot escape the feeling that life should have not only meaning, but *more* meaning than is currently visible. C. S. Lewis famously said "If we find ourselves with a desire that nothing in this world can satisfy, the most probable explanation is that we were made for another world."[24] This craving Lewis describes seems to express an instinctive leaning toward meaning, and an impulse away from meaninglessness. It becomes our impetus to write, to reflect, and to pursue theology.

BETWEEN DISTRUST AND TRUST

Paul Tillich explains that "the fall" has separated human beings from God, our "Ground of Being."[25] Separation from the ground of being, from God,

---

23. Thompson and Fujimura, *Soul of Desire*, use these four words to describe secure attachment.

24. Lewis, *Mere Christianity*, 136–37.

25. Tillich, *Theology of Culture*, 15.

has left us deeply anxious in the face of extinction and the uncertainty that comes from being between life and death. Our ultimate concern, says Tillich, "is then the meaning that gives meaning to all meanings."[26] We experience this ultimate concern at both a universal and a personal level. Only in God, who is the "meaning which gives meaning to all meanings," can humans make sense of life in liminality. He agrees with Blaise Pascal, who describes the human condition as a loss of true happiness. It is not loss of frivolous pleasure, but happiness that "is neither without us nor within us. It is in God, both without us and within us."[27] He sees in himself and others a deep sense of longing that cannot be satisfied by the things of this world. In liminality, we try to fill this emptiness with the things around us, but this is futile since these things cannot provide real happiness. In his view, only God can fill this "infinite abyss."[28] He longs for that attachment to God, just as a newborn baby instinctively grasps for its mother in the first moments of life.

I propose, in the in-between spaces of life, we long for a deep attachment to God. We live by faith. God is "the only trustworthy and wholly lovable reality."[29] We want God to see and soothe us. We yearn to feel safe and secure in his presence. Faith in God as our primary, covenanting other is essential for living in liminality. It is the "courage to be"[30] in the space between what has been and what is yet to come. I do not mean by faith that God will answer my prayers or save me from or destroy my enemies. I refer to faith as *"belifan,"* an Old English word that means "to hold dear," or to love or to cherish, or to experience a deep affection. This was the original meaning of faith.[31] Faith in liminality means we also hold God dear, "be-holding" or trusting him.

For Cantwell Smith, who agrees with Tillich, faith in God enables humans to recognize and grasp meaning in our lives and as such "it is a quality of human living" that "enable[s] one to feel at home in the universe, and to find meaning in the world and in one's own life, a meaning

---

26. Tillich, *Courage to Be*, 47.
27. Pascal, *Pensées*, 9.
28. Pascal, *Pensées*, 45.
29. Niebuhr, "Man the Sinner," 276.
30. Fowler, *Stages of Faith*, 5. We will need to return to his theory in a later chapter.
31. Only after the sixteenth century did belief become an affirmation of a proposition as true. For a detailed study of the evolution of the English word *belief* see Cantwell Smith, *Faith and Belief*, 105–18.

that is profound and ultimate, and is stable no matter what may happen."[32] For him, faith is an orientation of the personality that shapes the way individuals see and relate to themselves, others, and the world around them. This orientation of the personality sounds very similar to what attachment theory describes "as internal working models." Smith, however, sees faith as a total response, a way of perceiving and engaging with reality that goes beyond the mundane and personal. Faith is a capacity to live at a higher level, to experience and understand the world in transcendent dimensions. This means that faith is not limited to the physical world, but rather allows individuals to live in between the natural and supernatural aspects of reality integrated beings.

According to James Fowler, the "supernatural aspect of reality" functions as "centers of supraordinate value which have the power to unify his or her experiences of the world, thereby endowing relationships, contexts, and patterns of everyday life, past and future, with significance."[33] Fowler emphasizes that this is not merely an abstract idea, as we put our faith in "people, causes, institutions, or gods"[34] simply because they exist. Rather, we have faith in them because they have "an intrinsic excellence or worth"[35] for us, and because they "promise to confer value on us."[36] Faith is deeply personal and dynamic, as it is our affective way of being with the transcendent, with God, who has our best interests in the forefront of his intentions. Fowler is helpful when he adds that faith is "the realization of trust and loyalty to the transcendent, about which concepts or propositions—beliefs are fashioned."[37]

Faith is first experienced in liminality as an affection of trust, as *fiducia*.[38] Humans are fiduciary beings, says Fowler, which is the same as saying we are moral beings who make and break promises. When we trust we commit, but in distrust we fracture pledges and shirk commitments.[39] As humans we are suspicious of other beings, says Fowler, but God's disclosure in human history has turned this around. Our "distrust

---

32. Cantwell Smith, *Faith and Belief*, 12.
33. Fowler, "Faith and the Structuring of Meaning," 25–26.
34. Fowler, *Stages*, 18.
35. Fowler, *Stages*, 18.
36. Fowler, *Stages*, 18.
37. Fowler, *Stages*, 11.
38. For an explanation of this distinction see, Moreland and Craig, *Philosophical Foundations for a Christian Worldview*, 18.
39. Fowler, *To See the Kingdom*, 142.

is turned to trust," he says, "and we respond with loyalty to the cause to which the covenanting one is faithful. We dare to trust that there is fiduciary texture to reality."[40] So, we dare to trust so that we can find meaning in this world.

In the same way, children feel affection when they sense warmth, fondness, and love when they are emotionally connected with their caregivers who are emotionally attuned with them, who become the covenanting one for them. I believe that affection results from a sense of attachment and attunement. In these bonds of affection we learn to trust our caregivers and the world we find ourselves in. The essence of faith can be seen in a child who learns to trust his or her parents. These children may not understand the logic behind it, but learn through experience that they feel secure and comfortable when they do. Fowler remarks that this faith is globalized and stretches beyond the caregiver. For him, faith is a human search for meaning, an "overarching integrating and grounding trust" that is capable and sufficient "to give our lives unity and meaning."[41] Victor Frankl, as a psychiatrist and a Holocaust survivor, observed in the Nazi concentration camps that those prisoners who were able to find meaning in their suffering were more likely to survive and less likely to give up hope, even in the most dire of circumstances.[42] There is little doubt that meaning is essential for psychological well-being and can provide individuals with a sense of purpose, direction, and fulfillment in life.

BETWEEN MEANING AND MEANINGLESSNESS

We started with a childhood memory that inspired a discussion about living in the spaces between moments. However, the land we were living on when my father handed me my first wristwatch was the land that my forebearers migrated to: the Cape of Good Hope in the 1750s. A century earlier, Dutch East Indian Company sailors left these Dutch farmers on the southern tip of Africa to cultivate gardens. Although these settlers did not have the language to express themselves in the way we have done in this chapter, they nonetheless found themselves in an in-between space.

---

40. While reflecting on H. Richard Niebuhr's work, Fowler, *To See the Kingdom*, 142–43.
41. Fowler, *Stages*, 5.
42. Fowler, *Stages*, 34.

Although this was an in-between space of uncertainty, disorientation, and ambiguity, it was also an opportunity to begin a new life. As they stood on the picturesque but dangerous shores of Africa, the otherness of the world they had come to inhabit must have confronted these Dutch settlers. They were now forced to face the unfamiliarity of their new environment and the challenge of understanding and living in a strange land. This led them to reexamine the pillars of their faith as a way to make sense of the unknown and to explain the circumstances of their journey. This exploration of faith ultimately shaped how they interacted with the world they encountered and the decisions they took. As we will see in this book, they turned to their faith to make sense of their new situation.

This book is about doing theology in the face of uncertainties, just like the early settlers on the southern tip of Africa. In its first half of the book, we explore how these Christian settlers coped with being alone in the middle, and how their theological choices led to apartheid (ch. 1). We trace this theology back to Europe, seeking to understand how theologians place theory and Christian beliefs in the middle (ch. 2). This approach to theology, which moves from theory to practice, has been critiqued by those advocating for practical theology as the best way to engage with theology in the middle (ch. 3). My own experience in the middle has shown the inadequacies of the theory-practice binary, revealing that, ultimately, the heart, not the head and the hands, is in the middle of doing theology (ch. 4). God, the most moved mover, is the very ground of all beings (ch. 5). As image bearers of God, we were created to live with him in the middle (ch. 6), but our choices have left us with perpetual anxiety between birth and death (ch. 7). Fortunately, this is not where the book ends. In the second part, we explore the Christian practice of doing theology amid life's brokenness. Because God is with us in the middle (ch. 8), we become conscious of his desire to share life with us (ch. 9). As we commit ourselves to doing theology in union with God, the way we belong (ch. 10), communicate (ch. 11), love (ch. 12), serve (ch. 13), and grow (ch. 14) is transformed by God who is present with us in the middle. I invite those interested in theological method to join me in the post script for a brief exploration of how I do and teach theology in the middle.

We always do theology between this moment and the next; in the uncertainties of life, there is no escape. And just as my ancestors turned to their theology when their ships crept toward that distant horizon, we will do the same through the pages of this book.

PART A

Alone in the Middle

1

Afrikaner

INITIALLY, DUTCH SETTLERS ON the southern tip of Africa were stationed there as a waypoint for the Dutch East India Company's sailors to rest and recuperate. The new land was abundant and treacherous, with challenges like droughts, pests, and adapting to a new environment. To survive, the settlers had to learn to build shelters, cultivate crops, and engage the local people. This was the tricky part. They viewed the Khoisan as a primitive and inferior people based on their own beliefs and prejudices. European societies of the seventeenth century believed in the superiority of European culture and civilization and the notion that non-European peoples were racially and culturally inferior. "So these settlers imposed their own cultural and religious beliefs on the Khoisan and the local inhabitants, which led to the loss of many aspects of their traditional way of life."[1] As Archbishop Desmond Tutu famously observed when the colonizers and the missionaries came to Africa: "They had the Bible and we had the land. They said 'Let us pray.' We closed our eyes. When we opened them we had the Bible and they had the land."[2]

In this in-between state of existence, the settlers' faith significantly shaped their identity and understanding of the world. It provided them

---

1. This treatment of the Khoisan was a manifestation of the wider system of colonialism and slavery that existed in the Cape Colony, which treated the Khoisan and other non-European peoples as resources to be exploited and oppressed. This was also the experience of other indigenous peoples around the world and the legacy of this kind of treatment continues to impact the descendants of indigenous peoples to this day.

2. This quote is attributed to Desmond Tutu; see Maluleke, "Postcolonial Mission," 503–28.

with comfort, stability, purpose, a moral code to guide their behavior, and a sense of collective identity as Boers—the Afrikaans word for farmers. That is what they were and how they understood themselves. Through faith, they could perceive and engage with reality in a way that transcended the mundane. They believed that their lives were part of a larger narrative and thereby found meaning and hope in uncertainty. They believed God had chosen them specially and loved them exclusively, much like Israel, and saw themselves as having a divine mission to establish a godly nation in the land. In contrast, they did not consider indigenous people in this same light, regarding them as theologically recalcitrant, undesirable, and not their equals. For this reason, they believed that God placed the indigenous population under their guardianship. These beliefs led to the creation of a theological system that advocated for racial purity and separation at all costs. This was how they practically integrated the affective and cognitive aspects of their faith, but this was soon to change.

As the British took control of the Cape Colony from the Dutch in 1814, they found themselves in the middle between the past and the future. Anna Steenekamp, the niece of the first Boer governor, Piet Retief, explained to her family why they were leaving the prosperous Cape Colony and joining what would come to be known as the Great Trek. She felt that placing reprobate Africans on an "equal footing"[3] with Afrikaners was unacceptable. If Afrikaners were the chosen and elect of God, how could there be racial equality in this political system? And if God loved Afrikaners and punished Africans for their wickedness, how could the new law break the bonds of master and servant? In her opinion, it was unthinkable for "any decent Christian to submit to such a yoke."[4] Thus, their love for God required them to leave the colony and avoid the danger of racial mixing or intermarriage, which would violate God's law against being unequally yoked. Citing the Old Testament, they feared God's punishment for disobedience and were determined to remain pure. As a result, the decision to leave was clear. They would become trekkers.

In 1835, their affection for God and nation inspired more than one thousand Boers to embark on the Great Trek from the Cape. Like the settlers before them, they faced another in-between situation. But this journey was also similar to the Israelites' exodus from Egypt; they were caught between two worlds. The British governor was the modern-day

---

3. Bird, *Annals of Natal*, 2:459.
4. Bird, *Annals of Natal*, 2:459.

Pharaoh, the Boers' leader, Piet Retief, was Moses, and Andries Pretorius was Joshua, who became leader after Piet Retief and his men perished at the hands of Zulu king Dingaan.[5] The Great Trek played a defining role in sharpening the identity of the Boers as the people of God in the middle.

BETWEEN A RIVER AND ZULU WARRIORS, A COVENANT IS MADE

Perhaps the most nation-defining battle happened nine months after Piet Retief's death in 1838. As a young Afrikaner boy, I knew the legend of the battle of Blood River as well as the stories of the Bible. Even as I write, I can recall the many times I heard this story and retold it with pride; how it evoked in my childhood heart a deep affection for God, country, and nation. It settled a deep conviction that God had chosen us and that he was on the side of my people, the Afrikaners. This battle was the final and decisive encounter in the war against Dingaan's Zulus. The Boers were once again outnumbered and realized their dependence on God. Before the impending conflict the two most prominent Boer leaders agreed they should swear a vow that Afrikaners would become a holy nation if God delivered their enemies into their hands. Just as Hannah pledged to give her boy to his service if God allowed her to have a son, so this clan would devote themselves to God as a priestly people. This oath left an indelible mark on my young Afrikaner mind, and shaped my affections as I matured into young adulthood and prepared myself to pursue theology as a vocation.

On December 7, 1838, Charl Cilliers made this vow on behalf of the Boers, that if God "will be with us and protect us, and deliver the enemy into our hands so that we may triumph over him, that we shall observe the day and the date as an anniversary in each year, and a day of thanksgiving like the Sabbath."[6] Just nine days after they made this vow, four hundred Boers faced their deadliest foe. Like waves thundering onto a beach, Dingaan's army of warriors launched attack after attack to break through the Boer defense. Despite their best efforts, the attackers continually failed to overwhelm the Boers, because, according to Cilliers,

---

5. See Van Jaarsveld, *Afrikaners*, 9–10, quoting the history of C. P. Bezuidenhout, *Geskiedenis van het Afrikaansche Geslachtvan 1688–1882*, written in 1882.

6. Bird, *Annals of Natal*, 2:244–45.

"the Lord was with us."[7] When the Zulu warriors realized they were not going to succeed they refused to follow their commander's orders any longer. As they retreated, a small Boer army pursued them. According to Cilliers, three thousand Zulu warriors died that day fighting for their king, Dingaan, because the Lord's blessing commanded them "to flee before his face."[8]

BETWEEN SUFFERING AND HOPE, A VOLK IS BORN

The Dutch settlers, trekkers, generals, and later twentieth-century theologians such as J. D. Du Toit, turned to doctrine for guidance and relied on the Bible to provide answers and certainty in their ambiguous world. Du Toit was a Calvinist theologian, Bible translator, and a poet who wrote under the alias Totius. It is unlikely that the Great Trek inspired any other Afrikaner theologian as much to integrate the affective and cognitive aspects of Afrikaner faith in practical ways as did Du Toit. He wove a tapestry of devotion for God, nation, and country with his powerful words. As a high school student, his poetry about the sufferings of the early Afrikaners, as well as the women and children who died in Boer War British concentration camps, deeply moved me. Since my ancestors suffered this indignity, I also felt the pain acutely and personally.

His writings frequently mention Rachel, Jacob's wife, as well as a young Afrikaner girl, Rachel de Beer, a trekker heroine who gave her life that her younger brother might live. As the archetypal mother of Israel, Rachel is "weeping for her children in Ramah,"[9] but she is also the mother of the Afrikaner people.[10] Afrikaners have traditionally viewed themselves as members of God's family, with mothers like Rachel whose loved ones died in battle, from disease, or other misfortune. As the spiritual daughter of Israel's matriarch, Rachel de Beer also sacrificed everything for her sibling. Her memory would give strength to all Afrikaner mothers who stood between life and death, at the open graves of their parents, husbands, and children.

According to Totius, Rachel's suffering on behalf of Jacob foreshadows Christ's suffering on behalf of the entire world. Israel's suffering

---

7. Bird, *Annals of Natal*, 2:246.
8. Bird, *Annals of Natal*, 2:246.
9. Jer 31:15 (NIV).
10. Hexham, "Just like Another Israel," 7.

through history foreshadows Christ's suffering, who becomes God's suffering servant in the New Testament. As God's servants, he believed, the Afrikaners suffered for their loyalty to God at the hands of God's enemies.[11] In order to participate in God's redemptive initiative in Africa, they had to make sacrifices of their own, suffer, and even be willing to die. As such, Afrikaner hardships, sufferings, and victories became a contextual part of redemptive history.[12]

Even so, Totius believed that Afrikaners were never victims but remained resilient under all circumstances. He told the story of an ox-wagon's wheel crushing a young thorn tree growing beside the road. Although nearly destroyed, the small tree found the strength to grow again, bearing the scars of the ordeal.[13] As Totius saw it, the Afrikaners were called upon to bear their scars just as Christ did, because ultimately God is in control. Through this strong Calvinist belief in God's sovereignty,[14] they were able to perceive and engage with reality in a way that transcended mere physical survival. Their faith provided a lens through which to view the world and life with certainty.

Totius reminded Afrikaners that just as Israel was instructed never to forget its origins, Afrikaners too must never forget their God or deny their identity as God's chosen people. He feared any form of compromise or any sign of unfaithfulness to God and nation would lead to God's rejection of the Afrikaner race as a whole, a sentiment that he shares with Anna Steenekamp. This also ruled out any desire to reconcile with South Africans of British descent, since they were part of the empire that caused untold suffering during the Anglo-Boer War.

Totius published a famous series of poems in 1908 addressing the subject of the *volk*.[15] He attacked the policies of the South Africa Party, which wanted to unite the interests of the British and the Boers. His deep anti-British animus saturated his verse, inspiring Boers who feared that their sacrifice would be forgotten, and serving as a clarion call to nationalism. A similar summons also rang in the ears of Germans in Europe at that time. He reminded Afrikaners that if they forgot their suffering under British domination, their history would become meaningless.

---

11. See Hexham, "Just like Another Israel," 8.
12. See Hexham, *Irony of Apartheid*, 33–46.
13. See Du Toit, *Versamelde Werke*, 1.
14. Hexham, "Just like Another Israel," 5.
15. In Afrikaans, *volk* is an interchangeable term for "the nation" or "the people."

BETWEEN THEOLOGY AND POLITICS, A NATION IS FORMED

His writing ignited a nationalistic flame in the hearts of his readers and subsequent generations of Afrikaners. The theology that guided the Afrikaner people through uncertainty became a political movement when General J. B. M. Hertzog, the Anglo-Boer War hero, answered this call for Afrikaner nationalism. In 1914, he created the National Party,[16] and in 1948 this political organization formed the first all-Afrikaner (and all-male) cabinet under the leadership of Daniel Malan, a Dutch Reformed Church minister and theologian. Piet Meyer, an Afrikaner cultural architect and philosopher with a Calvinist worldview, said that the Afrikaner nation could boast it was the only nation in the world conceived and formed by Calvinism.[17] Meyer later helped to establish an Afrikaner university that would shape Afrikaner minds within this Calvinist mindset. That academy, the Rand Afrikaans University, was where I would later study. This university, like so many Afrikaner institutions, was now able to develop and propagate the theological, ideological, social-scientific, and legal rationale for apartheid through the organs of the state.

At the 1944 National People's Congress, Totius declared that the Bible, not a specific text, justified segregation.[18] He argued that the biblical narrative supported the Afrikaner's desire to remain separate and pure for the purpose God had preordained for them. Totius saw nations, not empires, as the way God intended the world to be. He believed that God created nations and condemned empires, which were the amalgamation of nations. This perspective was based on the idea that while we should not separate what God has joined together, we also should not join what God has divided.[19] The theological integration of the affective and cognitive aspects of Afrikaner faith led to the creation and justification of apartheid policies. In reality, it led to the segregation and subjugation of people on the basis of their race and provided the grounds for racial separation and oppression.

16. He fell out of favor with significant theologians like Daniel Malan when he merged his National Party with the rival South African Party of Jan Smuts in 1934 to form the United Party.

17. See Prinsloo, "Dr Piet Meyer in Johannesburg."

18. Du Toit, "Godsdienstige Grondslag." Totius said, if someone asked him for a text to justify segregation, he would say, "I do not have one"; instead, he said, "I have the Bible."

19. Du Toit, "Godsdienstige Grondslag."

Afrikaner theologians also leaned heavily on Dutch theologian and politician Abraham Kuyper for support in their theo-political endeavors. Kuyper believed that God, as the divider,[20] had drawn lines of demarcation throughout the world and established "sovereign spheres" in creation. According to E. P. Groenewald, whose work was mandatory reading in many theological courses in South Africa, God had divided nations and separated every aspect of life accordingly.[21] Totius shared this view and saw the unification of nations as the problem, not national segregation. He believed that the "Babylonian spirit of unification"[22] was hindering the Afrikaners' desire for independence and that *apartheid* policies and doctrines of racial segregation were necessary to defeat this global evil.

In the build up to the 1948 election, Groenewald reminded Afrikaners of the Tower of Babel, where humans attempted to rival God by building an empire. God divided the nations. The theological integration of the affective and cognitive aspects of Afrikaner culture followed a clear path. God had instructed Afrikaners to separate themselves from all others and establish boundaries to protect their purity. Subjugation of African races was seen as a logical outcome in this theo-political progression, with Afrikaners accepting as their duty the task to guide "less-civilised" African races to maturity.[23] This guardianship was not to be a demonstration of superiority, but rather a responsibility to help and nurture the African people. Groenewald used Paul's idea of trusteeship to justify this relationship.[24] Afrikaners had to show restraint as informed, benevolent guardians. Indigenous Africans must exhibit respect and gratitude that the Afrikaner people were helping them mature as a race.[25]

Unification would lead to racial equality but, more alarmingly, interracial marriage and the blending of bloodlines. Totius warned Afrikaners in stark and what today would be considered offensive language that Africa was a "black swamp"[26] and that entering it would result in their

---

20. Abraham Kuyper, "Blurring of the Boundaries," in *Abraham Kuyper*, 368. Kuyper believed that in the Hebrew Scriptures God is called Hammabdi, the divider, because God is the first to draw lines "between Himself and the created world, and then throughout the entire domain of the created world. He has drawn lines of design, lines of demarcation, lines of distinction, lines of separation, lines of contrast."

21. Groenewald, *Regverdige Rasse-Apartheid*, 43.

22. Du Toit "Godsdienstige Grondslag."

23. Du Toit "Godsdienstige Grondslag."

24. See Gal 4:2.

25. Groenewald, *Regverdige Rasse-Apartheid*, 64.

26. Translation of his phrase "*swart moeras*"; see Du Toit, "Godsdienstige Grondslag."

disappearance. Totius warned that nations had been "always swallowed up by Africa—and eventually disappeared."[27] Consequently, it could not be a sin for Afrikaners to seek racial purity; rather it was a sin for them to mix races and to "bastardize" Afrikaners.[28] The Dutch Reformed Church noted in 1935 that Afrikaners' fear of racial equality was rooted in their "aversion to the idea of intermarriage."[29] The church mailed a booklet opposing interracial marriages to all Dutch Reformed Church members in the Orange Free State, one of South Africa's provinces. This was a matter of life and death for the Afrikaner people. The booklet's author suggested that Afrikaner survival depended on a strict apartheid in social life, and that mixed marriages should be prohibited and interracial intercourse severely punished.[30] And with that, the matter was concluded: only a vote for the Nationalists could be justified biblically and theologically.

BETWEEN AFFECTIONS AND AVERSIONS, RACISM TAKES HOLD

It is wise to pause here for a moment to reconsider the Dutch Reformed Church's admission that an "aversion to the idea of intermarriage" motivated apartheid policies and gave credence to the church doctrines that supported these strategies. This is an admission that affections, attraction, or aversion inform and shape our beliefs, both theologically and practically: we sense before we make sense. The affections of attraction or repulsion can drive and influence how people perceive and interpret their beliefs, both in the theological sense and in practical matters. In other words, a person's beliefs are not just based on logic or reason but also on the emotional or affective aspects of their experiences. This can result in a situation where a person's emotions, such as love or hate, are able to sway their beliefs and actions. We will revisit this theme throughout this book.

27. Du Toit, "Godsdienstige Grondslag."

28. Du Toit, "Godsdienstige Grondslag." "There can never be racial equality, but there can never be racial bastardization . . . Scripture is opposed to all unnatural mixing as evidenced by the civil laws given by Moses at the command of God: 'You shall not sow your vineyard with two kinds of seed, lest the whole yield be forfeited, the crop that you have sown and the yield of the vineyard. 10 You shall not plow with an ox and a donkey together. 11 You shall not wear cloth of wool and linen mixed together.' (Deuteronomy 22:9–11)."

29. See Stoker and Potgieter, *Koers in die krisis*, 228.

30. Strydom, *Rassevraagstuk* , 28.

The National Party of General Hertzog defeated the South African Party on May 26, 1948. In 1960, Hendrik Verwoerd, the first prime minister of the Republic of South Africa, declared that Afrikaners could not only see their vocation as "establishing Christian civilization in" but it "must become the firm base" from which the white man can again advance" when he has his back to the wall."[31] Every act of parliament from this point on was crafted specifically to preserve purity, establish the position, and advance the cause of Afrikaners, creating a land filled with opportunity for Afrikaners like me but turning Africans into landfill.

The people who were denied opportunity and resources, who were subjected to guardianship, understandably rejected these theo-political justifications for white privilege. In no time at all, people were talking about revolution. In every corner of South Africa, fires of resistance and outright revolts flared. At no time in my young life was I unaware of the political tensions, or ignorant of the unsettled majority awaiting its moment of liberation. But as a young and devout Afrikaner, I felt an urgent obligation to defend the apartheid regime. I saw it as a way to preserve the resources and power of my people and to resist the looming threat of communism. Determined to further my understanding of theology and bolster its defense, I enrolled at Johannesburg University, then known as the Rand Afrikaans University, an institution dedicated solely to educating young Afrikaners like myself.

BETWEEN CERTAINTY AND DOUBT, A MIND IS TRANSFORMED

Before my time at university, I struggled to articulate the principles of apartheid and to understand why black people were forced to live in a segregated society. My upbringing and community had instilled in me a certain way of seeing the world, a form of implicit knowledge that was so deeply ingrained it felt like second nature, or a "social imaginary" as Charles Taylor would put it.[32] My faith and my beliefs were intertwined with *apartheid*, and I could not imagine my God outside the confines of apartheid policies and theology. Apartheid was the theological integration of the affective and cognitive aspects of my faith. At Johannesburg University, I was able to delve deeper into the biblical exegesis and theological

---

31. Van Jaarsveld, *Afrikaners*, 25.
32. See Taylor, "What Is a 'Social Imaginary'?," 23–30.

system that shaped my beliefs, and to turn my implicit understanding into a more focused, conscious knowledge. In the words of Michael Polanyi, my tacit knowledge had become my focal knowledge[33] and doctrine.

As a young and ambitious theological student, I was embarking on a journey of intellectual and theological exploration. My education was not limited to the intricacies of apartheid theology, but also explored the highly regarded principles of modernity and its grip on twentieth-century theology. The modernist approach to theological education emphasized a meticulous examination of the underlying foundations of our beliefs. Not all beliefs were created equal though, as the sovereignty, impassibility, and righteousness of God were considered more important than his compassion, creativity, and grace. This rigidity of beliefs, like a house of cards, made it imperative for every truth to stand in precise order. If a single principle was seen to be in error, the whole structure was at risk of collapse. What I believed to be my pristine theological system would soon face disruption.

In September 1979, a delegation of British MPs visited South Africa, which included David Owen, who was invited to speak at the Rand Afrikaans University. However, as students, we were informed that Owen refused to visit our campus unless he was accompanied by the newly appointed bishop of Cape Town, Desmond Tutu. Even more disturbingly, he insisted that Tutu be allowed to address the students in attendance. Until this point in my life, I had not had a conversation with an African man, and I had certainly never been addressed by one. Additionally, Tutu's reputation for provoking political turmoil, his reported support for communism, and his sympathy for the banned African National Congress roused me to join those who sought to disrupt his lecture. In my mind he was certainly only a Christian in name, and his opinions would poison our minds. But within moments of taking the stage, Tutu captivated me with his charming charisma, sharp wit, and fearless spirit. His words were both challenging and invigorating, and, despite his small stature, he reared as a giant and valiant depository of truth. Desmond Tutu's lecture that day exposed the glaring discrepancies between the rhetoric and the reality of apartheid. I felt as though a veil was torn from my eyes. It was as if Morpheus's words in *The Matrix* trilogy had come to

---

33. Polanyi, *Tacit Dimension*.

life: "There's something wrong in your world, and you don't know what it is. But you can feel it like a splinter in your mind, driving you mad."[34]

Through Archbishop Tutu's piercing assessment of the injustices of apartheid, I received my first shame-stained glimpse into the suffering of those whom this theo-political system oppressed. Tutu spoke of the immense distress faced by millions of indigenous Africans who were forced into poverty-stricken ghettos and exploited as cheap labor. Tutu shared his firsthand experiences visiting these areas. I particularly recall his recounting a heart-wrenching story of a young girl who described her companions filling their stomachs with water when food ran short.

It suddenly seemed unforgivable to think that people were starving in a country overflowing with record crop surpluses, all in the name of God. It was as if I could see these people for the first time. I longed for them to be safe and secure. The shift in me was not in my mind, but in my heart. I could no longer provide a theological justification for my thoughts. My rational resistance waned as his words opened my ears and my heart. I sensed that something was wrong, before I could make sense of my new realization. From that day forward, my life took a dramatic turn as my affections began to shift, and I found myself in a state of personal liminality. It was as if I had received a new wristwatch and I was once again mesmerized, not so much by time but by the spaces between the seconds.

I do not want to jump ahead of myself. Still, after the encounter with Bishop Tutu, I began to notice racism in myself, my family, friends, and every aspect of society, including the church. I remember one lazy Sunday afternoon in early 1980, when the screeching tires and the ominous sound of crushing metal disturbed our peace, drawing my family out onto our front lawn. As the dust settled, we noticed two cars involved in a collision. One car, driven by a big Afrikaner man, had clearly forced the other off the road. Adrenaline pumping through our Sunday legs, we rushed over to the accident scene. I have never forgotten what I saw there. The Afrikaner man was physically assaulting the African driver of a badly damaged car. I knew him to be a police officer from high school, although he was in plain clothes at the time. He had smashed the window and was dragging the badly injured body of his victim through the window, shouting: "You must learn to obey the white man, *kaffir*."[35] As soon

---

34. See Lawrence, *Like a Splinter in Your Mind*, for a beautiful exploration of this idea.

35. The origin of the word is Kafir in Arabic and it literally means one who conceals or who is an unbeliever. In the South African context it was used as a racial slur.

as the police arrived, the victim of this crime was cuffed and bundled into the back of the mortuary vehicle, which, for some reason, served as the police vehicle that day. I insisted that we report the off-duty policeman's behavior, which we did, but after a high-ranking policeman's visit to our home later that week, we never spoke of the incident again. But I knew then that there was something seriously wrong with my world; I had seen it firsthand.

After another few years of university, I received a scholarship to study theology in the United States of America. While I will need to return to this story later, it is sufficient to say that during this time, I had to face my own racism head-on. After our return from Cleveland, Tennessee, and my national military service as a non-combatant, we decided to move to the Western Cape. It was a radical move; we chose to embrace change by adopting English as our first language. I refused to serve in the military, a stance that could bring me into immediate and hostile conflict with the authorities. And I accepted an invitation to teach theology first at Chaldo Bible Institute, the college for so-called colored students of the Full Gospel Church of God in South Africa. After eighteen months, I joined the faculty of the Cape Evangelical Bible Institute on the Cape Flats in Athlone.

BETWEEN LOOKING FOR ANSWERS AND NOT FINDING IT, WE LEARN TO DO THEOLOGY

Under apartheid, the Cape Flats was one of the notorious ghettos, liminal spaces of poverty and suffering that Archbishop Tutu spoke about so passionately. At this interracial college—illegal at the time under apartheid law—I found myself once more positioned as the boy in the middle, surrounded by forces poised to strike from all directions at any given moment. I was fortunate to have as a mentor an empathetic black principal, Allen Jansen. Through his guidance and the support of my colleagues and students, I was able to develop a deeper understanding of theology and its power to transform human hearts. They taught me to practice theology from the inside out, rather than from the top down. Through our shared experiences of pain, oppression, and resilience, I learned to appreciate the beauty of diverse perspectives and to honor the rich cultural heritage that makes up our communities. My life transformed, and I am forever grateful for the lessons I learned and the relationships I formed during my time at this remarkable institution.

From the campus, I witnessed the brutal realities of the apartheid system, watching armored military vehicles storm the school just across the way, shooting at the families and friends of our students. I saw young people taking to the streets, stoning cars and expressing their anger and frustration through acts of violence. It was a challenging environment, but it taught me lasting lessons and gave me an intimate understanding of the difficulties faced by those whom the pitiless apartheid regime brutalized in turn.

At this college, I learned that good theology starts with reordered affections—the love *of* God, love *for* God, and love for our fellow human beings, regardless of their race or background. Here I was introduced to the words of Lloyd Alexander, the author of many beloved children's books, who once said, "We learn more from searching for answers to questions and not finding them, than from finding the answers themselves."[36] This was a turning point for me. I realized that the best way to approach theology is not by seeking to impose our own answers and beliefs, but by asking questions with open hearts and minds.

Our emotions often prompt our actions before rational thoughts do. When faced with danger, we instinctively respond based on gut reactions, making decisions that can impact our lives significantly. This raises the question: What if we approached theology with the same insight, putting our heart, emotions, and affections at the center of our theological pursuits? Jesus himself spoke about the importance of love and the ordering of our affections, instructing us to love God, our neighbors, and ourselves. As theologians we ought to display competence in our doctrines and actions through Christian practices. But in my experience, we often overlook our affections as if they have no contribution to make. If we do live in liminality, this could be a serious oversight when our senses are heightened, and our affections could mean the difference between life and death.

In uncertainty, we can walk the walk of doing theology in a room half-lit. But we do not practice alone. The Holy Spirit as a divine advocate promises us help to make sense of both the physical and the metaphysical. We do not engage in theology only as rational beings capable of theoretical formulations. We do not turn to theology as beings capable only

---

36. Alexander, *Book of Three*, 15.

of action in the here and now. We apply theology as living souls here on earth in union with God. We live in liminality, but the Holy Spirit walks with us through our days, surprises us with its rhythms, and dares us to try new steps and explore optional avenues. It invites us to find new integrations between our affective and cognitive relationships with God, so that our choice of modes of living can differ radically.

How could South African history have differed for the Dutch settlers, trekkers, generals, prime ministers, theologians of apartheid, and generations of South Africans? What if they and we in turn possessed sufficient courage to admit that our integration of the affective and cognitive connections with God was toxic? If we allow the Holy Spirit, who is the bond of love, to order our affections, we can trust God in the in-between spaces of life. If we had opened our minds to allow the Holy Spirit to lead us into universal rather than selective truth, we would have found that God, the ground of *our* being, was the ground of *all* being. Were not the Khoisan, the indigenous people of Africa, and the Dutch and British settlers all image bearers of God?

Theologically, we need the Holy Spirit to help animate our affections and cognition.

It will be helpful at this point to clarify how theology has battled over the centuries to integrate the affective and cognitive dimensions of faith and to measure what practical results it has achieved.

2

Head

THE PHILOSOPHER JAMES K. A. Smith once said, "We inhabit the world not primarily as thinkers or even believers, but as affective, embodied creatures who navigate life through our emotions and sensations."[1] It means that as human beings, we experience and interact with the world not primarily through our thoughts or beliefs, but rather through our emotions and physical sensations. Before exploring theological beliefs or acting on theological convictions, we long for God, to be at home with God. Stephen Wanta, a Walpiri leader in Australia, taught me about home in his language. He said that we are fully human when we are "at home-within."[2] We will need to return to the idea that as humans we are image bearers of God and our home is within him.

The early Christian church faithful found themselves embodied in an in-between state. In those initial days of the church, even when they hid behind locked doors, they knew that Jesus prayed that they would be in him and him in them. Jesus was no longer the external figure but an internal representation of attachment, the covenanting one.[3] Therefore, their theology was a daily act of devotion and heartfelt fellowship with the resurrected Jesus of their faith. Early Christians acquired their

1. Smith, *Desiring the Kingdom*, 47.
2. See Pawu-Kurlpurlurnu, Holmes, and Box, "Ngurra-kurlu," 7. "The Warlpiri word ngurra can mean 'camp,' 'home,' or 'residence.' Kurlu is a suffix meaning 'with,' 'having,' or 'about.' Ngurra-kurlu is therefore translated as 'about home,' 'with home,' and 'home within.'"
3. See chapter 1 where I have proposed that an attachment figure in theological terms is a covenanting one.

knowledge of God through communal practices of devotion that shaped their feelings, thoughts, and behaviors. They were at home with God, through Jesus, in the power of the Holy Spirit. Edward Farley calls this a *theology habitus*.[4]

BETWEEN HEART AND HEAD

The Greek term *habitus* refers to an ability acquired by habit.[5] Therefore, *theology habitus* describes theology as affective disposition, which refers to our emotional and intuitive responses to various experiences. It includes our emotions, feelings, attitudes, and values that shape our perception and response to the world. In the context of theology, affective disposition can therefore refer to our emotional response to God, such as love, reverence, awe, and gratitude. According to this view, theology is not simply a matter of acquiring knowledge or understanding but is also a continuing process of spiritual growth and transformation. It involves a personal relationship between the individual and God, and requires a way of being or habitual behavior of the whole person. We understand this habit as wisdom, which is the capacity to discern truth, to understand the nature of God, and to live in accordance with divine principles.[6]

While members of the early Christian community dedicated themselves to the apostles' teachings, fellowship, the breaking of bread, and prayer, they demonstrated those beliefs in their lives.[7] For these believers, their faith and their theology were not ends in themselves, but a means to attain a deeper understanding of God and to cultivate a closer relationship with God through Christ in the power of the Holy Spirit.

According to Farley, theology also has a second meaning. In addition to *habitus*, as affective dispositions that enables us to navigate competently within our normal habitat, to be at home, it can also refer

---

4. Farley, *Theologia*, 31. I agree with Farley when he observes that "it may seem misleading to speak of theology in the period of the first eleven centuries of Christianity. The term itself rarely occurs, and when it does it refers to pagan authors, like Orpheus, who dealt with religion." *Theologia*, 33. See also Farley, "Theology and Practice," 22.

5. *Habitus* is the Latin word for the Greek term ἕξις, or "habit."

6. Farley, *Theologia*, 23.

7. Fowler, *Faith Development and Pastoral Care*, 14.

to critical reflection[8]—a cognitive way of being.[9] He observes that the term "theology" was "appropriated from Hellenic philosophy by early Christianity, and its initial use did not differ significantly from that of Plato[10] and Aristotle."[11] Here we encounter theology early in Christian history as "*episteme*, a *scientia*, an act or cognitive disposition in which the self-disclosing God is grasped as disclosed."[12]

The two meanings of theology were therefore not contradictory since we can describe theology in essence as both an affective and epistemic disposition toward God. In other words, in these early days, theology was an affective disposition or posture of the whole person that was also cognitively and insightfully disposed toward attending to knowing a dutiful understanding of God. This means that theology was not merely concerned with acquiring knowledge or understanding, but was rather a way of being in the world that is oriented toward living in accordance with God's will and purposes for humanity.

In the early days of the Christian faith, believers grappled with the weighty question of who could be trusted and who was a potential traitor. The painful memory of Judas Iscariot, the infamous betrayer who sold out Jesus, loomed over the community like a storm cloud. Despite being part of Jesus's inner circle of disciples, Judas was ultimately seduced and turned his back on his Lord. The Gospels portray Judas as being at odds with Jesus on multiple occasions, and his heart was no longer with the Christ he once followed so closely.

The story of Judas serves as a stark reminder that the workings of the human heart are a conundrum and that our affections can change. No one can ever be entirely sure what someone else is thinking or feeling; or that uncertainty could spell the difference between life and death for the early Christian community. The colonizing Romans were hostile to this new religion, and its believers faced persecution and even death if

---

8. Rational disposition, on the other hand, refers to our cognitive abilities, including our capacity for logical reasoning, critical thinking, analysis, and problem-solving. Rational disposition involves using reason and evidence to evaluate and understand various phenomena, including religious beliefs and practices. In the context of theology, rational disposition can refer to our ability to use reason and evidence to interpret religious texts, doctrines, and traditions.

9. Farley, *Theologia*, 22.

10. *Theologia* as a term dates back to Plato's *Politeia*. Plato, *Politeia*, II 379a in 375 BC. Here the term refers to a study of the nature of the divine.

11. Farley, *Theologia*, 22.

12. Farley, *Theologia*, 22.

discovered. With that in mind, the question of who belonged to the faith and who was an intruder became a matter of mortal importance.

But how could they know? If someone like Judas, so close to Jesus and so attached to his mission, could turn defector, who could a loyal follower trust? The underground community had to find a way to distinguish between the faithful and the suspect. Here, theology as Farley's *episteme*, a *scientia*, an act or cognitive disposition, provided great comfort and security. The accepted explanation of the faith became the basis for determining who belonged. If someone agreed with the core tenets of Christianity, then they could be considered part of the community. Of course, this was not foolproof, and there were undoubtedly those who hid their true beliefs or motives.

According to Westar scholars, diversity, encompassing a broad range of beliefs and practices, marked the first two centuries of the "Jesus movement."[13] In 1 Cor 11:18, Paul raises and expresses concern about divisions (*schismata*) in the church, whereas in 1 Cor 11:19, he speaks of factions (*haireseis*) but does not show the same level of disquiet. The reason for this difference could be that he is using these terms differently in each case. *Schismata* typically refers to a physical or material division such as a tear or a split. In this context, Paul may be referring to actual divisions within the church community, such as disagreements over leadership or worship practices. These divisions may have been causing practical issues and tensions within the community, which would explain Paul's concern. *Haireseis*, on the other hand, usually refers to differences of opinion or belief within a group rather than practical divisions. In this context, Paul may be acknowledging the existence of different groups or schools of thought within the church but not necessarily seeing them as a source of conflict or a threat to the unity of the movement.[14] He even suggests that factions may be necessary.

Paul is not advocating for division or conflict within the church. Instead, he may be acknowledging the reality that differences of opinion and belief are inevitable in any group and that these differences can

---

13. Christian Seminar started in 2013, to rewrite the history of the early Christian church. Scholars in the seminar have unraveled a number of disparate movements in the first four centuries before Christ. Using textual, epigraphic, and archaeological evidence, they aim to uncover the connections between these disparate movements and draw conclusions about the nature and development of early Christianity as a whole. In 2021, these religious historians published their first major book, the best-selling publication by Erin Vearncombe et al., *After Jesus, before Christianity*.

14. See Eph 4:3.

serve a constructive purpose. By recognizing and engaging with different perspectives and beliefs, the community can better discern what is genuine and true. In fact, Paul may be suggesting that the existence of schools of thought can lead to greater clarity and conviction among those who hold a particular belief or position. When debate demands people explain and defend their beliefs in the face of opposition, they may gain a refined and strengthened understanding of their values and their place in the community.

Despite their diverse interpretations of Jesus's teachings and the significance of his life and death, early Christians' shared affection for Jesus Christ as a savior and teacher of wisdom initially united them. But as the faith became more organized and hierarchical, standard sets of beliefs and practices won preference "over keeping the bond of peace."[15] This led to the creation of orthodoxy and the condemnation of heresy.

Heresy was no longer a school of argument, but a fixed and definitive set of beliefs that contradicted what had become the mainstream view. The search for orthodoxy—the correct and accepted opinion about Jesus—became more urgent in the third and fourth centuries.[16] Theologians such as Tertullian and Augustine stand out among those who sought to create a clear and distinct set of beliefs that would separate orthodoxy from heresy and provide a unified framework for Christian thought and practice.

BETWEEN INFORMAL AND FORMAL

The emergence of this fixed and definitive set of beliefs was closely tied to the institutionalization of Christianity and the development of hierarchical structures of authority within the church. Inevitably those who interpreted the teachings of Jesus differently from the standard view at that time began to emerge. They were now labeled as heretics and their ideas were often viewed as a threat to the established order, leading to their excommunication, or worse.

Theology was not simply a matter of personal belief or spiritual *habitus*, but also a scholarly pursuit aimed at protecting the truth about Jesus and his teachings. This truth was seen as universal and

---

15. See Vearncombe et al., *After Jesus*, ch. 13.
16. Placher, *History of Christian Theology*, 44.

unchanging—believed everywhere, always, and by all.[17] It produced an urgency to protect the integrity of the faith, ensuring it was transmitted authentically from one generation to the next.

As the church grappled with questions of orthodoxy, in time it agreed on a list of authoritative sacred texts, began to form creeds, and began to create a clergy that served under the oversight of other spiritual leaders.[18] This allowed the church to establish a hierarchy of authority and to guarantee consistent interpretation of doctrine. Creeds were to provide clear and consistent understanding of Christian faith in propositional statements. The propositions were considered essential to their sense of identity and served as a unifying force for Christians all over the world.

While credal statements today may sound like mere propositions that we agree with intellectually, this was not the experience of these early believers. Creeds were (and still are) more than mere affirmations of doctrine. They are an exquisite blend of the two meanings of theology, reflecting an affective and cognitive disposition toward God. To proclaim "I believe" as part of a creed is to make a profound commitment.[19] It is a pledge to love and serve God above all else, and to be faithful to his teachings. The intellectual concord between self and doctrine is rooted in a deep love for God, and it is this love and loyalty that sustains the faith over time. Creeds are the artifacts that faith communities created by integrating their affection for and knowledge of God.

In addition to creeds, the need for formal leadership such as bishops and presbyters became more important as the church expanded over the globe. The leadership structures of the church were intended to oversee its administration and ensure that its teachings and practices remained consistent across different congregations and regions. However, the history of the early church shows that the exercise of power and authority could sharpen to a double-edged sword, and that the appointment of leaders could sometimes lead to unintended consequences and conflicts.[20]

---

17. Many years later Vincent of Lerins, in the *Vincentian Canon*, AD 434, defined catholicity (think orthodoxy) as *Quod ubique, quod semper, quod ab omnibus* ("holding to that which has been believed everywhere, always and by all").

18. MacCulloch, *Christianity*, 127–28.

19. Cantwell Smith, *Faith and Belief*, 13.

20. These included controversies over the requirements for gentile converts to Christianity, the existence of secret knowledge in Gnosticism, the full divinity of Jesus in Arianism, the validity of sacraments in Donatism, and the role of grace in salvation in Pelagianism. These conflicts were often bitter and prolonged, but contributed to

BETWEEN WOMEN AND MEN

Before we proceed to discuss the emergence of leadership, we should note that there was also a growing belief that orthodoxy rested in the hands of the male followers of Jesus. Women were pivotal to the spread of Christianity and the development of Christian theology in the early church. But as the church became more organized, women's voices were slowly silenced and their contributions were pushed aside.

The Nag Hammadi discoveries provide evidence of the existence of alternative and diverse Christian traditions in the early centuries of the church.[21] The texts included in this find give us a glimpse into the different beliefs and practices of early Christians, including those of women. For instance, in the Gospel of Mary Magdalene, we find Mary Magdalene as a prominent disciple of Jesus, teaching, challenging, and encouraging the followers of Jesus as one of the apostles. In the fragment of the Gospel that has survived, Mary delivers a message of reinforcement to the disciples following Jesus's crucifixion. But we read that several of the male disciples, including Peter and Andrew, express skepticism about Mary's teachings and question her authority to speak on spiritual matters. However, other disciples, such as Levi, defend Mary and acknowledge the value of her insights. In the Gospel of Mary Magdalene, we receive a closer interpretation of the inner tensions through the words of Levi:

> Peter, you have always been hot-tempered, and now we see you repudiating a woman, just as our adversaries do. Yet if the Teacher held her worthy, who are you to reject her? Surely the Teacher knew her very well, for he loved her more than us. Therefore let us atone, and become fully human [Anthropos],so that the Teacher can take root in us. Let us grow as he demanded of us, and walk forth to spread the gospel, without trying to lay down any rules and laws other than those he witnessed.[22]

Jesus's teachings and actions were radical for his day, and he challenged many aspects of patriarchy that were taking hold of the church. The transformation of Mary of Magdalene into a penitent prostitute was

---

the development of theological and ecclesiastical structures that sometimes helped to clarify the early Christian church's beliefs and practices.

21. The Nag Hammadi discoveries refer to a collection of ancient texts that were found in 1945 near the town of Nag Hammadi in upper Egypt. The discovery included thirteen leather-bound codices (books) containing over fifty different texts, some of which were previously unknown or thought to be lost.

22. In Vearncombe et al., *After Jesus, before Christianity*, 81.

sealed in the sixth century when Pope Gregory the Great declared in a homily in Rome that Mary Magdalene, Luke's unnamed sinner, and Mary of Bethany were in fact the same person. While it is not the aim of this book, it is important to note that the stifling of Mary Magdalene might be the first in the church's history, but it certainly was not the last time a woman would be silenced. I will comment on this from time to time in the following pages.

BETWEEN THEOLOGY AND PHILOSOPHY

But back to the bishops, who were exclusively male. They consulted biblical teaching, the writings of the apostles, and the apostolic fathers to resolve conflicts and defend Christianity. What is perhaps most surprising is that they also turned to philosophy for answers.[23] Justin Martyr, a Christian apologist in the second century, believed he had discovered the perfect philosophy in Christ after studying various contemporary belief systems.[24] He thought that philosophy was important because it carried the "seed of the divine Logos," providing a "glimpse of the truth."[25] Justin's writings reflect his love for true philosophy and are still helpful to students of theology. However, his love for Christ is even more evident as he admits that his affection for the prophets and followers of Jesus took hold of him while he was pondering the Scripture.

Clement of Alexandria also believed that philosophy and the law of Moses served as guides to lead people to Christ. But they were not teachers of fact, rather of wisdom and virtue, which was only possible through a genuine relationship with Christ. For Origen, Jesus, the anointed one of God, is present in all beings and serves as an intermediary between God and the world.[26] In other words, when we put our faith in Jesus, and set our hearts and minds on Christ the eternal *logos* (Word), we gain access to the sum total of all reason and truth, which enables us to understand and live in accordance with God's will.

---

23. As we have already noted, earliest reference to *theologia* in reference to the critical reflection on the nature of God can be found in Plato *Politeia* II 379a, written in ca. 375 BC.

24. Justin, *Dialogue with Trypho*, 3:15.

25. Justin, *Dialogue with Trypho*, 3: 15.

26. For an in-depth discussion see Todorovska, "Concepts of the Logos in Philo of Alexandria," 37–56.

The second-century apologists were ardent advocates of their faith and believed that philosophical argumentation could elucidate and support their love for Christ. However, Tertullian, whom we mentioned before and who was a contemporary of these apologists, was wary of the influence of Greek philosophical categories and concepts on the church's teachings. In his famous question, "What are the similarities between Athens and Jerusalem? What do the Academy and the Church have in common?," he challenged the compatibility of philosophical inquiry with religious truth.

Despite this, the earliest versions of the Apostle's Creed likely met Tertullian's standards by avoiding philosophical language. However, as the church faced new challenges and theological debates, theologians increasingly relied on sophisticated philosophical concepts and arguments to clarify the nature of God as Father, Son, and Spirit. Tertullian would have struggled with the Nicene Creed's reliance on philosophical terminology, if he was still alive to attend the Council of Nicaea in AD 325.[27]

BETWEEN EAST AND WEST

As the early church grew and theological debates became more complex and political, the need for theological instruction increased. This led to the establishment of schools such as the one founded by Augustine in Hippo, to teach the principles of Christianity and provide a platform for theological debates. These schools provided a structure for teaching and learning and they also served as a meeting ground for theological ideas. This was important in helping the early church to solidify its beliefs and formulate doctrines that would shape the course of Christianity for centuries to come.

Theologians such as Gregory of Nyssa recognized the importance of catechetical teaching and worked to expound the foundational doctrines of the Nicene Creed. In his *Catechetical Orations*, Gregory explained the intricacies of the Trinity, using the term *perichoresis*[28] to convey the dy-

---

27. While Greek philosophical concepts and categories found their way into the church's creeds, Constantine was eager to resolve disputes between fighting factions in the church. After the first failed attempt to unify the church in AD 313, he summoned a council in Nicaea where he himself introduced the Son as of "one substance," *homoousios*, with the Father, and not of "similar substance," *homoiousios*, as Arians and their followers contended. This sparked endless debates and many more councils and the matter was settled at the second council of Nicaea in AD 325, which then sparked further questions about the humanity of Christ and the nature of the Holy Spirit. The details of the various debates of the fourth century extend far beyond the scope of my argument here.

28. Torrance, *Christian Doctrine of God*, 198. We will return to this term in chapter

namic and reciprocal relationship between the Father, Son, and Spirit. These were not simple concepts, and most believers were not schooled in philosophy, so there was a great need for works like "On Instructing the Unlearned," written in approximately AD 400, or Augustine's *Handbook of Faith, Hope, and Love*, in which he provided answers to the questions of Laurentius. These works served as invaluable resources for instructing the unlearned and reinforcing the essential doctrines of the faith, ultimately shaping the course of Christian theology for centuries to come.

Yet the pursuit of theology in Christianity still involved more than just intellectual tasks; it required a personal connection to God as Father, Son, and Holy Spirit. While doctrine and philosophy could help clarify divine concepts, they served only as a means to an end. The ultimate goal was then and is now to cultivate an intimate relationship with God and experience a profound sense of connection and purpose in life with God. For instance, Athanasius of Alexandria believed the heart is the locus of communion with God.[29] In the same tradition, Basil believed that prayer "imprints a clear idea of God in the soul."[30] The lover of God, says Basil, withdraws into God. Even Augustine of Hippo, who is perhaps best known for his intellect, did not completely neglect the role of the heart. In his *Confessions*, he famously wrote, "The thought of you stirs us so deeply that we cannot be content unless we praise you, because you made us for yourself and our hearts find no peace until they rest in you."[31]

Augustine is often considered the "father of Western theology." His ideas on original sin, grace, predestination, and women, among others, have had a lasting impact on Christian theology and have shaped the way many Western Christians understand and approach their faith. Augustine's works, such as *Confessions* and *City of God*, are intellectual and rational monuments in theology that helped to shape the Western tradition of theology, Western philosophy, and intellectual history.

Reading Aristotle's works heavily influenced Augustine's approach to theology, especially his emphasis on reason and intellect. In his view, reason was a powerful tool for understanding God's nature and the

---

6. Miroslav Volf explains that *perichoresis* is the view that "every divine person as a subject, the other persons also indwell; all mutually permeate one another, though in so doing they do not cease to be distinct persons." Volf, *After Our Likeness*, 209.

29. Anatolios, *Athanasius*, 46.

30. Basil, "Letter 2," §4.

31. Augustine, *Confessions*, 1.1.5. I have changed the singular pronoun to make the statement more inclusive.

universe he created. Therefore, human reason could help us understand God's existence, as well as interpret Scripture and doctrine. Many scholars and theologians adopted his ideas, and his works became foundational texts for the study of theology in the West. The intellectual and philosophical framework of Western theology is largely attributed to Augustine's emphasis on reason and the integration of Christian doctrine with classical philosophy. In particular, during the medieval era, Augustine's knowledge of Aristotle and emphasis on reasoning in theology had a profound effect on the church at that time.

As we have seen, in the early centuries of Christianity the church fathers used Greek philosophy, particularly Platonic and Aristotelian thinking, as a means of understanding and articulating Christian doctrine. However, the Eastern and Western churches had different philosophical influences, which led to divergent theological views. The Eastern church, influenced by the Greek-speaking East, emphasized the mystical and contemplative aspects of Christianity, and relied heavily on the philosophy of the Greek church fathers. The Western church, on the other hand, was influenced by the Latin-speaking West and relied on the Neoplatonic philosophy of Augustine.

This philosophical divide contributed to several theological differences between the two churches. For example, the Eastern church emphasized the mystery and ineffability of God, while the Western church emphasized the rational understanding of God. Additionally, the Eastern church rejected the use of philosophical language in describing the holy Trinity, while the Western church relied on the Latin terms to describe the relationship between the Father, Son and Spirit.[32]

Rather than seeking a synthesis with philosophical traditions, Eastern churches in communion with the Patriarch of Constantinople looked to the apostolic fathers for guidance. They did not think rationalistic syllogisms were useful for understanding God's mysteries, and they were unwilling to let reason lead in matters of the heart, or to reduce mystery to words only. Simply put, they did not share the Western church's faith in rationalism. They preferred to let the heart have the final say.

---

32. *Filioque* is a Latin term that means "and the son." It refers to a phrase that was added to the Nicene Creed in the Western church, which asserts that the Holy Spirit proceeds from the Father and the Son. This addition was not accepted by the Eastern Orthodox Church, which holds that the Holy Spirit proceeds from the Father alone. The *filioque* controversy was one of the theological disagreements that contributed to the Great Schism between the Eastern and Western churches in AD 1054.

These and other differences ultimately led to the Great Schism. On a summer afternoon in AD 1054, Cardinal Humbert and two other representatives of the pope entered the Church of the Holy Wisdom in Constantinople during a church service and placed a sealed papal document known as a "bull" on the altar. It declared Constantinople's patriarch and his associates excommunicated, no longer in communion with the church, and no longer permitted to partake in the sacraments. The message was clear: The churches of the East and West were no longer in communion. Christians now belonged to two different churches and they no longer ate at the same table.

The distance between the churches grew wider in the eleventh century as Western Christian armies reconquered parts of Europe. At the same time, ancient manuscripts, including Aristotle's works in Latin, were discovered, and made available to Western scholars. In his *Metaphysics*, he observed that theology (*theologikē*) or metaphysics contained knowledge of non-physical and divine origins. It was the pinnacle of all theoretical knowledge and even surpassed mathematics and physics.[33] His philosophical synthesis presented a logical view of life independent of revelation. This caused a "crisis of conscience"[34] and a transition from the heart to the head in Christian theology.[35]

BETWEEN MONASTERY AND SCHOOL

So intense was the struggle been the head and the heart, that Anselm of Canterbury, a monk of the eleventh century, prayed, "I do not seek to understand so that I may believe; but I believe so that I may understand."[36] Anselm still believed that faith preceded understanding, that it arose from the heart, and that the search for understanding followed. He was inspired to search for understanding because understanding required living faith, and living is loving faith.[37] For him it was still true that to say, "I believe," was to say, "I belove." So he prayed as one who understands that his best ideas about God were still as "one who looks in a glass darkly." "I do not try, Lord, to attain Your lofty heights," he declares, "because my

---

33. See Aristotle, *Metaphysica* F 1026a, 19; K 1064b, 3.
34. Cantor, *Civilization of the Middle Ages*, 358.
35. Fowler, *Faith Development*, 14.
36. Anselm, *Proslogium*, in Anselm, *Major Works*, 87.
37. Anselm, *Proslogium*, in Anselm, *Major Works*, 87.

understanding is in no way equal to it. But I desire to understand Your truth a little, that truth that my heart believes and loves."[38]

He was not alone, and many would follow the same path of theology *habitus*; for instance, Francis of Assisi, who emphasized poverty, humility, and service to others as central aspects of Christian discipleship. He saw love as the foundation of the Christian life, and believed that by loving and serving others, we can experience the love of God more deeply. We can easily add Bonaventure, Meister Eckhart, and Thomas à Kempis to the list of medieval theologians who prioritized their affection for God as they sought to make sense of how to be with God in this world.

During the medieval period, female theologians also made significant contributions to Christian thought and spirituality, but many of their works have been overlooked or forgotten.[39] Despite the challenges and barriers experienced by their gender, women such as Hildegard of Bingen left a legacy that continues to inspire people to consider their affective way of being in the world with God.

Mysticism and contemplative prayer, as well as the importance of love, humility, and detachment from worldly desires as a means of drawing closer to God, are common themes that emerge in the writings of many of these medieval female theologians. They also challenged patriarchal norms and power structures of the time. These theologians emphasized humility and self-denial as ways to draw closer to God and wrote about the unity of God's love and the interconnectedness of all things in creation. They also frequently recorded their personal encounters with God. Many of these theologians believed that our love for God should shape our thinking and inspire us to live virtuously. They frequently emphasized the importance of putting that love into action through compassionate service to others as the foundation of Christian life.

Peter Abelard would agree that it is beyond our ability to comprehend the depths of God's being. For him, it was a "matter of reason that God far exceeds what can come under human discussion or the powers of human intelligence."[40] Nevertheless, he also held the view that we could believe nothing unless we first understood it.[41] Unlike Anselm, Abelard

---

38. Anselm, *Proslogium*, in Anselm, *Major Works*, 87.

39. Julian of Norwich, Mechthild of Magdeburg, Hildegard of Bingen, Clare of Assisi, Teresa of Avila, Catherine of Genoa, Angela of Foligno, Margery Kempe, Gertrude the Great, and Hadewijch of Antwerp.

40. MacCallum, *Abelard's Christian Theology*, 68.

41. *Nec credi posse aliquid nisi primitus intelligetis* is perhaps a direct disputation of

believed that theology was not faith seeking understanding but rather rational arguments seeking satisfaction through the church's claims on faith. He lamented in *Sic et Non* that some statements, even those of the holy fathers, appeared to differ from and even contradict one another.[42] Theology's task was to resolve these contradictions and to confirm or reject these assertions.[43] As a scholastic philosopher, he believed in the use of reason to understand theology and emphasized the importance of logic and rational argument in theological discussions.

Abelard believed that faith and reason were not opposed, but rather complemented each other. However, he believed that the mind took precedence over the heart, and that theology was no longer a matter of internal comfort but rather intellectual satisfaction and rational certainty.[44] Abelard felt we found truth when human reason and Christian revelation reconciled. Therefore, unlike Anselm, he believed that we needed to scrutinize faith with human rationality before we could believe it.[45] For Abelard, knowledge and not affection leads the way, and, specifically, theoretical knowledge was the path to faith. He judged we should deploy reason to analyze and comprehend theological concepts rather than relying solely on faith.

Hildegard of Bingen was a vocal critic of Peter Abelard. She professed that divine love is an all-encompassing force that pervades all of creation and unites everything into a harmonious whole. She criticized Abelard's approach to theology, which she saw as overly intellectual and disconnected from the spiritual and mystical aspects of faith. She argued that the use of reason alone could not fully capture the divine mysteries, and that a more holistic approach was needed, incorporating both reason and intuition.

However, Abelard's approach prevailed. In time he revolutionized theology in the West and his method became the standard. For instance, Peter Lombard (1150s), the bishop of Paris, used the *Sic et Non* to reconcile doctrinal differences in his four-volume collection called the *Sentences*. This work became the standard theological text for students throughout medieval Europe, and a commentary on the *Sentences* was

---

Anselm's motto, *fides quaerens intellectum*. See Nielsen, "Peter Abelard and Gilbert of Poitiers," 107.

42. Abelard, *Sic et Non*, "Prologue."
43. Brown, "Medieval Theology," 134. See Clanchy, *Abelard*, 5.
44. Abelard and Heloise, *Letters of Abelard and Heloise*, 78.
45. For a detailed account of this history, see Marenbon, *Philosophy of Peter Abelard*, 26–32.

required to become a master of theology.[46] During this period the practical and theoretical strands of Scripture were regarded as separate, with the *Sentences* serving as authoritative statements on the latter. As a result, a clear hierarchy emerged in which biblical scholars were seen as practical and less academic, while sententiaries (or aphorists) were the true authorities on theology because they could provide commentary on Lombard's *Sentences*. Despite initial resistance to Lombard's approach, the momentum soon swung to the sententiaries who were considered the experts in dealing with the theoretical complexities of theology. As Abelard's theological method took hold, the stage was set for theology to take its place as an intellectual discipline rather than a habit of the heart.

The awakening of the high Middle Ages in Europe, particularly in the twelfth and thirteenth centuries, saw a renewed interest in classical learning and a revival of scholarship and innovation, characterized by a focus on reason, empirical observation, and the pursuit of knowledge for its own sake. Its emergence paved the way for the development of modern science and philosophy, as well as the promotion of universities as centers of learning. The church and the university recognized that the European development was irreversible and that they could harness reason to advance orthodox religion.[47]

BETWEEN THEOLOGY AND THE SCIENCES

Thomas Aquinas, a professor at the University of Paris and a student of Abelard, emerged as a formidable theologian at this time. He sought to understand God's creation and to pursue knowledge as a noble end in itself. In the mid-thirteenth century, the University of Paris declared theology the Queen of Sciences, with a carefully crafted curriculum that aimed to promote personal transformation through mental exercises. Students began their studies with natural philosophy, followed by mathematics, before delving into transcendental and immutable issues, thus creating a hierarchy that placed theology above all other studies.[48]

---

46. Scholars who read lectures, or commented, on the *Sentences* of Peter Lombard. See Asztalos, "Faculty of Theology," 409. She explains that those biblical scholars could graduate to become sententiary scholars who lectured on the *Sentences* of Peter Lombard.

47. Rubenstein, *Aristotle's Children*, 285.

48. See Zakai, "Rise of Modern Science," 126.

Aquinas famously identified two types of science, the first the product of the "light of the intellect," while the second relied on "principles made known by the light of a higher science, namely the science of God."[49] And since theology was about God, it was speculative and not practical.[50] It was also not a theology that started as a habit of the heart. Instead, his scientific method of learning and applying theology relied on the human ability to formulate propositions, identify logical objections against and arguments in favor of the proposition, and the human capacity to make rational decisions.[51] John Duns Scotus disagreed with his contention that theology was a science. For him, the aim of theology, or sacred doctrine, was not scientific knowledge, as we have seen from Aquinas. Instead, theology developed the human mind's ability to love God. He believed that the more we learned about God, the more we would incline toward loving him.[52] Giles of Rome also disagreed with Aquinas, contending theology was neither speculative nor practical but rather an affective science. He is fond of quoting Augustine, who said: "You have made us for yourself, and our hearts find no peace until they rest in you."[53] Scientific theology did not satisfy the restlessness of the human heart.

This is not to suggest that Aquinas had no place for affection in his theology. The opposite is perhaps true. He saw love as the source of all human action, and argued that the highest form of love is love of God, which leads us to seek our ultimate happiness and fulfillment in him. But when we compare his approach to Hildegard, we can see that he prioritized the cognitive over the affective way of being with God in the world.

By way of contrast, Aquinas primarily used reason and rational arguments in his theological writings, whereas Hildegard relied more heavily on mystical experiences and revelations from God to inform her understanding of theology. While Aquinas believed that emotions such as love and desire were important for experiencing God's love and grace, he emphasized the importance of using reason to control and moderate

49. Thomas Aquinas, *Summa Theologiae* Q1, art. 2, in Pegis, *Saint Thomas Aquinas*, 6.

50. Thomas Aquinas, *Summa Theologiae* I^a q. 1 a. 4 s. c. "*Non ergo est scientia practica sed magis speculativa.*" I translate this as "Therefore it is not a practical science, but rather a speculative science."

51. See Grant, *God and Reason in the Middle Ages*, ch. 5, for a description of the scientific approach of the scientific method of scholasticism. Aquinas followed this nearly step by step. His insistence that the decision was subject to church dictates is perhaps less scientific.

52. Cross, *Duns Scotus*, 9 (*Ordinatio* prologue, part 5, qq. 1–2).

53. Augustine, *Confessions*, 21 (bk. 1.1).

our emotions so that they do not lead us astray. In contrast, Hildegard saw emotions as a vital part of the Christian life, and believed that they could help us to connect with God and experience the fullness of his love.

BETWEEN CATHOLIC AND PROTESTANT

But a larger split was looming again, and the theological pendulum was on the move once more. The renaissance of the fourteenth century brought renewed interest in Aristotle's teacher, Plato, who maintained that there was more to the world than we can see or experience. With advances in science and technology, humans could now see what was previously invisible. The telescope and microscope pointed to new realms formerly beyond the reach of the human eye. Humans realized that reality was greater than objects in plain sight. It was more mysterious, complex, and wonderful, and humans were not at the center of this world. With this came a renewed appetite for ideas and scholarship. The invention of eyeglasses and the movable type printing press created a whole new generation of restless scholars.

The church was also restless. Academically astute but morally corrupt priests often led congregations. This is the context in which the German monk Martin Luther made his appearance. As a man of his times he too wanted to return to the earliest sources. But in his case he chose not Plato but the Bible. Luther believed Scripture, not the church, was the final authority, and that by God's grace people received salvation through faith. Deliverance for Luther was a relationship with Jesus who was able to bring us into a right relationship with God our Father. So, the purpose of human life, of all that we say and do, even in theology, was to the "glory of God alone."

The reformation began in AD 1517 when Martin Luther published his *Ninety-Five Theses*. They criticized certain practices of the Catholic Church, among them the authority of the pope and the church's teachings on issues such as the role of faith and works in salvation, the interpretation of the Bible, and the use of sacraments. They rejected certain Catholic practices, including the veneration of saints, the use of Latin in worship, and the celibacy of the clergy. Luther's ideas spread quickly, and other reformers, such as John Calvin and Ulrich Zwingli, also emerged, each with their own ideas for reforming the church. This resulted in the second divorce known as the Protestant Reformation.

During its early stages Reformation theologians sought to establish a clearer understanding of biblical authority to undergird their commitment to *sola scriptura* (Scripture alone). In the medieval Roman Catholic Church, the authority of Scripture was understood to emerge from not only the Bible itself but also the interpretation of the church's *magisterium* (teaching authority) and accumulated tradition. Luther rejected this understanding and insisted on the sole authority of Scripture. He believed that the Bible contained all necessary truth for salvation and that it was the ultimate source of authority for Christians. For him the Bible was the cradle that held Christ, meaning that the Bible was the story of God's plan to bring salvation to sinful humanity through the life, death, and resurrection of Jesus Christ.

One of the most important and frequently overlooked aspects of the Protestant Reformation of the sixteenth century was its emphasis on the renewal of the heart, or biblical *pietas*, which was one of John Calvin's major themes. Piety is the correct disposition of the human heart toward God. Theology is the study of who and what God is, and it leads to attitudes and behavior that please him. Calvin remarked, "I call 'piety' that reverence joined with love of God which the knowledge of his benefits induces."[54] For him, "The whole life of Christians ought to be a sort of practice of godliness."[55] Theology comes from the heart and renews the human heart that finds its rest in God.

Theological differences between Catholics and Protestants further divided communities and nations, leading to a growing sense of unrest. During this period, science emerged as a new source of certainty and stability. As people looked for answers and explanations for the world around them, science offered a novel way of understanding the natural world based on empirical observation and experimentation. It paved the way for the scientific revolution of the seventeenth century, transforming how people thought about the natural world and leading to many significant advances in practical knowledge and technology.

BETWEEN REASON AND REVELATION

For a philosopher like John Locke, reason no longer had to seek the permission of the church and its beliefs to express itself freely. While the

---

54. Calvin, *Institutes*, 1.2.1.
55. Calvin, *Institutes*, 3.19.2.

church endured the uncertainty of its second divorce, science was building itself a cohesive and internally consistent system of thought empowered by reason and not beliefs. It promised certainty in a liminal world that had descended into theological chaos. So, Locke could assert with great confidence that "if anything shall be thought revelation which is contrary to the plain principles of reason, and the evident knowledge the mind has of its own clear and distinct ideas; there reason must be hearkened to, as to a matter within its province."[56] As this conviction grew, theology as a science superior to all other sciences became untenable.

According to Immanuel Kant, the eighteenth-century German philosopher, human reason is the source of the moral law that underpins our belief in God, our right to individual autonomy, and our hope for an afterlife. Theology was known as the Queen of all Sciences, and this honorific title was given because God was the subject of theology, but now Kant wryly observed, "in accordance with the fashion of the age, the queen proves despised on all sides."[57] In his *Critique of Pure Reason*, he makes a case that philosophy, not theology, should be "the bearer of Enlightenment rationality and a vindication of its right to freedom of expression, the right to have its members' rational arguments answered by rational arguments rather than by coercion or appeals to religious authority."[58] Now, the stage was set for theology to reinvent itself once more, but this time as a science among sciences. This new form of theology was instrumental in the establishment of theology faculties at Western universities and provided the intellectual foundation for modernism.[59]

Protestant scholasticism that emerged in the early stages of the Protestant Reformation was the church's response to the growing influence of science. This movement aimed to clarify and solidify the doctrine of *sola scriptura*, which is the idea that the Bible is the only authority in matters of faith and doctrine. To achieve this, Protestant theologians sought to establish a clearer understanding of the authority of the Bible, elevating its divine origin above its human authorship and treating it as accurate in every detail. They saw the Bible as a storehouse of revealed propositions and sought to systematize its teachings into a coherent

---

56. Locke, *Essay concerning Human Understanding*, bk. 4, ch. 18, sect. 4.941.
57. Kant, *Critique of Pure Reason*, 99.
58. Kant, *Critique of Pure Reason*, 25.
59. For more detail see Toward, *Protestant Theology*. I follow him closely in this section.

theological framework. As a result, theology came to be viewed as the attempt to establish a system of irrefutable doctrine based on the teachings of Scripture.

BETWEEN SPECIALIZATION AND INTEGRATION

In 1810, Friedrich D. E. Schleiermacher, a philosopher, theologian, and university leader, published *On the Establishment of the Theological Faculty*, which provided a blueprint for the faculty of theology at the University of Berlin. Despite opposition from some who believed theology had no place at the university, and others who suggested it be housed in the faculty of philosophy, Schleiermacher argued that since the Lutheran Church in Germany was a state church, and the government indirectly employed pastors, it made sense to conduct their training at the university. However, since graduates would work in churches, their training needed to be in the faculty of theology.

A few years later, in his *Brief Outline of the Study of Theology*, he clarified that the purpose of the faculty of theology was to train clergy,[60] and the various theological sciences—biblical studies, church history, dogmatics, and practical theology—were discrete academic fields. He proposed that professors of the Bible, history, and dogmatics teach practical theology together, reasoning that this would integrate theoretical knowledge with practical application. However, this attempt at amalgamation resulted in specialization, with each discipline developing a primary loyalty to the secular field from which it drew its methods and legitimacy. As specialization continued, professional guilds of scholars in various theological disciplines generated both confidence in and isolation from one another.[61] Each discipline developed its own methodology, assumptions, and modes of inquiry, which led to a fragmentation of theology as a unified field of study.[62]

Theological disciplines, like other academic pursuits, relied on reason to construct rational arguments to support their claims to truth. This was possible because theology accepted the premise that God created a rational world and humans developed the tools required for scientific investigation. In this new world, the professors who taught theology were

---

60. Farley, "Theology and Practice," 25.
61. Farley, "Theology and Practice," 25.
62. Farley, "Theology and Practice," 25.

themselves primarily academics who had to produce scholarly works to gain academic recognition and so secure tenure.

This emphasis on academic scholarship rather than spiritual formation meant that while theological faculties were training students to be great thinkers, they were less attuned to an affective way of being with God in the world. Consequently, students who excelled in these academic environments were not necessarily the best candidates for ministry. In this fragmentation of theology,[63] theologians no longer felt they needed to believe and behave as if they were "holding God dear," as they made their way through liminality. This, in Schleiermacher's view, was the fragmentation of theology.[64]

In America, nineteenth-century Princeton theologians were worried about the challenges they faced with scientific developments and new forms of biblical criticism that emerged in their era in Europe. Prominent among them, Charles Hodge responded to these questions by developing a theological method that mirrored the empirical scientific approach. He believed that theology and science shared a common line of inquiry and patterned his work on uncovering theological facts in the Bible following the model of a scientist.[65] Hodge also assumed that the theological propositions he drew from the Bible stated universal facts, similar to how natural scientists of his time assumed that their scientific propositions represented globally recognized beliefs.

BETWEEN THEORY AND PRACTICE

The ground was fertile for systematic theology to emerge as a new normative genre of theology.[66] In response to the challenges of modernity, which called into question traditional religious beliefs and practices, a desire for a comprehensive and internally consistent system of theological thought and life arose.[67] While the systemization of theology was primarily a nineteenth- and twentieth-century phenomenon, we can trace the desire for a coherent system back to the reformers, the *Sentences*, the *Summa*, and even to the writings of some apostolic fathers. However, systematic

---

63. See Farley, *Theologia*, 99–124.
64. Taken from Farley, *Theologia*.
65. Hodge, *Systematic Theology*, 1:18.
66. Fowler, *Faith Development*, 14.
67. Farley, "Theology and Practice," 23.

theology now emerged as "a comprehensive, coherent, and contextual system."⁶⁸ "A theological system," says Paul Tillich, "is supposed to satisfy two basic needs: the statement of the truth of the Christian message and the interpretation of this truth for every new generation."⁶⁹ And so theology students in the early twentieth century, and clergy and academics, turned to the works of theologians such as Karl Barth, Emil Brunner, and Paul Tillich to find the answers to their theological questions.

According to Farley, systematic theology was now no longer a sub-discipline of theology; it was "simply the one, single science, on par with philosophy, rhetoric, and astronomy, with its object and proper method."⁷⁰ In his view, systematic theology took over the mantle as the queen of the theological disciplines. Other sub-fields of theology may have contributed to the construction of systematic theology. Systematic theology, however, used exegetical insights, archaeological findings, and historical timelines, and systematic theologians gathered practical applications as they constructed the system of thought. Systematic theology was as "scientific" as theology could ever hope to be.⁷¹

In South Africa, Afrikaner theologians, in the early twentieth century, also created a system of theological thought to justify support of apartheid. It is true that the architects of apartheid in South Africa drew upon theological ideas and interpretations to justify their policies, and some of those ideas and interpretations did originate in Europe. European Protestant theology, particularly the theology of Abraham Kuyper and the Dutch neo-Calvinist tradition, influenced many prominent South African theologians and church leaders. Among them were D. F. Malan and Hendrik Verwoerd, who were both prime ministers of South Africa.

Neo-Calvinism, which emphasized the sovereignty of God in all aspects of life, heavily influenced the theological system that supported apartheid in South Africa. This worldview held that God controls all things, including politics, economics, and culture, and that it is the

---

68. See Fackre, "Revival of Systematic Theology," 229–41 (esp. 230.) He describes the features of systematic theology as follows: For all the differences in perspective, what makes a systematics is fourfold: 1. comprehensiveness, the coverage of the standard places of Christian teaching; 2. coherence, a clear demonstration of the topics' interrelationships; 3. contextuality, the interpretation of the sweep of doctrine in terms of current issues and idiom; 4. conversation, a feature that marks classic and classical works engaging the whole spectrum of historical and contemporary points of view.

69. Tillich, *Systematic Theology*, 5.

70. Farley, "Theology and Practice," 23.

71. Hall, "Does Systematic Theology Have a Future?," 253–56.

church's role to transform society according to God's plan. These theologians of apartheid believed that the gospel had implications for all areas of life, and sought to create a comprehensive Christian worldview that understood and engaged with the complexities of South African society. This approach was reminiscent of the theological method of Charles Hodge, who saw parallels between the study of theology and the empirical scientific method. In seeking to uncover the theological facts found within the Bible, apartheid theologians aimed to provide a modern and rational basis for their beliefs, grounded in a systematic and scientific approach to Scripture interpretation. However, their own cultural biases and political goals profoundly swayed their interpretation of the Bible, leading to a distorted and oppressive view of society that justified discrimination and segregation on racial grounds.

The systematic theology that underpinned apartheid and perpetuated it for over four decades serves as a warning not to approach theology as a rigid structure or immutable system of thought. This kind of theology prioritizes intellectual coherence, or even obedience, over the lived experience of faith, often disregarding the complexities and nuances of theological truth that language alone cannot fully capture.

Apartheid theology was steeped in historical and cultural biases that favored certain perspectives and marginalized others. It excluded and demonized theological voices that challenged the status quo. Such exclusionary practices reflected the power dynamics and hierarchies that were prevalent in church, state, and society at large, where certain elect voices were amplified while others were silenced.

Apartheid's theology was more concerned with providing politically compliant answers than exploring the questions that arose from the lived experiences of people of faith. This focus on logical coherence led to a reductionist approach that failed to account for the intricate realities of life in South Africa. This reductionism also perpetuated the injustices of the apartheid system; theological justification was dragged in to support the oppression of certain groups.

We should recognize that theologians are not immune to their own biases, assumptions, and personal affections. These factors can color their understanding of their calling and manipulate—sometimes unconsciously—how they construct theological systems. Therefore, theologians must engage in critical self-reflection and question their own assumptions. They must ensure they do not perpetuate harmful or outdated ideologies that reinforce existing power dynamics and hierarchies whose validity might have waned.

Over time, all theological systems risk stagnation if they fail to consider new knowledge, experiences, and questions. This was particularly true of apartheid, which co-opted rigid religious doctrine to justify the dehumanization of an entire race of people. Moreover, theology should not be a closed encyclopedia of dogmas that provides set answers to set questions. Rather, theology is a dynamic, ever-evolving Christian practice that integrates our affection for and knowledge of God as we try to live this human life wisely in union with that same God. Theology is a disposition or a way of being in this world that is ingrained in us, though not all may sense or devote thought to it. This vision for theology sees it not just as an intellectual pursuit or an emotional experience, but as a practical, lived-in, and acted-out reality. The everyday experiences of real people ground theology in their lives, and the lives of those who have come before us and those who will follow us. It should seek to facilitate a partnership between humanity and the divine. Theology in this sense is not merely a theoretical exercise, but an active engagement with the world and with God's work in it. This practical orientation of theology aligns it with the ultimate purpose of our existence—to live in relationship with God and to work toward the betterment of ourselves and the world around us.

BETWEEN SYSTEMATIC THEOLOGY AND PRACTICAL THEOLOGY

For some, this means we should approach theology practically and that its ultimate purpose is to guide us to a deeper understanding of God and, ultimately, to salvation. A fine example of this is how Farley describes *theology habitus* as a "cognitively, insightfully disposed posture that attends salvation, a knowledge of the self-disclosing God. As such it is for the sake of God, but that means for God's appointed salvific end of the human being. Theology in this sense cannot be anything but practical. *Theologia practica* is simply the *habitus* viewed as to its end."[72]

This is not new, as we have seen. A movement toward a "bottom-up" approach to theology has formed, where "bodily practices—such as acts of care, worship, proclamation, and transformation—take precedence

---

72. Farley, "Theology and Practice," 27.

over abstract doctrines and concepts."[73] This approach recognizes that our embodied experiences of life are as important as our intellectual understanding of it. As we advance, it is vital to explore this practical approach to theology in liminality, acknowledging that our experiences of transition and change require a theology that can adapt and respond to fresh challenges. This means being open to contemporary perspectives, questioning our own assumptions, and recognizing the limitations of our own knowledge. Only by doing so can we create a theology that truly helps us navigate the complexities of the world and live out our faith in meaningful ways. This is what we will turn to now.

---

73. Graham, "On Becoming a Practical Theologian," 3.

3

Hand

THE STUDY OF THEOLOGY can help us develop a secure attachment to God as the covenanting one, especially since we live in liminality. But the question is: How does this happen? In church history, we have seen many examples of believers who have integrated their affective and cognitive ways of being with God in such a way that it has led to personal and practical knowledge of God. These people possessed the wisdom of God, because they were more than book-smart or street-savvy; they knew how to live wisely. In this view, all theology is practical, leading to a personal and practical knowledge of God.

Toward the end of the last millennium, the answer to liminality relied on a theological system. It provided a comprehensive and integrated set of ideas or beliefs that were logically interconnected and supplied a framework for understanding the world. Ancient Greek philosophers such as Plato and Aristotle, medieval thinkers like Thomas Aquinas, and enlightenment philosophers such as Immanuel Kant have all attempted to provide systems for understanding the world.

From the middle of the nineteenth century to the middle of the twentieth century, modernist thinkers sought to create unified systems of thought that could explain all aspects of human experience, often incorporating scientific methods and principles into their work. In theology, systematic theology provided such systems of propositions that were comprehensive, coherent, and contextual. It proceeded from imaginary questions and answered these questions within the confines of the system it had created. In this view, theology is a set of doctrines working together to create a complex whole. However, as we have seen from the case study of South Africa, theological systems can be ill-conceived and become rigid, causing great misery for all. Instead of it providing a way to find our way through the complexities of life in liminality, it can become a tool of oppression, disconnecting people from one another and preventing meaningful dialogue and engagement.

According to Bonnie Miller-McLemore, in the 1950s, scholars in various fields began to turn to "practice and daily life as a site where knowledge accrues."[1] A growing understanding in professions such as law, medicine, nursing, and ministry held that "expert practitioners in the professions possess a kind of wisdom that escapes the quantifiable, technical, rule-bound restrictions of theory alone."[2] This shift was also taking place in theological discussions. Instead of focusing solely on the study of doctrines and their potential applications, there was a growing recognition of the significance of religious practices in daily life.

Theologians increasingly wanted to wrestle with real-life situations and questions, and therefore the starting point was not a theory but rather the practice of theology. According to Elaine Graham, theology shifted from a narrow focus on "applied theology" to a broader emphasis on theological reflection on practice.[3] The task of theological reflection requires that theory, or principles derived from other theological disciplines, be used to assess and understand the pastoral situation, but it does not supersede the experience of the practitioner. In this proposal, it is not theories, propositions, or even doctrines that guide practice of the minister. Instead, it is the practice that gives rise to a new cycle of theological reflection.

Throughout this book, I present theology as the integration of affection and knowledge of God as the figure of attachment, the covenanting one, who sees and soothes us and with whom we sense that we are safe and secure. We try to make sense of our affection through cognitive processes, which we direct toward the goal of understanding God as the one who is with us[4] in liminality and who is reconciling us to him.[5]

1. Miller-McLemore, "Contribution of Practical Theology," 2.
2. Graham, "On Becoming a Practical Theologian," 1.
3. Graham, "On Becoming a Practical Theologian," 1.
4. "For in him we live and move and have our being" (Acts 17:27–28 NIV).
5. "All this is from God, who reconciled us to himself through Christ and gave us the ministry of reconciliation: that God was reconciling the world to himself in Christ, not counting people's sins against them. And he has committed to us the message of

As such, theology is a way of understanding the relationship between humanity and God and how God's revelation affects our understanding of ourselves and our place in the world. This involves not only intellectual inquiry but also a willingness to reflect on personal experiences and emotions in light of theological concepts. "Theology in this sense cannot be anything but practical."[6]

BETWEEN REVELATION AND HUMAN EXPERIENCE

According to Don Browning, all theology starts with practice and is fundamentally a practical discipline.[7] He believes that every part of theology begins and ends in practice and that humans never really move from theory to practice, even when it seems we do. "Theory is always embedded in practice."[8] Theology is no different; it too has a "practice-theory-practice structure."[9] For Browning, theology is a recursive process: practitioners constantly intertwine theory and practice to mutually shape each other, rather than following a linear process of moving from theory to practice, and doctrine to application. Therefore, the lived experience of believers should be the starting point for theological inquiry as well. Theological ideas have their roots in the practical concerns and experiences of the community.

Browning's approach to theology differs from most theological systems of the twentieth century, which had a theory-practice structure. For example, Karl Barth, a prominent Protestant theologian of the twentieth century, believed that theology must begin with God's self-revelation in Jesus Christ rather than with human experience. This emphasis on revelation and the authority of Scripture led Barth to a theory-practice structure in his theological system. Barth believed that we can only gain access to the content of God's word through systematic study of revelation, and only then can we discover what should be proclaimed in everyday life.

To understand Barth's approach, we need to understand his broader concern that the "liberal" theology of his day was turning theology into a

---

reconciliation" (2 Cor 5:18–19 NIV).

6. Farley, "Theology and Practice," 27.
7. Browning, *Fundamental Practical Theology*.
8. Browning, *Fundamental Practical Theology*, 9.
9. Browning, *Fundamental Practical Theology*, 9.

"human concern."[10] Barth thought that theologians like Friedrich Schleiermacher were absolutizing human nature[11] because they started from subjective human experience instead of God's concrete act of revealing himself in Jesus Christ. According to Browning, however, Barth's theological approach "leaves no role for human understanding, action, or practice in the conception of God's self-disclosure."[12] He contends that since God's revelation is applied to our daily circumstances in the most direct and pure way possible, this transforms practical theology into applied theology.[13] Barth's understanding of the centrality of revelation as the origin and goal of theology adds further weight; it is through revelation that God graciously chooses to disclose himself to us.

According to Browning, he and Barth take two very different approaches to theology.[14] Barth's angle on theology moves from revelation to practice. He starts with the idea that God has revealed himself to humans and then tries to understand how this revelation should inform human behavior and action. In other words, Barth's approach is focused on understanding how to apply theological concepts in practical, everyday situations. On the other hand, Browning argues that all practice is theory-laden:[15] an underlying belief or theory influences every action we take. Consequently, his approach to theology is more focused on understanding the underlying beliefs and assumptions that inform human action. Browning's view starts with an understanding of practical actions and then seeks to understand the underlying beliefs and theories that inform those actions. As such, he believes that all theology is fundamentally practical theology, which requires four movements of theological reflection.

---

10. Barth, *Church Dogmatics* (*CD*), 2:1. Later in Barth's writing, he acknowledged that he might have misread Schleiermacher. See Barth, *Theology of Schleiermacher*, 274–75. He asked this question of his critique of Schleiermacher: "For have I indeed understood him correctly? Could he not perhaps be understood differently so that I would not have to reject his theology, but might rather be joyfully conscious of proceeding in fundamental agreement with him?"

11. Barth, *CD*, 2:1, 73.

12. Browning, *Practical Theology*, 5.

13. Browning, *Practical Theology*, 5.

14. See Scalise, "Book Review: Fundamental Practical Theology," 445–46. According to Scalise, Browning stereotyped Barth's hermeneutics and ignored the narrative approach used in his later work, as theologians such as David Ford and Hans Frei highlighted. Furthermore, Browning also does not give enough weight to the postcritical aspects of Barth's hermeneutics, discussed by Rudolf Smend and others.

15. Browning, *Practical Theology*, 6.

BETWEEN DESCRIPTIVE AND SYSTEMATIC THEOLOGY

The first movement of *descriptive theology* highlights the importance of recognizing that all practices carry embedded theories. Every practice carries with it a set of underlying beliefs, values, and assumptions that inform how we understand and engage in that belief or behavior. In this first movement, the theologian recognizes these embedded theories and examines them carefully as a necessary part of theological reflection.[16] By doing so, we can gain a deeper understanding of the practical questions that arise from our experiences and the theories that underpin them. Ultimately, *descriptive theology* reminds us that beliefs and values influence all practices and we must consider them in any theological reflection.

Historical theology, the second movement in Don Browning's model of theological reflection, explores "normative texts and the monuments of the Christian faith—the sources of the norms of practice."[17] This includes biblical studies, church history, and the history of Christian thought. *Historical theology* seeks to provide context for understanding the development of Christian thought and practice over time, and to identify the sources of the norms of practice that guide the Christian community. By exploring the history of Christianity, theologians can gain insight into how historical and cultural contexts have shaped Christian beliefs and practices, and how they have been interpreted and applied in different times and places. This understanding can inform and enrich contemporary theological reflection by providing a deeper appreciation of the diversity and complexity of Christian thinking and action. Ultimately, historical theology reminds us that theological reflection should ground itself in a careful and critical examination of the historical and cultural contexts that have shaped the Christian tradition over time.

Browning's third movement, *systematic theology*, is part of a practical framework that helps us better understand our current practices and the vision they may reveal. There is a place for *systematic theology* in Browning's proposal, but it is a component in a functional structure in which it "tries to look at the big, all-encompassing themes of our current practices and vision latent in them."[18] It does this by organizing and synthesizing theological insights from various sources, such as Old Testament and New Testament studies, biblical exegesis, church history, and

---

16. Browning, *Practical Theology*, 47.
17. Browning, *Practical Theology*, 49.
18. Browning, *Practical Theology*, 51.

contemporary intellectual trends, into a coherent and systematic whole. By doing so, *systematic theology* can help us identify underlying patterns, principles, and values that are present in our current practices and experiences. It can also help us articulate a coherent vision of what we believe, why we believe it, and how it relates to our practical concerns. Ultimately, systematic theology can help us to better understand the practical implications of our theological beliefs, and how they might shape our actions and attitudes in the world.

Strategic practical theology, the fourth movement, deals pragmatically with church disciplines, contributing to the life of the church, and the common good beyond it. Here theologians think practically about church disciplines such as "religious education, pastoral care, preaching, liturgy, social ministries, and so forth."[19] The movement seeks to develop practical strategies and frameworks for addressing the needs and concerns of the church community and the wider society. *Strategic practical theology* emphasizes the importance of engaging with real-world problems and opportunities and of contributing to the life of the church and society. By doing so, it seeks to bridge the gap between theoretical reflection and practical action, and to ensure that theology is relevant and responsive to the needs of the world. Strategic practical theologians may work closely with practitioners in various fields to develop and implement workable solutions to complex problems. They may also engage in interdisciplinary research and collaboration with scholars from other fields, such as psychology, sociology, and anthropology, to gain insights into the social and cultural contexts in which church practices and beliefs are embedded. Ultimately, *strategic practical theology* aims to equip the church community with the knowledge, skills, and resources needed to engage in meaningful and effective action in and with the world.

Don Browning's proposal for practical theology involves a practice-theory-practice movement that enables theologians to gain a practice-led understanding of the Christian faith. This approach emphasizes the importance of recognizing that theology is both practice-laden-theory and theory-laden-practice, and that theory and practice should be integrated into a pattern of action and reflection. Practical theologians use the term *praxis* to describe this dynamic interaction between theory and practice and strive to keep them in creative tension while integrating them into

---

19. Browning, *Practical Theology*, 8.

a coherent whole.[20] However, before exploring the concept of *praxis* further, it is important to clarify what is meant by practice.

BETWEEN CHRISTIAN PRACTICES AND VIRTUES

Alasdair MacIntyre's definition of *practice* as "any coherent and complex form of socially established cooperative human activity" has been influential in theological discussions about Christian practices.[21] He proposes that practices are essential to developing virtues, and it is through participation in these practices that individuals become more virtuous. However, merely committing to Christian practices is not enough to achieve true virtue, as Paul warns against having a form of godliness but denying its power.[22] Craig Dykstra and Dorothy Bass argue that the belief in God's active presence in Christian practices is crucial. Christian practices are not just activities that Christians do, but they are the embodied beliefs behind shared behavior that "Christian people do together over time in response to and in light of God's active presence for the life of the world in Christ Jesus."[23] According to Elaine Graham, "God is embodied in faith-filled practices" for Christians, implying that God is present and active in the practices and actions of believers.[24] This understanding has inspired Christians throughout history to live out their faith by participating in religious activities and rituals.

God's active presence is manifested in the Christian practice of being a pastor, or pastoring, according to Jacob Firet.[25] This understanding has significant implications for how pastors and other Christian leaders

---

20. I have reflected on *praxis* "as a creative ability to keep theory and practice in tension, although it does more than only keep these in tension; it also integrates them into a pattern in which action and ongoing reflection mutually indwell each other." De Kock, *Out of My Mind*, 136.

21. MacIntyre, *After Virtue*, 175. The full definition is: "any coherent and complex form of socially established cooperative human activity through which goods internal to that form of activity are realised in the course of trying to achieve those standards of excellence which are appropriate to, and partly definitive of, that form of activity with the result that human powers to achieve excellence, and human conceptions of the ends and goods involved, are systematically extended." This definition caught the attention of prominent theologians such as Craig Dykstra. In *Reconceiving Practice* (2007) he uses MacIntyre's definition as his point of departure.

22. See 2 Tim 3:5.

23. Dykstra and Bass, "Times of Yearning, Practices of Faith," 5.

24. Graham, "On Becoming a Practical Theologian," 4.

25. Firet, *Dynamics of Pastoring*, 15–18.

approach their work. Instead of simply imparting information or advice, they answer the call to become conduits of God's presence and power, mediating his word and facilitating transformation in the lives of other believers who are trying to find their way in liminality. The "pastoral dynamic" these practices create cannot be manufactured or replicated through human effort alone.[26] Rather, it is a result of God's presence and power working through the faithful endeavors of pastors and other leaders. Therefore, they share in the commonly held understanding that God is embodied in the faith-filled practices of pastoral care, in which God's grace and love can be experienced.

BETWEEN *POIESIS* AND *THEORIA*

This brings us back to the importance of *praxis* for theologians, since they are generally interested in Christian practices that have the ability to transform individuals from the inside out, and changing their way of being in the world.[27] *Praxis* is a central concept in Aristotle's understanding of human activity and is closely related to other key concepts in his philosophy, such as *poiesis* (knowledge of making), and *theoria* (knowledge of ideas).[28] *Praxis* can be seen as the integration of theoretical and practical knowledge to produce something new or effect real-world change, but it does not operate in a theory-practice direction only. It involves a cyclical process in which theoretical knowledge informs practical action, and practical experience informs theoretical understanding. In Aristotle, *praxis* refers to practical activity with an end or goal that involves making choices and taking action in the world.[29]

---

26. Firet identifies three ways in which the word comes and is mediated: *kerygma*, *didache*, and *paraklesis*. In Christian tradition, *kerygma* signifies the essential proclamation of the gospel message—an eloquent declaration that encapsulates the core tenets of faith. It is the announcement of a new reality. While *didache* embodies the teachings or doctrines that guide believers, constituting a doctrinal framework for understanding and living out Christian principles, it also points to the spiritual growth and development of people of faith. Lastly, *paraklesis* conveys the idea of encouragement or consolation, emphasizing the supportive, comforting aspect of spiritual counsel and community.

27. James Fowler describes *praxis* as "the basic concern of practical theology." See Fowler, *Faith Development and Pastoral Care*, 16.

28. I have found Fowler, *Faith Development and Pastoral Care*, 13–17, and the preface of Bernstein, *Praxis and Action*, very insightful in my attempt to define the meaning and importance of *praxis*.

29. For Paulo Freire, *praxis* is "reflection and action upon the world in order to

As our discussion deepens, we come across another inflexion point. Instead of regarding practice, as a mindless activity, it is vital to understand it as a form of knowledge. Every action we take involves some form of knowledge or understanding, whether conscious or subconscious. In the same vein, all practice is theory-laden, just as theory is practice-laden. This insight challenges the traditional notion that theory is a domain of knowledge and practice is not. Instead, we must recognize that theory and practice are both domains of knowledge and are intimately connected to inform one another. Theories are born out of practical experiences, and practical experiences, in turn, shape theories. In this way, we can deepen our understanding and cultivate a more holistic approach to learning, knowledge, and behavior.

Praxis is a unique type of knowledge that integrates theory and practice continually. It transcends mere action and becomes a way of knowing and being in the world. The idea behind *praxis* as a way of knowing where theory and practice are not separate but interconnected, interdependent, and mutually indwelling is intriguing. It suggests that our understanding of a theory should inform our actions and that our actions should inform our understanding of a theory. This means that as we engage in practices or actions, we should reflect on how these behaviors align with our understanding of a theory and, if necessary, adjust our understanding. Similarly, as we reflect on a theory, we should consider how it applies to our behaviors and, if required, adjust our actions to align with our understanding of the theory. This is a constant cycle of reflection and action that leads to personal and communal growth and transformation. Additionally, it calls for a holistic approach where we consider and engage both the cognitive and practical aspects of human change. There is no theory without practice and no practice without theory. In this way, *praxis* is the integration of theoretical and practical knowledge that leads to transformation.

This is also true of our knowledge of God. Even our knowledge of God is *praxis* since it is never purely theoretical. The experience of those who brought this theoretical knowledge to us in the first place always mediates the theories or doctrines we have about God. As we have seen above, they are practice-laden. These experiences could be personal experiences of individuals, the experiences of a particular community, or the experiences passed down through religious traditions. In other words, the

---

transform it." Freire, *Pedagogy of the Oppressed*, 33.

experiences of those who have come before us and have influenced our beliefs and practices always shape our understanding of God. Therefore, our knowledge of God is not just theoretical but also practical because it is grounded in the lived experiences of individuals and communities. So it makes sense that Charles Gerkin insists that practical theology takes place in the midst of *praxis* and is prompted by the situation of being "in the midst of" Christian actions.[30] Accordingly, theology is performed in the crosshairs of theory and practice; it is the embodiment of the theories we hold and the practices to which we are committed. Theologians allow the practice of being "in the midst" of these actions to shape theoretical theological understandings.[31] This bring us back to Aristotle's view that *praxis* as a practical activity is directed toward some end or goal, and that involves making choices and taking action in the world.[32]

BETWEEN *PRAXIS* AND *PHRONESIS*

Practical theology, according to James Fowler, is what the church does in the "praxis of its mission" as it responds to God's work in the world.[33] The choices that the church makes either enable or hinder "ongoing modifications and development of the ways in which the church shapes its life to be in partnership with God's work."[34] Theology assumes that God is actively present in local communities, and the ability to make wise choices enables local churches to respond to the specific needs of the people in their communities and the ever-changing world around them in partnership with God. According to Fowler, "this kind of knowing that praxis requires is often taken as synonymous with *phronesis*, which translates as prudence—a practical wisdom that informs action."[35] However, some hold the view that *phronesis* is a unique virtue that encapsulates *praxis*. This is because it involves a range of cognitive and affective faculties, including rationality, intuition, empathy, and experiential knowledge.[36]

---

30. Gerkin, *Widening the Horizons*, 60.
31. Gerkin, *Widening the Horizons*, 60.
32. See Freire, *Pedagogy of the Oppressed*, 33.
33. Fowler, *Faith Development*, 17.
34. Fowler, *Faith Development*, 17.
35. Fowler, *Faith Development*, 15.
36. Dunne, "Virtue, Phronēsis and Learning," 49.

While rational choice captures some aspects of *phronesis*, it is not the most comprehensive translation of the term. As we saw above, *phronesis* involves more than just rationality; it also embraces our cognitive and affective capabilities, which are not necessarily captured by the term *rational choice*. It straddles the divide between our affections and rationality,[37] or colloquially, our hearts and minds. It is more about being reasonable than being rational. It involves a deliberative judgment which takes into account factors such as context, emotions, and intuition. It suggests a standard of behavior or decision-making that is fair, justifiable, and acceptable to others, rather than one that is based solely on individual self-interest.

Theologically, reasonableness is acquired over time through the Christian practice of doing the theological work of integrating our hearts and minds as we live this human life wisely in union with God. This involves constantly engaging and modifying our understanding of God's work in the world and following God in heart and mind. Our current understanding of God's work is limited and temporary, but our future understanding will be unimpeded by human limitation. Therefore, theology must be carried out in a way that acknowledges our own limitations and the constant movement and activity of God in the world. As Christian travelers on a journey with God, we can become more reasonable and wiser if we perform the theological work of integration faithfully and lovingly, as we have seen. If so, theology will enable us to make wise choices that lead to modifications and developments in the ways we shape our lives to be in partnership with God's work.

BETWEEN SACRED QUESTIONS AND ANSWERS

In the previous chapter I mentioned that I used to think that the goal of theological education was to teach students the right answers that fit into a certain system of beliefs. I then believed that understanding this system would allow them to apply it in their own context and that knowledge would empower them to change the world. But as I submerged myself more in the work of theologians like James Fowler, I felt empowered

---

37. According to Duane, Aristotle views *phronesis* as a unique virtue that straddles the categories of character and intellect, making it an essential ingredient for practical wisdom. Although Aristotle sometimes categorizes *phronesis* as a virtue of both character and intellect, its centrality in his philosophy is undeniable. He emphasizes the importance of right reason in *phronesis* and intimates that it is closely related to wisdom.

to set aside my doctrinal certainties and to embrace the questions that emerged from the issues that my students were facing in their communities on the Cape Flats. I saw that the people there were suffering under a theo-political system of racial segregation and oppression. This system of theological and political doctrines provided answers but forbade and punished questions. It silenced the voices of the oppressed and justified violence against them.

Theology should be comfortable with questions, because it is through questions that we can discern what God is doing in our midst and what our response should be. Browning believes that questions animate thinking[38] and theological reflection. Questions, not propositions, help us understand what God is doing, because we ask questions from a place of vulnerability and uncertainty as we open ourselves to learning and attempt to discover the best answers we can find. We could say that these questions emerge as we discern what partnership with God would mean in changing situations. Emerging questions are inquiries of significance. They are sacred. They need to be answered wisely. David Dark explains it beautifully.

> I believe deliverance begins with questions. It begins with people who love questions, people who live with questions and by questions, people who feel a great joy when questions are asked. . . .When we're exposed to the liveliness of holding everything up to the light of good questions—what I call 'sacred questions'—we discover that redemption is creeping into the way we think, believe and see the world. The re-deeming (re-valuing) of what we've made our lives, a redemption that perhaps begins with the insertion of a question mark beside whatever feels final and absolute and beyond questioning, gives our souls a bit of elbow room, a space in which to breathe and imagine again, as if for the first time.[39]

In our always-changing world, it's becoming more and more important for theology to do more than just give answers. Instead, it needs to focus on helping people articulate the sacred questions of their time and place. Through the rich and rewarding work of theological inquiry, we are called to integrate our love for God with what we know about him and learn how to live wisely with him in the midst of life's uncertainties. In this way, we cultivate the virtue of reasonableness, which, as we have seen, is

---

38. Browning, *Practical Theology*, 55.
39. Dark, *Sacredness of Questioning Everything*, 14.

the ability to make wise choices when the path forward is not clear. Paul encouraged the Christians in Philippi to do this when he said, "Let your reasonableness in judging be clear to everyone. The Lord is present with you."[40] This non-anxious gentleness, or reasonableness in the way we live, is rooted in a deep and abiding awareness of the presence of God in our lives and a recognition of the importance of living in union with him.

Living this human life in the presence of God is not a passive endeavor, but an active and intentional pursuit. It requires us to approach life with wisdom, discernment, and a willingness to learn and grow. Through the practice of doing theology, we develop the ability to be reasonable in the face of uncertainty and to act with integrity and compassion in all circumstances. The transitions, uncertainties, and challenges of life often leave us with more questions than answers and so feeling anxious. As we have discussed earlier in this chapter, reasonableness is not an innate quality we possess, but rather a skill we hone through intentional and continuous practice. Central to the proposal of this book is that we acquire reasonableness over time through practicing the theological work of integrating our affection for and knowledge of God as we live this human life in union with God. It is time for us to take a closer look at this claim.

---

40. My translation of Phil 4:5. According to Rienecker, *Linguistic Key to the Greek New Testament*, 560, *epieikes* (τὸ ἐπιεικὲς) can be translated as "reasonableness in judging. The word signifies a humble, patient, steadfastness, which is able to submit to injustice, disgrace, and maltreatment without hatred or malice, trusting in God in spite of it all."

4

Heart

FOR MANY YEARS, CHRISTIAN theology in South Africa supported apartheid and agreed that it was a reasonable political solution. This "reasonableness" came from the idea that God, who was seen as the great divider, had made the world so that nations would stay separate and no empire would rise that would threaten his power. In this view, the practical thing to do was to create laws that kept black and white people apart and prevented interracial marriage. This theologically driven position gave rise to the system of apartheid, a theo-political *praxis* that enforced racial segregation and discrimination. Those who benefited from this system praised it as reasonable, claiming it ensured people of different races could be separate but equal. However, those whom the new policy disempowered, stealing their human dignity and self-worth, saw no reasonableness in the outcome. They were denied basic rights and opportunities solely on the basis of their skin color, a practice that was both unjust and inhumane.

When we think about the effects of apartheid, we have to wonder how Christians could have thought that such an unfair system was theologically sound. After all, we should learn to be reasonable by integrating our hearts and minds as we live this human life in union with God. Yet, in the case of apartheid, theology was used to justify oppression and inequality rather than to promote justice and compassion. This prompts us to reconsider our conception of what it means to live in union with God and poses significant questions about what we mean by practicing theology as an integration of our affection for and knowledge of God.

My first experience with the challenge of integration came when I was in my first semester at seminary. As I have written before in *Out of My Mind*, it was a few days before Christmas when my young bride, Marian, and I arrived in Cleveland, Tennessee, a sleepy little town in the southeastern United States. We were little more than children, stepping into a world completely different from our home country of South Africa. But I had a scholarship to study theology at the seminary, and we were determined to make the most of the opportunity. A wall of cold air and a blanket of glistening snow greeted us as we opened the curtains on the first day of our new reality. The icy mantle had transformed the landscape into something otherworldly, a lustrous, wonderland that dazzled us with its ethereal beauty. We marveled at the snowflakes falling gently from the sky, fluffing the ground in a pristine eiderdown of white. We did not know then that this winter nirvana would rapidly deteriorate into a much harsher truth for us.

BETWEEN TRAILER AND SEMINARY

As the weeks wore on, the whimsy of winter faded, giving way to the cruel reality of its icy grip. Our new home was a caravan in a crowded trailer park. This was a massive step-down from the comfortable homes we grew up in. I had received a scholarship, but it was a work bursary that only paid for half of my seminary expenses. To make ends meet, I had to work as a janitor at the seminary. I recall vividly the long nights spent cleaning toilets and urinals, vacuuming floors, and wiping windows while my mind raced with theological doubts and worries about what I had exposed me and my young bride to. The biting cold seemed to invade our bones, and the wind howled through our trailer like a ravenous wolf threatening to devour us whole. But as we struggled to make ends meet, working long hours to scrape together the bare necessities of food and warmth, we began to understand what it meant to live in poverty. I sensed a growing empathy for the little girl who had told Bishop Desmond Tutu that she and her companions drank water to fill their stomachs when there was no food to borrow or beg.

As a young, newlywed theology student, I spent my days attending lectures and getting used to marriage. At night, I worked as a janitor and wrote academic papers in English, a language I despised because of what it historically represented to me as a proud Afrikaner. Though some aspects of my experience may be common to many graduate students, I also had the added challenge of working the same shift as Cornelius Ugandele, another student and co-janitor from Uganda. I could not help but feel, as our ancestral trekkers once did, that we were not equals, despite our shared experiences as students and cleaners. But there we were, working, side by side, linked in indignity with our hands down public toilets. It represented everything that I and my Afrikaner people feared. It also made me question the purpose of my education and whether it was worth sacrificing my pride and self-respect for it. This was the leveling of races—and what Anna Steenekamp, Totius, and other Afrikaner theologians warned against. If this was reason enough for the trekkers to leave the Cape of Good Hope, it could have been reason enough for me to abandon my theological studies.

BETWEEN SEMINARY AND HOSPITAL

My struggle did not go unnoticed, and my troubled relationship with Cornelius caught the attention of the dean of field ministry, Robert Crick. In an emergency disciplinary meeting with him and other faculty members, they expressed concerns about my lack of empathy. They felt I was all head and questioned if I had the capacity to feel. In retrospect I realize they compared me to the Tin Man from *The Wizard of Oz*—all brain but lacking a heart. Crick, as a student of Charles Gerkin, believed that transformation was possible if the head and heart integrated, a phrase he often repeated. He believed theological education was pointless without this assimilation. He warned me that my academic achievements would be worthless, and I would find myself on a plane back to South Africa unless I was willing to bridge the chasm between my head and heart. His stern recommendation was to enroll in a three-month clinical pastoral education (CPE) program, which Anton Boisen, Charles Gerkin's mentor, pioneered. This program involved working as a chaplain in a hospital setting and dealing with patients facing potentially life-ending circumstances.

Looking back, I realize his advice emerged from Gerkin's belief that transformation occurs in the midst of Christian practice, where the head is of little value and the heart is exposed. Though I had no other choice, I enrolled in a basic twelve-week CPE program in the summer of 1983. Crick's wisdom and guidance, along with my eye-opening experience in clinical pastoral education, proved invaluable in not just shaping me as a theologian but transforming me as a human.

For the three months of the CPE program, I called the attic of an old church my home, consisting only of a single bed with a few broken springs and a stained foam mattress. This was another step down from the "comforts" of living in a trailer park. To add to my discomfort, Cornelius, my co-janitor at the seminary, was also my assigned roommate. I could not help but feel that the dean had made a deliberate choice, knowing how I preferred to avoid Cornelius. Looking back, I can see that my personal version of racism was on full display during my time in that church attic. But I could not have been ready for what I was about to go through at Egleston Children's Hospital in Atlanta, Georgia. The experience overwhelmed me, unforgettably. It was as if all the pent-up emotions that I had begun to process since I first became aware of the apartheid-poisoned splinter in my mind had finally come to the surface. As I walked through the corridors of the hospital, I saw children in pain, many fighting for their lives. I witnessed parents tormented by unanswerable sorrow. I stood in awe of stressed medical staff stubbornly waging an often-unwinnable war against what sometimes seemed like ungodly odds. The reality of desperately sick children, many from different races and cultures to my own, confronted me endlessly. I was locked in a battle with my own emotions. How could I find the right words to comfort them and their families? My own prejudices and biases were painfully obvious. I would soon be forced to face them head-on.

My interaction with James, a young Black boy who had fetal alcohol syndrome, exposed my deep-seated dislike of people of color. I recall hearing that alcohol is a teratogenic substance that can lead to birth defects in some children whose mothers consume it while they are pregnant. *Teratogenic* derives from the Greek word for monster, which emphasizes how serious the condition is. It applied to James; he had grim birth defects, including head, facial, and mental malformations. Seeing James in this condition was a daunting experience that brought all my prejudices to the surface. As much as I wanted to provide him with compassion, my biases made it difficult to see him as a boy in need of unconditional care. Working with children was already a challenge for me because I had to let my heart guide me. However, James—through no possible fault of his—made it even more difficult because my conditioning clouded my judgment. It felt impossible for me to see past his skin color and birth defects and render him the love and compassion that he deserved.[1]

---

1. This is not his real name; we were not supposed to use our names in our notes.

BETWEEN PHYSICAL AND SPIRITUAL DEFORMITY

A chance meeting with James in Egleston on a fateful day in the summer of 1983 changed the course of my life forever. I recently found a handpenned note I had written to capture what had happened between James and me. Even though I have reflected at length on this event, re-entering my memory through my own words brought back all the intensity of that time.

> Today was the day that changed everything. It all happened in the main corridor of the Egleston Children's Hospital in Atlanta, Georgia. A thunderstorm raged outside, and as I was walking down the hallway, I saw James. He's the little black boy with severe birth defects that [sic] I've been avoiding for some time. I didn't want to be near him, let alone touch him, but God had other plans. James was frightened by the thunder and came out into the corridor. He grabbed onto me, trembling with fear and drooling as he made unrecognizable sounds. I was overcome with revulsion for him and everything he represented. All I could think about was how I could free myself from his grasp and get away from him. But I knew that wasn't an option under the gaze of many onlookers. It took a lot of effort to get him back in his room and onto his bed, but not before his little fingers had wrapped themselves tightly around my arm. He was holding on as if I were his last hope. And yet I was frozen, unable to respond with any kindness or compassion. I felt like I was losing my limbs one by one, like Tin Woodman in *The Wizard of Oz*. Each time he reached out, it was as if an axe had severed another limb. I had no human arms to pick him up, no hands to hold him, and no fingers to wipe his face. The instant I finally succeeded in prying his fingers apart, he swung around and grabbed his stuffed animal, and I faded into the background. I became just another person who failed him, who was disgusted by his mere existence. In that moment, I realized that I was indeed a Tin Woodman with a heart made of tin. This little boy shone a spotlight on me today, and for the first time, I could see that I too suffer from a syndrome caused by the drug of racism and the doctrines of apartheid. He may have been born a "little monster" because his mother took a teratogenic drug, but my motherland and the church that fed me spiritually must have been high on hatred to give birth to me.

In the days following my encounter with James, I found myself urgently needing time and space to process the profound spiritual encounter at Egleston Children's Hospital. Conveniently located nearby, the Pitts Theology Library boasted a world-class collection of resources for theological studies. There, I unearthed publications banned in apartheid-era South Africa that exposed the atrocities committed in the name of the church and state. As I read these texts and examined photocopies of graphic images depicting government brutality and murder, I realized that the so-called reasonableness of apartheid—to keep races separate but equal—was nothing more than a sham. The theo-political justifications used to indoctrinate my generation served to conceal a deep aversion white people felt toward people of color, using religion and societal harmony as a smokescreen. These justifications perpetuated a system of inequality, oppression, and control, all while hiding the true, insidious motives rooted in prejudice and fear. Black people in South Africa were suffering, while those with my skin tone lived in privilege. It appalled me to think that individuals who resembled me and shared my language, culture, and faith were responsible for such violence. For the first time in my life, I felt a profound sense of guilt and shame for my inherited privilege and my complicity in perpetuating these injustices, as well as a deep desire to help dismantle the system that caused such suffering.

So we return to the question: How could such an unjust system be seen as theologically reasonable by Christians who supported it, including myself? After all, we should learn to be reasonable by integrating our hearts and minds as we live this human life in liminality in union with God. An obvious answer would be that apartheid theologians were in theological error; that they simply got it wrong doctrinally. Of course, it is evident that the distortion of religious teachings and the exploitation of fear allowed Christians, like me, to rationalize an inherently unjust system, betraying the core principles of love, compassion, and justice that lie at the heart of the Christian faith. However, I contend that there is more to it.

BETWEEN UN-MOVED AND MOST-MOVED MOVER

The answer to this question is more complex than merely using doctrine to mask an unjust system. It is important to consider the role of our conscious pre-conceptual "pre-propositional affective mentalities"[2] that

---

2. As we have seen in chapter 1, see Panksepp, "On the Embodied Neural Nature," 158–84.

influence our perception and interpretation of the world around us. As Panksepp found, these affective mentalities move us to act and think, often without our explicit awareness. In the context of apartheid, those of us who supported the unjust system, myself included, were moved by our affective consciousness, which shaped our perceptions and responses to the situation in South Africa. Deeply ingrained prejudices and fears, operating at the level of affective consciousness, contributed to an emotional aversion towards people of color or those who threatened the status quo. This aversion made it more likely for us to accept theo-political justifications that aligned with our pre-existing emotions and biases. Panksepp has also shown that affective consciousness modulates rational consideration and the introduction of alternative perspectives, and this is the role that theology could play. But instead of modulating the pre-propositional aversion that the Dutch settlers to the Cape—and the many generations that followed them—felt toward the inhabitants of southern Africa, theology was used to justify that aversion in the name of God and nation. By acknowledging the interplay between affections, rational thought, and socio-cultural factors, we can gain a deeper insight into the complexities of human behavior and decision-making; we can work toward finding a way to practice theology in liminality that considers the whole person, both heart and mind.

Although affective neurology was not known to theologians throughout most of Christian history, the tradition that acknowledges the interplay between affection and rational thought in theology is traceable back to the early church fathers. As we have already seen, Augustine of Hippo, for example, emphasized the significance of the human heart in the pursuit of God. His famous phrase, "Our hearts are restless until they find rest in you," from his *Confessions*, illustrates the centrality of affective experience in his theological thought. Similarly, the Desert Fathers and Mothers, early Christian hermits and ascetics, focused on cultivating a deep, personal relationship with God through withdrawal, prayer, meditation, and contemplation, emphasizing the role of the heart in the spiritual journey. Medieval mystics such as Hildegard of Bingen and Bernard of Clairvaux, as well as theologian Thomas Aquinas all acknowledged the importance of love and affective experience in spiritual life. Bernard believed that love for God, experienced through mystical contemplation, should form the basis of theological reflection, while Aquinas emphasized the role of love as the primary virtue that unites the soul with God.

Since the enlightenment, theologians like Friedrich Schleiermacher, the father of modern theology, Søren Kierkegaard, an existentialist theologian, and John Wesley, the founder of Methodism, have each placed significant emphasis on religious experience and feeling in theological reflection. These figures believed that personal encounters with God—rooted in a passionate, inward relationship—were essential for a genuine understanding of God. Influential Puritan theologians Jonathan Edwards and John Owen both highlighted the importance of religious affections as signs of true conversion and genuine faith. Edwards, in his work *A Treatise concerning Religious Affections*, argued that true religion consists of holy affections such as love for God and joy in spiritual matters. The Pietist movement, led by figures such as Philipp Jakob Spener, August Hermann Francke, and Count Nikolaus Ludwig von Zinzendorf, further emphasized the need for a personal, affective experience of God's grace. They advocated for a more experiential and practical approach to the Christian faith, focusing on individual piety, practical godliness, and personal relationships with Christ. Collectively, these theologians and thinkers underscore the importance of affective experience in shaping theological reflection, highlighting the need for heartfelt devotion and inward transformation in the Christian life.

People of faith should not be overly surprised that humans can be deeply moved because we bear the image of a passionate God. Abraham Heschel, a famous Jewish theologian, philosopher, and social activist of the twentieth century, says that God interacts emotionally with the world, including by feeling pain. Heschel does not believe in a God who is far away from creation. Instead, he shows a God who is very close to it. Contrary to Aristotle's concept of an unmoved mover, Heschel presents God as "the most moved mover,"[3] affected by our actions and responding passionately to evoke the best emotional response from us. It is beautiful to imagine that God, the "most moved mover," spoke creation into existence, and humans as his image bearers are moved by love and passion for his creation.

BETWEEN GOD AS A CONCEPT AND GOD AS A PERSON

According to Jürgen Moltmann, creation reveals the inner movement in the Trinity. "The Father creates the world out of his eternal love through the Son, for the purpose of finding a response to his love in time, in the

---

3. Heschel, *Between God and Man*, 25.

power of the Holy Spirit, which binds together what is in itself different."[4] God is moved to create the world out of his eternal love for the Son. This movement in God is made possible by his love for the Son and his longing for his "other," which is humanity. Moltmann explains it beautifully: "In his heart, God has this passionate longing, not just for any, random 'other,' but for 'his' other—that is, for the one who is the 'other' for him himself. And that is humanity, his 'image.'"[5] The love that moves the Trinity is the love that moves creation. The divine life is love, and so the creation of life is an emanation of love. Moltmann establishes that the love within the Trinity is the basis for the love present in creation. He argues that God's love is not only the reason for creation but also the sustaining force that continuously nurtures and upholds it.

Heschel thought that you cannot learn theology through ideas and concepts, as the prophets in the Hebrew Bible showed. Instead, theology emphasizes the divine-human relationship, and we can only know God within this intimate context. While logical methods such as syllogism and deduction are undeniably important, in theology they assume a secondary role to the pre-propositional knowledge that we gain through direct encounters with the divine presence. In Heschel's view, the theologian's knowledge of God is not primarily acquired through reason or rationality but through "fellowship" with him and "a living together" with him. This knowledge of God is, therefore, intuitive, and theology begins with conscious, pre-conceptual, "pre-propositional affective mentalities" that enable theologians and believers alike to discern and understand their encounters with God in the uncertainties of life. The result is an intuitive understanding that binds a lover and their beloved—not merely knowledge about God but a profound connection that unites them.[6]

However, God's love has been tested throughout the course of human history, with humanity often questioning God's intentions and trustworthiness. As any Bible reader knows, the creation account in Genesis, where the serpent tempts Adam and Eve, is a prime example of this testing. The serpent's question, "Did God say . . . ?" prompts the primal couple to analyze and scrutinize God's intentions rather than trusting in his love for them. In the Judeo-Christian narrative, the so-called fall of humanity significantly impacted the relationship between humans and

---

4. Moltmann, *Trinity and the Kingdom*, 114.

5. Moltmann, *Trinity and the Kingdom*, 45. I edited the translation to read "humanity" instead of "man."

6. Berkovits, "Dr A. J. Heschel's Theology of Pathos," 67–104.

God. Not only did it introduce a spiritual separation and sever the direct communion once shared in the Garden of Eden, but it also diminished humanity's capacity to know and understand God. This diminished capacity resulted from the moral corruption sin caused, the shift to more limited and indirect modes of divine revelation, and the fear of death that led humans to prioritize self-interest. Not only did they have to deal with thorns, thistles, and labor pains, but their connection with God became increasingly distant, less approachable, and seemingly impassable, meaning incapable of feeling pain or suffering. As humans tried to navigate the uncertainties of life, questions about God and their relationship with him became more pressing and consequential. The story of Cain and Abel illustrates this well, as Cain, in competition for God's affection and not knowing what God wants, kills his brother in a homicidal rage.

Before God revealed himself to Abraham, humans experienced reality as a living garment of God, in which all aspects of creation were intimately connected to and infused with divine presence.[7] An interconnected, organic view of the divine's relationship with the world characterized this perception of reality. However, the Abrahamic understanding introduced a shift in perspective, presenting a more distinct, personal God who enters into relationships with humans through covenants, such as the one formed with Abraham. This transformation marked the beginning of the Judeo-Christian tradition, which places a greater emphasis on faith than religion. In this context, according to theologian Hendrikus Berkhof, we see faith as a trust transcending experience, living by a promise, and maintaining a connection to the divine even in the face of uncertainty.[8] We should again remind ourselves of the very personal meaning of faith: "to hold dear, to love, or to cherish."[9] In this covenantal view, theology not only requires a personal knowledge of God and a desire for him to know us, but it implies that theologian and believer alike cherish God and hold him dear as the covenanting one.

---

7. According to Hastings, *Seeing All Things Whole*, 90.
8. Berkhof, *Christian Faith*, 16.
9. See the introduction of this current volume.

BETWEEN DETACHED INQUIRY AND COVENANTAL KNOWING

Within a covenantal framework, loving and knowing become two parts of the same reality, especially when it comes to how we know God personally. This point of view says that knowing covers relationships and that love for God and trust in him are important parts of the quest for understanding. By recognizing that love and knowledge go together, we can deepen and change our relationship with God and the world around us. According to Esther Meek, knowing in a covenantal sense "is relational knowing, and the better we are at cultivating the knowing as an interpersonal relationship, the better we will be at knowing."[10] Drawing from Michael Polanyi's epistemology, Meek emphasizes the concept of subsidiary-focal integration as a key aspect of knowing.[11] Polanyi used this concept to describe the process by which our attention shifts between focal and subsidiary awareness when engaging with a subject. Focal awareness refers to the explicit, conscious focus on an object or idea, while subsidiary awareness involves the implicit, background knowledge that supports our understanding. They are "palpable, rooted in our embodiment and rooting us in the world, concretely enacting the guidance of guiding words. They are palpably felt, the way our bodies are palpably felt to be our own. That palpable feel makes the subsidiary wonderfully ordinary."[12] As such, subsidiaries represent what we have called our affective way of being in the world as humans.

Esther Meek proposes that knowing is an act of love and a journey that involves cultivating an interpersonal relationship between the knower and the known. "The knower riskily and creatively scrabbles to indwell clues to achieve a focal pattern. It takes love and commitment."[13] This way of knowing not only informs but also transforms the way the knower views the known. Her approach to knowing differs significantly from the traditional understanding of knowing through facts. The traditional view often emphasizes the acquisition of discrete, objective pieces of information, where knowing equates to accumulating facts or mastering a subject through memorization and intellectual analysis. This

---

10. Meek, "Covenant Epistemology."
11. Meek, "Covenant Epistemology."
12. I follow Esther Meek closely in this section. See Meek, *Little Manual for Knowing*, 50.
13. Meek, *Little Manual for Knowing*, 52.

approach tends to prioritize objective, detached, and analytical methods of inquiry. In contrast, Meek proposes that knowing is an act of loving and a journey that involves cultivating an interpersonal relationship between the knower and the known. It is not about collecting objective facts but about a journey that begins with "puzzlement or wonder."

Instead of collecting facts and data, we create focal patterns as a way of organizing the particulars or clues into a coherent structure to make sense of the subject that has puzzled us or filled us with wonder. Indwelling forms these focal patterns, which requires the knower to "rely on clues subsidiarily to shape a complex focal pattern."[14] This involves shifting from "looking at" the clues (focal awareness) to "looking from" them (subsidiary awareness of what we know tacitly), but we can only do one of these actions at a time. "All knowledge and knowing have a 'from-to' structure: It has two connected levels: the focal and the subsidiary. Each is what it is in relation to the other. We are aware of the subsidiaries as they bear on the focal pattern. The pattern makes sense of the subsidiaries. The relationship between focal and subsidiary is like whole to part."[15]

As knowers experience moments of insight, or epiphanies, they feel a sense of recognition and connectedness with the known, what Meek calls an encounter. She argues that this experience of knowing through love is an encounter or, drawing on the work of Martin Buber, an I-thou relationship, between the knower and the known. The knower gives themselves in love to the subject, and the subject responds in kind, revealing its truths and transforming the knower's understanding of reality. In her covenant epistemology, Meek asserts that our relationship with God serves as the subsidiary awareness that makes focal knowledge of God possible. In liminality, we cultivate a deeper understanding of God and our relationship with him. "We give ourselves in a loving pledge to pilgrimage in the half dark, navigating by a dimly understood, half-hidden star. We are giving ourselves, and at that point we have no guarantee of eventual light. And, in fact, there is no guaranteed link between subsidiary and focal."[16] This process requires us to embrace the unknown and be willing to dwell in uncertainty and ambiguity as we seek to know God.

As we walk this path of loving the God we want to know, we may not be assured of a clear and definitive subsidiary-focal integration, but although there is no guarantee, "we may find ourselves graciously blessed

---

14. Meek, *Little Manual for Knowing*, 48.
15. Meek, *Little Manual for Knowing*, 51.
16. Meek, *Little Manual for Knowing*, 63.

with integration—with insight and understanding."¹⁷ From her work I have identified these signs that integration has occurred:

1. Depth and richness of the integration: The sense of contact with reality comes from the depth and richness of the newfound understanding. A successful integration not only makes sense of the original puzzlement and wonder but also reshapes the questions and transforms the knower's reality.

2. Retrospective and prospective richness: Retrospectively, the integration makes sense of past experiences and puzzles. Prospectively, it opens up hopes and possibilities for the future, which Meek calls "indeterminate future manifestations."

3. A profound transformation: When the knower comes into contact with reality, it has a deep effect on his or her journey. The integration does not merely fit into the person's pre-existing sense of reality. Instead, it reshapes their understanding and places them in a new world, the world of the known.

4. Excitement: A successful integration generates a sense of excitement in the knower, accompanied by "indeterminate future manifestations." These ministrations represent the endless possibilities and prospects that stem from the encounter with the real. This excitement and anticipation of future possibilities indicate that contact with reality has been made.

5. Pledge-based verification: People know they have made contact with reality when they later confirm their original sense of rightness and conviction about the informal and personal integration through formal testing and verification.[18]

Even though it is hard to know exactly how Old Testament prophets and other religious figures experienced subsidiary-focal integration, we can guess based on what they did and how they lived. Although the prophets of old would not have known the terminology of subsidiary-focal integration, the tell-tale signs are present. Prophets and religious figures in the Old Testament often received messages and insights directly from God through visions, dreams, or other supernatural experiences. These

---

17. Meek, *Little Manual for Knowing*, 63.
18. I have identified these tell-tale signs from my reading of Meek, *Little Manual for Knowing*, 63–70.

revelations might have served as "particulars" or clues, which the prophets would then need to interpret and integrate into their understanding of God and reality. While we cannot know the exact process of subsidiary-focal integration for Old Testament prophets and religious figures, it is reasonable to assume that divine revelation, prayer, meditation, knowledge of sacred texts and oral traditions, community and mentorship, and obedience to God all played a role in shaping their understanding of and relationship with the divine. These experiences likely contributed to moments of encounter and insight, similar to the "aha!" moments Esther Meek described in her framework of covenantal knowing.

They possessed a deep love and an intimate understanding of God and his people. Their tacit knowledge of God stemmed from their experiences, revelations, and personal relationships with the divine. This background knowledge supported their focal awareness, or explicit messages, which they communicated to the people. The prophets in the Old Testament believed it was possible for Israel to be at peace with God, and their tacit knowledge of God's love and mercy underpinned their messages of hope and restoration. They called upon the people to repent and return to God, assuring them of his forgiveness and willingness to reestablish a right relationship with them. Their tacit understanding of God's plan for salvation and the ultimate reconciliation of humanity with him also informed their prophecies regarding the future messiah. Throughout the challenges and setbacks faced by the people of Israel, the Old Testament prophets consistently conveyed God's unwavering desire to restore his relationship with them. This covenantal relationship was grounded in love, as God placed eternity in human hearts.[19] The prophets, as intermediaries between God and the people, demonstrated the integration of tacit and focal knowledge, emphasizing the importance of both types of awareness in developing a deep, transformative understanding of God and his intentions in the world.

A great example of subsidiary-focal integration is found in Eccl 3:11, in which the prophet declares that God "has made everything beautiful in its time. He has also set eternity [*olam*] in the human heart; yet no one can fathom what God has done from beginning to end."[20] The verse speaks to the beauty and mystery of God's plan for creation, recognizing both its inherent order and our inability to grasp its full extent.

---

19. See Eccl 3:11.
20. Heschel, "God of Israel and Christian Renewal," 467–68.

But, while *olam* refers to God and his attributes, it suggests also that the human heart possesses an inherent yearning for God himself. Understanding this passage through the lens of Polanyi's tacit knowledge and Meek's covenant epistemology, we can appreciate the human desire for a deeper connection with the eternal God who created us. Only through an intimate relationship with God can we satisfy our longing for meaning and purpose, which is rooted in our tacit awareness of the divine.

BETWEEN A NOTION AND A NAME

It is indeed interesting that *olam*, which signifies eternity or everlasting, is also a name for God in the Old Testament. As Abraham Heschel says, "The God of Israel is a name, not a notion."[21] A distinction exists between a "name" and a "notion." A notion encompasses all objects with similar characteristics, while a name pertains to a specific individual. A notion offers descriptions and definitions, whereas a name stirs emotions and connections. "A notion can be conceptualized, while a name is something you invoke."[22] His emphasis on invoking the name of God rather than a notion of God suggests a call for subsidiary-focal integration. There, our tacit knowledge of God—represented by the eternity placed in our hearts—is deeply intertwined with our focal knowledge of God, which we can express through a personal knowledge of God as *infinite*.

It is important to notice that it is in the human heart, the seat of his affections, where eternity resides and the integration originates. Jeremiah, the supposed author of Ecclesiastes, in his desire to know God, participates in and is absorbed into, as it were, God's words and the reality that these utterances produce. As he stands in the midst of everyday life, facing the challenges, victories, joys, and sorrows that come with being a prophet, what matters is that he knows God. But more importantly, God knows him,[23] or that he conducts his theology not only in the active voice but in the passive voice of being known.[24] It is a beautiful interplay between heart and mind in an eternal dance that declares the name of God as one who knows God, but in the full knowledge that God knows him and the people of Israel. This relationship reflects the intimate

---

21. Heschel, "God of Israel and Christian Renewal," 467–68.
22. Heschel, "God of Israel and Christian Renewal," 467–68.
23. This is based on the idea made famous by Packer, *Knowing God*, 37
24. Hays, *First Corinthians*, 139.

connection between the human and divine, emphasizing the profound significance of seeking both to know God and be known by God.

BETWEEN ATTENDING TO AND ATTENDING FROM

As I look at my life story through the lens of subsidiary-focal integration and think about how my life is changing, I can now see how indwelling, encounter and integration played a big part in answering my "puzzlement" about the theology that supported apartheid. And I can understand how I once thought it was "reasonable." Indwelling, for me, started with the challenge that Bishop Tutu presented all those years ago, when I was an undergraduate student of theology. Working as a janitor, living in an attic, and seeing so many very sick people in hospitals made the struggle for integration harder for me. But it was the experience with James that laid bare the condition of my heart, and for the first time I became aware that I was not purely rational and that I cannot think my way to a new means of being in the world. In the words of Panksepp, it was then that I realized that I, like everyone else, have conscious pre-conceptual "pre-propositional affective mentalities"[25] that influence my perception and interpretation of the world around me. These affective mentalities move me to act and think, often without my explicit awareness. Despite supporting an unjust system, our affective consciousness moved Christians like me. It shaped our perceptions and responses to find our way through the liminality of life on the southernmost tip of Africa. Deeply ingrained prejudices and fears, operating at the level of affective consciousness, contributed to an emotional aversion toward people of color or those who threatened the status quo. We can easily explain this through the lens that Meek provided, by noting that the focal pattern apartheid theology provided—the apparent reasonableness of that system—was the product of the subsidiary-focal integration of the Afrikaner culture that I inherited. This in itself was not wrong; what was and is wrong is that the church and state prohibited anyone from questioning the focal pattern that was preached as gospel and enshrined in law.

What South Africa needed, and what I found in Egleston, was the opportunity to give my subsidiary awareness focal attention. I followed Meek's advice to "revert to attending *to* what we have been attending

---

25. Panksepp, "On the Embodied Neural Nature," 158–84.

from," since subsidiary awareness operates without focal knowledge.[26] In addition, subsidiary-focal integration never really stops, and so the influence of subsidiary awareness grows in size and influence, and as a result shapes how we perceive the world. Since subsidiary and pre-conceptual and pre-propositional mentalities operate automatically, we may maintain a flawed, inadequate integrative pattern, or one that harbors disordered affections.

So as I began to attend *to* what I had been attending *from*, I experienced a profound sense of loss at first, as if I were a stranger in my own body and mind. On my best days, it felt "uncomfortable, disconcerting, unnatural, and risky."[27] As I inhabited my disordered affections, I wandered through a dimly lit path with no promise of finding light at the end. I knew there were no guarantees that exploring these subsidiary affections would bring about an integration of my head and my heart, but indwelling eventually led to breakthrough moments, and my heart began to shift. I could see a new picture emerging as I sensed a deeper connection with and understanding of what was truly real. My most profound realization was that I too had a birth defect, that I too was a victim of the embryo-damaging drug of racial superiority masquerading as Christian virtue. It became clear to me that I needed God's grace, "the gracious inbreaking deliverance, the possibility of a new being—the Holy."[28] But how can a finite human being encounter an infinite God without inadequately representing or comprehending the vastness of his being? This is what we need to turn to next.

---

26. Meek, *Little Manual for Knowing*, 55.
27. Meek, *Little Manual for Knowing*, 56.
28. Meek, *Little Manual for Knowing*, 67.

5

Being

AT THE HEART OF the promise of new being lies a question that humans have grappled with for centuries: How can finite human beings encounter an infinite God without inadequately representing or comprehending the vastness of his being? Despite the challenges and apparent contradictions that may arise, the idea of this encounter has remained a central and enduring question throughout human history, driving our curiosity and our search for meaning. Therefore, before we can understand what it means to live in the world, we have to have a better understanding of the Being who is the ground of our being. In this undertaking, it is important to ask how we can even begin to understand God, who is infinite, if we are not. How can a mortal life fathom the depths of immortality? Our search is complicated because we are neither gods nor beasts; we are somewhere in the middle.

BETWEEN ZIMZUM AND TIKKUN

In many religious and philosophical traditions, the idea of the finite encountering the infinite sits within the belief in that underlying unity or interconnectedness of all things. This unity, often referred to as the "divine essence" or "ultimate reality," suggests that a point of connection between the finite and the infinite exists, even if it may not be immediately apparent. For instance, in the Lurianic doctrine of the metaphysics of Judaism, Rabbi Isaac Luria explains how creation has been filled with the divine presence of God descended to this world, making it possible for people to have an understanding of God. According to this doctrine, the world was created in three stages: *Zimzum*, *Shevirah*, and *Tikkun*. *Zimzum* is the stage where God contracts himself and makes room for the creation of other beings. In *Shevirah*, which is often translated as "brokenness" or "shattering," God's presence returns to the world, but the earthly vessels meant to hold divine light break, causing the *Shekhinah* to be scattered as shards of light throughout creation. According to this idea, the world was originally created as a perfect and unified whole, but this unity was shattered and scattered throughout creation as a result of human rebellion. The shards of light that were scattered throughout creation represent the divine sparks that are present in all things. The task of human beings is to gather these sparks and restore the original unity of creation. In Jewish thought, the ultimate goal of human existence is to come closer to God and to participate in the ongoing processes of creation and redemption. *Tikkun* refers to the restitution of the vessels, which can only be achieved through the arrival of the messiah, the restoration of the broken vessels, and the reunification of God's presence in the world.[1]

BETWEEN GOD AND THE CREATION

In Christian theology, *analogia entis*, or the analogy of being, was the solution that Thomas Aquinas proposed to explain how humans could even begin to understand who God was. With this idea, he proposed a similarity or analogy between God's being and the being of creation, while maintaining the fundamental distinction and difference between the two. This analogy allows us to understand and speak about God in a meaningful way without reducing him to a mere creature or equating him with the created world. It acknowledges that while there are similarities between God and creation, there is also an infinite qualitative difference between the creator and the created.

Erich Przywara explains it well when he says, "Within every similarity, however great, is an ever-greater dissimilarity."[2] With this, Przywara highlights the core idea of the analogy of being by emphasizing that while there is a resemblance between creaturely being (created beings) and God's being, the differences between them far outnumber the similarities. It acknowledges that creatures have some aspects of their being that

---

1. For a detailed discussion, see Scholem, *Kabbalah*, 128–44.
2. Przywara, *Analogia Entis*, 234.

reflect or are analogous to God's being, but at the same time, the essential distinction between the finite and the infinite is maintained. The similarities allow us to comprehend and speak about God in a meaningful way, using aspects of creation as a basis for our understanding. However, the recognition of the vast differences between God and creatures reminds us that our language and understanding of God are always limited and cannot fully capture the essence of the divine.

The analogy of being is a way of speaking about God that acknowledges both his transcendence and his immanence, or permanent pervasion of the universe, while also recognizing that our language and concepts are limited and imperfect when it comes to understanding the divine nature. For Paul Tillich, because God is "the ground of our being,"[3] our individual existence is not separate from the divine or ultimate reality; "we all know," he says, "that we are bound eternally to it but rather that it is an integral part of it."[4] However, humans experience alienation from God as separation from the ground of being, and therefore we are anxious beings who face the prospect of non-being.[5] Faith in the light of non-being is the "courage to be" in the face of possible annihilation and to find meaning in the midst of this reality. For him, this understanding of the relationship between the individual and the divine has profound implications for how we view ourselves and our place in the world. In another sermon, "Escape from God," he reminds listeners that "the centre of our whole being is involved in the centre of all being, and the centre of all being rests in the centre of our being."[6] He believed that true spirituality requires a deep engagement with the world and its problems and that the call to justice and compassion is a demand that comes from the eternal presence of God in the world. This makes sense because there is an "ultimate unity of all beings" that is "rooted in the divine life from which they emerge and to which they return. All beings, non-human as well as human, participate in it. And therefore, they all participate in each other."[7]

---

3. Tillich, *Shaking of the Foundations*, 160.
4. Tillich, *Courage to Be*, 157.
5. Tillich, *Courage to Be*, 157.
6. Tillich, *Courage to Be*, 47.
7. Tillich, *Eternal Now*, 45.

BETWEEN BEAUTY, GOODNESS, AND TRUTH

David Bentley Hart sees creation as the product of God's free and unconstrained act of love, through which he guides us by his infinite wisdom and goodness.[8] He uses the metaphor of light to describe how the Spirit refracts or differentiates the radiance of God into an infinite variety of forms and colors. According to Hart, the Son perfectly reflects the image of the Father, and therefore, God is "always somehow analogous."[9] For his part, the "Spirit forever 'prismates,'" refracting the radiance of God into an infinite array of beautiful and harmonious forms.[10] This means that every aspect of creation, no matter how small or seemingly insignificant, can reveal something of God's truth. Hart believes that the Spirit's refraction allows every finite slice of creation to become a possible disclosure of God's truth. In other words, the beauty and wonder of the created world, whether it be the majesty of a mountain range or the delicate intricacy of a flower, can all be seen as reflections of the infinite beauty and wonder of God's being. Furthermore, Hart argues that the Spirit "projects" the trinitarian being into the created order. This means created beings, both visible and invisible, that reveal something of the nature of God. This projection of the trinitarian being into the world means that we can see every place as a site of beauty and wonder we can trace back to the infinite source of being.[11]

But not everything is beautiful in the world. We should ask the hard questions about war zones, natural and personal disasters, cruelty and crime that are sites of suffering and ugliness. Hart does not shy away from this; for him, this all happens in God. This view emphasizes that God is not a distant and aloof being, but rather that he is intimately involved with the created world. Everything in the world is interconnected and has a relationship to God. This interconnectedness is often described as a "oneness" or a "unity" that transcends individual things or beings. In this sense, God is understood as the "ground of being," the underlying source of all existence and the unifying force that gives coherence and meaning to the universe. From this perspective, our engagement with the world is

---

8. Hart's first major work, *Beauty of the Infinite* (2003), an adaptation of his doctoral thesis, received acclaim from theologians such as John Milbank. However, in more recent publications he has drawn criticism from scholars such as N. T. Wright.

9. Hart, *Beauty of the Infinite*, 186.

10. Hart, *Beauty of the Infinite*, 186.

11. Hart, *Beauty of the Infinite*, 191.

not just a matter of intellectual inquiry or observation, but rather a way of encountering and experiencing God. Through our engagement with the world, we can sense the interconnectedness of all things and the underlying unity that binds them together. This sense of interconnectedness and unity can lead to a deeper sense of awe and wonder at the beauty and mystery of the universe and can inspire a sense of gratitude and reverence for the divine presence that permeates all things. Therefore, the task of carrying out theology should be approached with a sense of awe and wonder, as we seek to understand and appreciate the divine presence that permeates all things. Theology, in this view, is not just an intellectual pursuit, but also a spiritual practice that requires an openness to the mystery and beauty of the world in which we dwell. Theological inquiry should seek to understand how we can live in relationship with God and with each other, and how we can work toward the flourishing of all things.

Four transcendental attributes reveal the interconnectedness and interdependence of all things, according to Hans Urs von Balthasar in *The One, the Good, the True, and the Beautiful*.[12] He refers to these attributes as transcendental because "they surpass all the limits of essences and are co-extensive with Being."[13] In other words, these attributes cannot be reduced to or be defined by any particular essence or substances. Rather, they are fundamental and universal aspects of reality that apply to all things, regardless of their specific nature or characteristics. They "run through all Being," they are the "interior to each other," which means that they are not independent qualities but are interdependent and inseparable from each other.[14] Something that is truly true is also truly good, beautiful, and one, and vice versa. The idea of truth and beauty as matched coordinates may first have been recorded in English in 1819 by the English poet John Keats (1795–1821). He concludes his famous "Ode to a Grecian Urn" with two iambic lines: "Beauty is truth, truth beauty,—that is all / Ye know on earth, and all ye need to know." Critics are divided on its value. Therefore, we cannot understand being without understanding the way in which these attributes mutually indwell each other as inseparable aspects of the very nature of reality. In this way, goodness is not just a property that exists on its own; it is the unity of truth and beauty. It therefore follows that beauty is the fusion of goodness and truth, and truth is the synthesis of goodness and beauty. Balthasar's proposal intrigues because he is explicit

---

12. Von Balthasar, "Résumé of My Thought," 468–73.
13. Von Balthasar, "Résumé of My Thought," 471.
14. Von Balthasar, "Résumé of My Thought," 472.

that the mutual indwelling of the attributes of being—beauty, goodness, and truth—is analogous to the mutual indwelling of the persons of the Godhead, "from whom all created beings originate and who, we surmise, is the supreme reality that pervades all finitudes."[15] Balthasar's proposal suggests that the interconnectedness and mutual indwelling of the Trinity can serve as a model for understanding the interconnectedness and interdependence of all created beings, and that the attributes of beauty, goodness, and truth are not just abstract concepts but concrete realities that shape our lives. This perspective offers a rich theological framework for exploring the nature of God, humanity, and the world we inhabit.

BETWEEN FATHER, SON, AND SPIRIT

Many contemporary theologians describe the three persons of the Godhead as a mutual indwelling. Thomas Torrance describes the Trinity as a "three-way reciprocity" between the Father, Son, and Holy Spirit, in what he calls "the perichoretic co-activity of the holy trinity."[16] This idea of *perichoresis* has a long history in theology, going back to the early Christian church to explain the mutual indwelling of God.[17] The word has two primary meanings: to go around, circle around, encircle; and, secondly, to permeate, pervade, imbue, penetrate through and through.[18] The second meaning, as permeation, was applied to explain the Trinity, where one being enters another and becomes present within that entire being, communicating or passing on its attributes to the being of another, thus leading to complete unity while preserving difference. This meaning reminds me of Paul's saying that the Holy Spirit saturates Christians "and we were all given the one Spirit to drink."[19] In both Christological and trinitarian debates, *perichoresis* expresses the idea of communication of attributes, which is a special and important effect of permeation. Slobodan Stamatović explains this well. "Their perichoretic conception could

---

15. Von Balthasar, "Earthly Beauty and Divine Glory," 202.

16. Torrance, *Christian Doctrine of God*, 198.

17. The Greek word for *perichoresis* is περιχώρησις, which comes from the verb περιχωρέω (*perichoreo*) meaning "to go around, move about, or to interchange." The root of the word is composed of two parts: *peri*, meaning "around," and *choreo*, meaning "to make room," "to contain," or "to move."

18. In this section I follow the lexicographic study of Stamatović, "Meaning of Perichoresis."

19. 1 Cor 12:13 (NIV).

be defined as a view by which two or more different entities create unity by entering into each other without blending or merging, but either of them remains what it is and, at the same time, participates in the other or others. Or more briefly: *Perichoresis*, or permeation, is the unity of the different, where the difference remains completely preserved despite the communication of one to the other."[20] This means that the three persons of the Trinity are in a perichoretic relationship with one another, constantly giving and receiving in a way that sustains the unity and coherence of divine life. This means that each person in the Trinity is actively involved in the lives of the other two, and that their actions affect each other in a dynamic and reciprocal way.

This word *perichoresis* helped theologians, then and now, to grasp a glimpse of a unique way of relating ontologically, while faith in the light of non-being is the "courage to be" in the face of possible annihilation, preserving the difference between beings. Miroslav Volf believes that "in every divine person as a subject, the other persons also indwell and mutually permeate one another without ceasing to be distinct persons."[21] Millard Erickson highlights that the Trinity is "bound together in agape love," the love of God for humans which unites them in the closest and most intimate of relationships.[22] This unselfish love makes each person of the Trinity more concerned for the other than for themselves. This mutual submission and glorification of one another reflects a deep and intimate unity that is grounded in love and shared life. As we have seen, Balthasar's proposal links the mutual indwelling of the transcendental attributes of being and the perichoretic union of the persons of the Godhead. For Balthasar, there is an analogy between the transcendentals, which are properties that are universally present in all things, and those that exist within God.[23] This suggests that the Trinity can be a model for understanding the interconnectedness of all beings, and the attributes of beauty, goodness, and truth shape our lives. It provides a theological framework for exploring God, humanity, and the world.

20. Stamatović, "Meaning of Perichoresis," 321.
21. Volf, *After Our Likeness*, 209.
22. Erickson, *God in Three Persons*, 331.
23. See Balthasar, "Résumé of My Thought," 471. Here he says: "If there is an insurmountable distance between God and his creatures, but if there is also an analogy between them which cannot be resolved in any form of identity, *there must also exist an analogy between the transcendentals—between those of the creature and those in God*" (italics mine).

BETWEEN THE FINITE AND THE INFINITE

Humans know that unity of beauty, goodness, and truth is the transcendental attribute of God's being, who is the ground of all being, because we have experienced glimpses of these qualities in human life. Any understanding of the metaphysics of being must start from our experiences of the world around us, which are always limited by our senses. For Balthasar, no "metaphysics of Being as such and its transcendental qualities can be separated from concrete experience, which is always of the senses." He goes on to explain: "'The True,' the disclosure of Being in its totality, only becomes visible where a particular thing is adjudged true. The goodness of Being is only visible where one meets with some good thing which both brings 'the Good' near and—through its finitude, fragility and relative 'badness'—causes it to retreat again. And we know that there is beauty from the sensuous experience which presents and withdraws it, reveals, and again conceals it, evanescent, in myriad layers."[24] We sense it before we even make sense of it.

So, we must ask, again, how can finite humans make sense of their encounters with God without inadequately representing or comprehending the vastness of his being?[25] Our sense of being comes from "being," or existing in relation to the formation of human self-consciousness and understanding of the world through our relationships with others. Balthasar suggests that our first conscious recognition of ourselves, our "I," as a being, forms through our relationship with another, namely our human parent, who we have already argued is the figure of authority, the covenanting other, in the liminal existence of the newborn baby.

"In that encounter, the horizon of all unlimited being opens itself for him, revealing four things to him: (1) that he is one in love with the mother, even in being other than his mother, therefore all being is one; (2) that love is good, therefore all being is good; (3) that love is true, therefore all being is true; (4) that love evokes joy, therefore all being is beautiful."[26] We see a very clear progression here; we move from sensing to making sense. Balthasar believes a mother's smile exemplifies the affection of love.

This view suggests that our understanding of reality follows a specific order, beginning with the beauty of an object, moving through the

---

24. Von Balthasar, "Transcendality and Gestalt," 34.
25. See Schindler, *Catholicity of Reason*, 58.
26. Balthasar, "Résumé of My Thought," 471.

goodness it represents, and finally arriving at the truth it embodies. The process starts with the encounter or presentation of a being; the beauty of this being captures our attention and stimulates our intellectual interest. Beauty acts as the initial spark that draws us into a deeper engagement with the object. As we indwell and experience the beauty of the being with which we share time and space, we start to appreciate the goodness of that being. The goodness serves as a conduit between beauty and truth, connecting these two qualities and deepening our desire to know, just as we believe we are known.

BETWEEN SENSING AND MAKING SENSE

This truth becomes the culmination of the process, where we fully realize our cognitive understanding of the object. In Balthasar's view, beauty, goodness, and truth are interconnected, with each attribute building upon the previous one. The beauty of an object captures our attention, its goodness adds depth to our understanding, and its truth brings the entire process to a close. By following this order, we gain a more profound and comprehensive understanding of reality, he argues. Today, we often prioritize thinking over experiencing beauty and goodness, which does not align with how our brains work.[27] Following Balthasar, Curt Thompson agrees that beauty is invitational and welcoming. Beauty leads us to worship and helps us see through the challenges of life, just as Thomas did when he encountered Jesus and touched his wounds. It again explains that we first sense things and then make sense of them. Beauty is what attracts us to goodness in the first place and ultimately to truth. Once we immerse ourselves in beauty and goodness, we can comprehend truth. But we too often focus on right thinking and cognition in our faith instead of what truly matters: the experience of beauty that captivates and draws us in. For beauty "pulls us in to the object of beauty (as an act of eros, where we simultaneously lay hold of and are laid hold of by the beautiful object), pulls us up towards the source of beauty (as an act of contemplation), pulls us outside of ourselves (as an act of ecstasy), and pulls us out towards others (as an *agapic* act)."[28]

---

27. For an in-depth discussion, see chapter 2 of Thompson and Fujimura, *Soul of Desire*.

28. Taylor, "Beauty as Love," §6.

Many would agree with this point of view, but, as we have seen, Karl Barth objects to any theology that starts from subjective human experience instead of God's concrete act of revealing himself in Jesus Christ. He rejected the Catholic concept *analogia entis*, the analogy of being, since he believed that it set up a common category of "being" between God and human beings, which risks placing "being" as a divine subject prior to God.[29] Being can then be seen as a reality or category that is independent of God's self-revelation in Christ or even the intra-relationship of the Trinity. In short, it risks placing God and his creatures on the same level, which would limit God's transcendence and freedom. This potentially makes "being" God's god, rather than recognizing God as the one who creates and sustains all being. However, Balthasar makes it clear that to *be* God and to *be* a creature "are utterly dissimilar, contrasting with each other in every way."[30] But in Jesus the Christ they become the same; in him is the unity of beauty, goodness, and truth that reveals who God is as the ground of being.

Humans, as image bearers of God, have a sense that there is the potential for beauty, goodness, and truth in everything, even in us. When we encounter something beautiful, we are drawn to it and experience a sense of love and awe. In the same way, when we see good qualities in other people, it makes us want to be better ourselves. And we seek truth to gain understanding and insight because we want to live free from falsehoods. These desires for oneness, beauty, goodness, and truth are fundamental to the human experience and are often seen as expressions of our spiritual or transcendent nature. They are the point to a deeper longing for meaning and purpose in life, and a sense that there is something that gives our lives significance beyond the material world.

From a theological perspective, we can see these desires as reflections of the divine nature. The Christian tradition holds that God is the ultimate source of all beauty, goodness, and truth, and that these qualities manifest not only in the created world but ultimately in the life, death, resurrection, and ascension of Jesus Christ. As such, we can understand our desire for these qualities as a longing for God and a recognition of the divine presence in the world. Our desires for beauty, goodness, and truth are not simply aesthetic or intellectual pursuits but rather expressions of

---

29. Barth, *CD*, 1:224.
30. Von Balthasar, *Theology of Karl Barth*, 286.

our deepest affections. For Christians, they represent our longing to live in union with God, in Christ through the Holy Spirit.

In the upcoming chapters, I will explore how we engage in theology as a Christian practice while living in union with God. However, it appears to me that this inquiry is intricately tied to even more fundamental questions: Who constitutes the "we" that exists in union with God? What defines our humanity? This also presupposes the possibility of union with God and suggests that our existence is inherently designed for such unity. It implies that, as human beings, we were intentionally fashioned for a harmonious connection with the divine.

The manner in which we respond to these inquiries carries profound implications for our understanding of the role and purpose of theology.

6

Human

WHAT DEFINES OUR HUMANITY? According to the ancient wisdom of Genesis, God's existence predates time and space, transcending our limited understanding of existence itself.[1] In the vast expanse of eternity, there was only God—a boundless, divine presence pulsating with the infinite potential of creation. Within the depths of his infinite divine essence, God conceived the magnificent idea to bring forth a wondrous universe, teeming with life, purpose, and interconnectedness. Yet, in contemplating this awe-inspiring notion, we come to realize that God was not merely a being harboring an idea; he was the very essence of that idea—the quintessence of creative power and divine intention. Through this divine idea, all aspects of existence find unity and harmony. God's creation becomes the manifestation of his own inner being—a dynamic expression of a social trinity, interconnected and interwoven in divine communion.[2] Within the fullness of his boundless being, God imagined

---

1. An idea that I have taken from Moltmann, *God in Creation*, 80.

2. This divine being, identified in the creation narrative in the plural form. Biblical Hebrew does not have a "royal we" for pronouns, but it does have a plural of excellence or majesty for nouns. If *Elohim* is indeed a majestic noun in Gen 1:1, we see that *Elohim* (אֱלֹהִים) refers to himself in Gen 1:26 as "us," a plural pronoun, which is not "royal we." "And God said, let us make [נַעֲשֶׂה] human beings [אָדָם] in our image, after our likeness [וַיֹּאמֶר אֱלֹהִים נַעֲשֶׂה אָדָם בְּצַלְמֵנוּ כִּדְמוּתֵנוּ]." *Elohim* (אֱלֹהִים) is a triune being. So early Christian interpreters described creation as a trinitarian event. As evidence of this, we could turn to Paul's teachings, but we can also find it in the writing of the earliest theologians, such as Irenaeus (AD ca. 130–202). In his book *Against the Heresies*, he writes, "Now humans were formed after the likeness of God, and molded by His hands, that is, by the Son and Holy Spirit, to whom also He said, 'Let Us make humans.'" Translation taken from Irenaeus, *Against Heresies*, bk. 4.20. I have changed the text to

human life, fashioning a space beyond himself to accommodate the unfolding of his creative vision for life that will be in a covenantal relationship with him.

In ancient times, these concepts would have resonated effortlessly with diverse cultures, for they too perceived that thoughts possessed an inherent urge to be given form and expression.[3] Thus, God's transcendent idea unfurls into a vibrant world where finite creatures in a web of life grow and evolve to be a reflection of his infinite being. God spoke into existence a cosmos pulsating with purpose and significance—a cosmos in which beings can find kinship, meaning, and a profound connection to the divine vision that birthed them.

The early theologians of the church frequently sought insight from Gen 1:26–27 to address one of the most basic questions that we have as human beings: Who are we? For the sake of easy reference, I will quote these famous words in full here.

> "Let us make human beings in our image, to be like us. They will reign over the fish in the sea, the birds in the sky, the livestock, all the wild animals on the earth, and the small animals that scurry along the ground." So God created human beings in his own image. In the image of God he created them; male and female he created them. (NLT)

BETWEEN GOD'S BREATH AND OUR BREATHING

Gregory of Nyssa, the youngest of the Cappadocian Fathers, calls his reader to recognize that Adam, as a person, had not yet come into existence in Gen 1; it happens in Gen 2.[4] From this perspective we consider a pre-gendered view of humans here.[5] He sees humanity, male and female, as one being. Imagine a single, sacred body, where every individual is intricately united, rejoicing in the presence of God. Therefore, the image of God refers to the harmonious unity, bound together by love, that reflects

---

be more gender inclusive. See also *Against Heresies* 4.20.1; 5.1.3; 5.6.1; 5.28.4. Basil the Great makes a similar claim, "Moreover, from the things created at the beginning may be learned the fellowship of the Spirit with the Father and the Son." Basil, "*De Spiritu Sancto*," §16.38.

3. "Myth" is an idea that has "an inner urge to express," according to Stählin, "μῦθος," 766–67.

4. Irenaeus, *Against Heresies*.

5. Irenaeus, *Against Heresies*, 22, 4.

the ideal image of God. To speak of the image of God "is the same as to say that He made human nature participant in all good; for if the deity is the fullness of good, and this is his image, then the image finds its resemblance to the archetype in being filled with all good."[6] It is a state of being where there is no division, no alienation among humanity. In this divine unity, humanity shines forth as a perfect and harmonious expression of the divine. Humans are permeated by God's Spirit which called it into existence. "For nothing in the world exists," says Jürgen Moltmann, "lives and moves of itself. Everything exists, lives and moves in others, in one another, with one another, for one another, in the cosmic interrelations of the divine Spirit."[7] God spoke, and creation manifested.

As humans, we can relate to the idea that God speaks. We know that our vocal cords vibrate as we breathe, causing the production of sounds when we speak. Our breath materializes as sound vibrations in the ear canal of the listener, causing their eardrums to move. As these sound vibrations make their way through the ossicles to the fluid in the cochlea, the auditory nerve eventually registers them and transmits them as a signal to the brain. In the same way, anthropomorphically, God speaks, producing a physical manifestation of his ideas. Just as our words become something else, through God's word, the cosmos exploded into existence. The breath of God, his *rûaḥ*, was exhaled as God spoke. In this sense, the narrator of the proto-story wants us to see how the infinite idea became a reality through God's creative act, his word spoken. Clark Pinnock explains, "The Son is the Logos of creation, the origin, and epitome of its order, while the Spirit is the artisan who by skillful ingenuity sees to it that creaturely forms arise and move toward fulfillment."[8] This was certainly the view of the psalmist when he wrote:

> When you send your Spirit, they are created,
> and you renew the face of the ground.
> . . .
> When you hide your face, they are terrified;
> when you take away their breath,
> they die and return to the dust.[9]

---

6. Irenaeus, *Against Heresies*, 16, 10.
7. Moltmann, *God in Creation*, 11.
8. Pinnock, *Flame of Love*, 60.
9. Ps 104:29–30 (NIV).

The psalmist wants us to delve into the wondrous act of creation, where God's very breath infused life into existence. Picture the scene: the Lord God meticulously forming a human from the dust of the earth, sculpting him with divine craftsmanship.[10] But the awe-inspiring moment comes when God leans close, tenderly infusing the breath of life into the newly formed nostrils. At that very instant, the dust becomes a living, breathing being.

This act of creation is radical, for it signifies that human bear the image of God himself. They carry within them the breath of the divine, a breath that grants them the ability to know God intimately. The intertwining of God's breath and human breath is not confined to the pages of Genesis alone. The prophet Isaiah beautifully portrays this interplay, using the words *rûaḥ* and *nᵉšāmâ* interchangeably, revealing that it is God who gives breath to the people and life to those who walk the earth.[11] Ezekiel further illuminates this divine connection, depicting the image of God's breath returning life to the slain, just as it did with Adam. The comingling of our breath and God's breath is evident, as Job declares that his integrity remains intact as long as God's breath and Spirit dwell within him.[12] It is the very idea of God that his life, his breath, would infuse human life with sacredness. Every form of life, from the smallest particle to the most complex organism, carries the indwelling divine breath. In this pristine state, there is no flaw or imperfection—only pure beauty and unbounded joy. Reflecting on this profound truth, we can trace our origin back to the mind of the maker.[13] We recognize a transcendent quality to human life as our spirits reach beyond ourselves in alignment with the divine. As Jürgen Moltmann eloquently expresses it, "Because God's Spirit is present in human beings, the human spirit is self-transcendently

---

10. Gen 2:7. For a detailed look at this scripture I have included the important Hebrew words. "Then the Lord God formed a man [אָדָם—*'āḏām*] from the dust of the ground [אֲדָמָה—*'ăḏāmâ*] and breathed into his nostrils the breath [נְשָׁמָה—*nᵉšāmâ*] of life [חַי—*ḥay*], and the man became a living being [נֶפֶשׁ—*nep̄eš*]." The word for "breath" is a different word, but is a synonym of the word for "spirit" in Gen 1:2. See Johnson, *Vitality of the Individual*, 27. "In the circumstances, it is not surprising that we should find a form of polarization in the significance of the term רוּחַ [*rûaḥ*] . . . In the former case רוּחַ [*rûaḥ*] came to be used with a purely physical connotation as a simple synonym of נְשָׁמָה [*nᵉšāmâ*], the ordinary word for 'breath.'"

11. Isa 42:5 (NIV).

12. Job 27:3 (NIV).

13. I borrowed this beautiful phrase from Sayers, *Mind of the Maker*, 27.

aligned towards God.[14] We are intricately woven into the tapestry of creation, resonating with the very essence of the original idea.

BETWEEN BEING SUBJECT AND OBJECT

Prior to the scientific revolution of the sixteenth and seventeenth centuries, individuals perceived themselves as integral components of, or intimately connected to, the world that enveloped them. Knowledge, during that time, manifested as a lived reality, a product of navigating an intricately interwoven existence within their surroundings. According to Owen Barfield, the medieval mindset did not experience the same degree of separation from the external world that characterizes our contemporary perspective. Consequently, acquiring knowledge did not necessitate the pursuit of objectivity. The medieval person, according to Barfield, was "integrated or mortised" into their environment, with each facet of their being intricately linked to different elements of the world through imperceptible threads. In this paradigm, the individual of the Middle Ages resembled less an isolated island and more an embryo in symbiosis with its surroundings.[15]

However, this profound connection underwent a seismic shift during the enlightenment, marked notably by René Descartes's philosophical contributions. Descartes introduced an epistemological discontinuity between the self and the world, altering the fundamental relationship between human consciousness and its surroundings. The once seamless integration was replaced by a conceptual separation, laying the groundwork for a more detached and objective approach to knowledge. He feared that what he thought was real could be the work of some evil power luring him into illusion. How could he be certain that what he thought he knew was in fact real? Since the senses are a primary link between self and the world, one of the primary ways through which Descartes accomplished the separation of self and world was by purging his senses from the knowledge process. He suspected that our tendency to accept knowledge of the world through the senses must be overcome, and he made a plan to do just that.

> Therefore, I will suppose that, not God who is the source of truth but some evil mind, who is all powerful and cunning, has

14. Moltmann, *Spirit of Life*, 7.
15. See Barfield, *Saving the Appearances*, 78.

> devoted all their energies to deceiving me. I will imagine that the sky, air, earth, colors, shapes, sounds and everything external to me are nothing more than the creatures of dreams by means of which an evil spirit entraps my credulity. I shall imagine myself as if I had no hands, no eyes, no flesh, no blood, no senses at all, but as if my beliefs in all these things were false.[16]

He displayed his doubt in this statement, through which he attempts to achieve a foundation of knowledge that cannot be doubted. By doubting everything, including the physical body and sensory perceptions, Descartes aimed to find indubitable truths upon which he could build his philosophical system. By imagining that everything external to him was the fabrication of an evil spirit, he sought an unshakable truth that could not be deceived. This skeptical stance allowed him to arrive at his famous declaration, *"Cogito, ergo sum"*—"I think, therefore I am," which became the starting point for his philosophy. From this self-evident truth, Descartes attempted to rebuild knowledge and establish the existence of God and the external world.

Descartes relied on reason, his ability to think. He sought a rational objectivity. He felt that only through detaching from the world could knowers obtain pure and undistorted knowledge. With this, he laid the foundation for the enlightenment and modernism. In this human epoch, separation from the world became the key to credible and verifiable knowledge and understanding. This became the preoccupation and the cornerstone of this time in human history. In this way of understanding, objects are always "other." There is an inner eye in this so-called Cartesian epistemology where we experience the world in our mind, through elevated reason. Reason is the deductive process of step-by-step analysis which yields clear and distinctive ideas and therefore brings about unquestionable understanding. If we were to rely on passions and allow emotions to enter into our attempt to understand the world, our minds would be clouded, and knowledge would be distorted.

BETWEEN ROMANTICS AND MODERNISTS

However, during the romantic period of the late eighteenth century, a renewed interest in metaphysics arose and a critical reevaluation of Descartes's ideas took place. The Romantics, influenced by philosophers such

---

16. In his *Meditations* 1; Descartes, *Meditations*, 15–16.

as Johann Wolfgang von Goethe, Friedrich Schelling, and Georg Hegel, sought to explore the nature of being and the interconnectedness of the world. In Hegel's philosophical framework, God is characterized by complete transparency to himself, emanating boundless self-awareness and consciousness.[17] As the pinnacle of existence, God freely unfolds his infinite creative spirit, perpetually engendering new forms of being and actualizing the full range of his divine potential.[18] As the absolute spirit, God encompasses the full spectrum of reality, transcending all limitations and encapsulating the unity and interconnectedness of existence. The Romantics rejected the Cartesian dualism that separated mind and matter, advocating for a more holistic and intuitive understanding of reality and what it means to be human. They emphasized the role of emotions, intuition, and subjective experiences in comprehending the world, in contrast to Descartes's reliance on reason and detachment. Romantics sought to reconnect with a sense of unity with the natural world and embraced metaphors as a means of capturing the ineffable aspects of human experience. Metaphors became a tool for expressing the interconnectedness of all things and exploring the depths of the human soul.

In contrast to the holistic and metaphysical perspectives of the Romantics and Hegel, modernists of the nineteenth and early twentieth century adopted a more skeptical stance toward metaphysics and a more empirical and scientific approach to understanding reality. They questioned the feasibility and relevance of unified, transcendent entities and instead focused on humans as objects to be studied. Artists and thinkers during this period sought to capture the fractured, chaotic, and rapidly changing nature of society, employing innovative techniques and exploring new possibilities. Modernism emerged as a response to the rapid changes and disruptions brought about by industrialization, urbanization, and technological advancements. It sought to reflect the complex but shattered and often frenzied nature of modern life.

In art and literature, modernism marked a departure from traditional styles and conventions. Artists rejected established forms and ventured into uncharted territories of experimentation. They aimed to reflect the intricate tapestry of modern life, incorporating unconventional forms, disconnected narratives, and subjective perspectives. Early twentieth-century writers like James Joyce, Virginia Woolf, and T. S. Eliot delved

---

17. Hegel, *Lectures on the Philosophy of History*, 1:150.
18. Hegel, *Encyclopedia of the Philosophical Sciences*, 3:29–30.

into the depths of the human mind, employing stream-of-consciousness narration, nonlinear storytelling, and rich symbolism. Through their works, they sought to convey the intricate layers of subjective experience and the disorientation prevalent in the modern era. The rise of modernism also brought forth a shift in philosophical thinking. Modernist thinkers challenged traditional metaphysical frameworks and advocated for a more empirical and scientific approach to reality. They questioned the feasibility and relevance of a unified, transcendent entity like Hegel's absolute spirit. Figures such as Friedrich Nietzsche, Søren Kierkegaard, and Martin Heidegger emphasized the limitations of human knowledge and the subjective nature of existence. Nietzsche famously proclaimed the "death of God," signaling a departure from traditional metaphysics and the need for individuals to create their own values and meaning in a secular and scientifically oriented world.

BETWEEN MODERNISTS AND POSTMODERNISTS

Within the realm of psychology, the advent of psychoanalysis provided a framework for understanding the complexities of the human mind. Sigmund Freud explored the depths of the unconscious and the influence of repressed desires and early experiences on adult life. His theories shed light on the hidden, irrational, and conflicting aspects of the human psyche. Carl Jung expanded upon Freud's ideas, introducing the concept of archetypes that shape human thoughts, behaviors, and cultural expressions. Jung's exploration of archetypes touched upon metaphysical elements, recognizing the presence of transcendental and timeless aspects within the human psyche. His approach emphasized the interconnectedness of the human experience, transcending the boundaries of empirical observation and individual perception. Behavioral psychologist B. F. Skinner took a different stance by rejecting metaphysics and focusing solely on observable human behavior. Skinner's radical behaviorism emphasized the role of external stimuli and reinforcement in shaping behavior, excluding subjective experiences and internal states. His rejection of metaphysical concepts aligned with the skepticism prevalent in modernism and deviated from the introspective aspects emphasized by psychoanalysts and other modernist thinkers.

Postmodernism emerged as a response to ontological anxiety, specifically during a time characterized by existential threats of the Cold

War era. The looming specter of nuclear annihilation, concerns about environmental degradation, and the uncertainty posed by technological advancements like artificial intelligence fueled existential anxieties. Postmodernism challenged the grand narratives and absolute truths of modernism, recognizing the fragility of human existence and the need to confront existential perils. By questioning traditional foundations of knowledge and authority, postmodernism allowed individuals to navigate the uncertain and disintegrating terrain of the postmodern world. It embraced the subjective, contextual, and socially constructed nature of knowledge and experience, acknowledging the complexities and anxieties of human existence in the face of challenges to survival.

BETWEEN WHAT WE KNOW AND DON'T KNOW

So, the question remains: Who are we? What do were really know about what it means to be human? This question is complicated, since we live in the aftermath of the cultural wars that have preceded us and the current battles that rage across our electronic screens and printed pages, in movies, television, political debates, and social media. We now navigate a disorienting landscape of diverse and conflicting viewpoints, contributing to a sense of epistemic uncertainty and ontological angst. The erosion of shared metaphysical frameworks and traditional belief systems has left individuals grappling with existential questions and a longing for coherence and meaning in a riven world. The longing for ontological grounding stems from a desire for lucidity, purpose, and a sense of belonging. It is fair to say that our understanding of what it means to be human causes deep anxiety and fear, leaving us with a renewed yearning to grasp our origins and perceive our destiny.

Many of us today long to reconnect with a more integrated understanding of what it means to be human. We seek an instructive orientation amid division. However, the challenges of reconciling diverse slivers of knowledge and perspectives in a search for unity and coherence persist. We lack, and do not trust, the overarching narratives, or grand metanarratives, that have answered our questions in the past. The certainties that once were prevalent, the ontological grounding and a deeper sense of connected and collective intelligence, evade us in an ever-increasingly fractured world.

We have created the problem and must address it. In order to advance, we need to examine where we have come from; perhaps we will find answers in ancient texts and cultures. There I believe we will rediscover the deeply held truth of human interconnectedness, a view of a unified and harmonious cosmos, a coherent understanding of reality, identity, and purpose. I find solace in the answers I find in the ancient Judeo-Christian culture in which I stand. Here I discover the value of all life, and human life, since God's breath animates all life. God breathed his life into clay that he gathered to make us living souls. Through God's breath of life we find our existence and sustenance. In this way, the natural and the supernatural are intricately intertwined, harmoniously coexisting as a testament to God's creative and sustaining presence. Every aspect of creation bears the imprint of the divine. It is not limited to extraordinary or miraculous occurrences, but it permeates the ordinary, happy, dull, and sad moments of our lives. In the mundane routines, in the ordinary tasks, in the depth of our emotions, and in the complexity of our experiences, we can find God's presence.

God's imprint in creation means that every encounter, every relationship, and every situation holds the potential for divine connection. In the joys of life, we glimpse the overflowing love and goodness of God. In the midst of monotony or struggles, we discover God's sustaining presence and the invitation to seek meaning beyond the surface. In the happy moments, we celebrate the blessings and experience a glimpse of the abundant life God desires for us. In the dreary and routine moments, we learn the value of perseverance, finding that even in the seemingly mundane, God can reveal hidden treasures and growth opportunities. In the sad moments, we find solace in the compassionate embrace of God. In times of grief, loss, or pain, God walks alongside us, offering comfort as one who knows the depth of our pain. Through it all, God's presence brings hope, resilience, and a reminder that we are not alone.

God does not separate himself from his creation. He wants to be known; he wants to share his life with us. This is embedded in the creation narrative. Humans were created to be able to know God, through the Spirit that indwells us. We were created to understand God's depths, to know the mind of the maker. The Spirit enables us to know his mind so we can experience the fullness and beauty of God's creation with pure joy. Because we have God's breath in us, we have tacit knowledge that comes from being once united with God in the universal humanity described in Gen 1:26–27. Our knowledge of God gives us the categories and schemata to appreciate his creation and to understand his original idea. The Spirit infused God's image bearers with meaning and understanding, flowing through the Spirit from the creator to image bearers and back again, in an eternal hermeneutical circle of meaning and understanding. Jeremy Begbie describes this as a priestly function in which "humans are to mediate the presence of God to the world and in the world, representing his wise and loving rule. But this is so that on behalf of creation humans may gather and focus creation's worship, offering it back to God, *voicing* creation's praise."[19]

However, there is also a sad reality that marks human existence, which we need to consider as we answer the question of who we are as humans. It is to this that we will now turn.

---

19. Begbie, *Resounding Truth*, 203 (emphasis mine).

7

Anxiety

Elie Wiesel told the awful story of a young Jewish boy who was executed by the Nazis. As death camp inmates watched the young boy die slowly on the gallows, one of the onlookers asked, "Where is God?" This has been a question on the lips of humans from our early beginning, since it reveals our ontological anxiety. From the first pages of the Bible we see evil is at work to obscure God as the ground of being, the creator of all. We see how evil broke relationships between humans, between humanity and nature, and between humanity and God. This separation or fracture manifests in various ways, including conflict and hostility, and physical, spiritual, and emotional distance. It impairs our ability to make sense of our senses. Throughout the Old Testament, we see examples of humanity's struggle with sin and its destructive consequences. The prophets spoke of God's judgment on sin and the need for repentance and reconciliation. The psalmists cried out for restoration and healing, acknowledging the pain and suffering sin and evil caused, and prompting the question: "Where is God?" That is the question humans ask in liminality; that lies at the heart of our ontological anxiety.

"Where is God?" has been a pivotal issue in the complex reality of human existence portrayed in the biblical narrative. We can trace our ontological anxiety back to the creation story when God spoke the world into being. In the early phases of creation, God enacted a series of separations, carving out light from darkness, day from night, water from land, and aquatic beings from terrestrial creatures. However, while these acts of separation were far from arbitrary or permanent, they foreshadow the emergence of an evil force in the biblical narrative that desires to separate God from his creation.

HUMANS BETWEEN GOOD AND EVIL

But for God, creative separation was not the end but the means to an evolving grand design, an elegant configuration. In subsequent creative acts of creation, God wove together all the disparate elements designed to coexist harmoniously. Humans found themselves intimately bound to the rest of creation, entrusted with the noble roles of stewards and caretakers. They were also bound to God as reflections of his divine image, and to one another as perfectly complementary beings.[1] Thus, in this grand orchestration of creation, the initial separation transmuted into an intricate web of connection, mirroring the complexity and simplicity of divine life. Jürgen Moltmann explains that God "goes creatively 'out of himself,' communicating himself to the one who is other than himself."[2] But because the idea is infinite, this action did not overwhelm God or overcome him with surprise. Instead, "to create something outside himself the infinite God must have made room for this finitude beforehand, 'in himself.'"[3]

Early theologians of the church, like Gregory of Nyssa, understood that humans had a very privileged relationship with God.[4] If God is the supreme good of all existence, then it follows that his divine essence represents the epitome of beauty and goodness, and the only being truly worthy of our love and adoration. Therefore, Gregory argues, humans as image bearers have a natural inclination toward what is beautiful and good, and we are ultimately drawn to God. It is as if there is an inherent pull toward this ultimate source of perfect union. The human mind, in its pure and aligned state, remains in harmony with the divine mind. It is like a mirror that, through its likeness to the divine archetype, captures and embodies that inherent beauty of God. The mind acts as a guiding force, shaping and giving meaning to the material world, while the natural world, in its reflective capacity, magnifies and expresses the beauty and goodness of the mind. Just as the mind reflects the beauty and goodness

---

1. Plantinga, *Not the Way It's Supposed to Be*, 29.
2. Moltmann, *Trinity and the Kingdom of God*.
3. Moltmann, *Trinity and the Kingdom of God*.
4. Gregory, *On the Making of Man*, 24:2, esp. 12, 8, and 9.

of the divine, this nature, in turn, is adorned with the beauty that the mind imparts. It becomes a mirror of the mind, mirroring the mirrored reflection, if you will.[5] But Gregory has a warning: that if the mind were to deviate from its alignment with the divine, if it were to stray from its mirrored reflection, it would become deprived of that inherent beauty. We will still look for beauty, but we will look for it in ourselves.

In the creation narrative, evil emerges as a serpent seemingly intent on causing an irrevocable separation between God and creation, especially between humans and God, fellow humans, our intrinsic selves, and the very fabric of creation. The biblical account offers a profound commentary on this transformative event. It exposes evil's innate tendency to sever connections, to isolate elements that were meant to be seamlessly integrated. Considering this, it is intriguing that the Greek term for evil, *diabolos*, is closely associated with the act of tearing things apart. The image evoked is of God and humanity, once bound in a harmonious relationship, wrenched asunder by malevolent forces.[6] At its core, *diabolos* connotes defamation and false accusation, providing an apt epithet for the devil as *diablo*, humanity's accuser. His malicious, deceitful allegations serve to deepen the chasm between God and his creation. Where unity was intended, separation has prevailed. The harmonious co-existence that was supposed to define creation is now marked by power struggles and dominance. A tragic tale unravels in the biblical story, showcasing how, in our state of separation, we not only strive for dominance over one another but also fall prey to our self-absorption. Men seek to dominate women, people attempt to assert control over the earth, and the planet retaliates, endeavoring to control its human inhabitants. In this maelstrom of ascendency and subjugation, the individual is drawn deeper into a

---

5. Gregory, *On the Making of Man*, 12, 9. Gregory writes: "And here, I think, there is a view of the matter more close to nature, by which we may learn something of the more refined doctrines. For since the most beautiful and supreme good of all is the Divinity Itself, to which incline all things that have a tendency towards what is beautiful and good, we therefore say that the mind, as being in the image of the most beautiful, itself also remains in beauty and goodness so long as it partakes as far as is possible in its likeness to the archetype; but if it were at all to depart from this it is deprived of that beauty in which it was. And as we said that the mind was adorned by the likeness of the archetypal beauty, being formed as though it were a mirror to receive the figure of that which it expresses, we consider that the nature which is governed by it is attached to the mind in the same relation, and that it too is adorned by the beauty that the mind gives, being, so to say, a mirror of the mirror; and that by it is swayed and sustained the material element of that existence in which the nature is contemplated."

6. Liddell, "Διαβαλλω," in *Lexicon Abridged*, 185.

vortex of self-obsession, an insight Augustine brilliantly captures in his term *"incurvatus in se."*[7] In this relentless pursuit of self-interest, our love for ourselves burgeons such that it eclipses our capacity to love others, driving us further down the path of self-absorption.

BETWEEN ONTOLOGICAL AND EXISTENTIAL INSECURITY

According to Flavius Josephus, a first-century Jewish priest, scholar, and historian, Adam and Eve in Gen 3 sacrificed their knowledge of God and the knowledge they shared with God, turning away from God and into themselves. A rupture occurred between creator and the creature plunging Adam and Eve into a profound crisis of conscience and understanding. According to Josephus, after humans listened to Satan,[8] God addressed Adam saying, "But now you have abused my purpose by disobeying my commandments; for you are silent not through virtue, but by guilty[9] conscience."[10] For Josephus, a guilty conscience is more than just feeling bad about something. The origin of the word for conscience is "shared knowledge," even more so, "privileged knowledge." In the garden, humans went about their daily lives while they shared intimate knowledge with God, while they had a privileged understanding of God and creation, but, sadly, now after this betrayal knowledge lost its currency.[11] Humans, from this point on, would struggle to interpret the particulars

---

7. See Jenson, *Gravity of Sin*, for a discussion of the development of the concept "*homo incurvatus in se*" through theological history. He discusses Luther's expansion of the concept beyond original sin to religious "man," as well as Karl Barth's broadening the concept for *homo religiosus* beyond pride and hubris.

8. The serpent persuaded, as Eve did Adam, to "incite or stir up by persuasion." This section also uses forms of πειθω (if they obeyed God) and περιπειθω (the serpent believed disobedience would bring trouble) and αναπειθω (disobey misled). There is this interesting semantic interplay between active and passive forms—πειθω, active, meaning "persuade" and πειθομαι, passive, meaning "obey." The serpent persuaded Eve, Eve persuaded Adam (moved to action by listening to), and as a result, they ceased to obey (listen to God).

9. The translation is mine. I believe that "guilty" is a more accurate translation of *ponērō*—πονηρω since it pertains "to guilt resulting from an evil deed." See "πονηρω" in Louw and Nida, *Greek-English Lexicon*, 1:776.

10. I also maintain that "conscience" is still the best translation of "συνειδοτι" in Louw and Nida, *Greek-English Lexicon*, 1:324. For the full Greek text, see Josephus, *Antiquities of the Jews*, bk 1, 48.

11. See πονηρω as "worthless" in Louw and Nida, *Greek-English Lexicon*, 1:776.

of their lives in the spirit of the whole; in fact the spirit of the whole will be seen as an obstacle to understanding.

For Paul Tillich, the entrance of evil into our lives has left an indelible mark, rendering us deeply anxious beings due to the profound separation we experience from the very ground of our being—God. This separation has engendered an inherent ontological and existential insecurity, a default mode of insecure attachment. We find ourselves not expecting to be truly seen, soothed, or secure in the presence of others and in the world, which leads us to embark on a lifelong quest to fill these voids from the very moment we come into existence. The cunning of evil has successfully achieved the separation of humanity from God, both in ontological essence and existential experience. This separation has isolated our existence on various levels, causing us to turn inward, detached from the harmonious interconnectedness that permeates the world around us. We become trapped within ourselves, isolated from genuine connection with others and the wider fabric of existence. This inherent insecure attachment compels us to take matters into our own hands, to secure our own lives, and to place our trust solely in ourselves. This according to Ted Peters is the very definition of pride.[12]

BETWEEN PRIDE AND MORTALITY

Pride, as Peters explains, fundamentally refuses to allow God to be God, instead seeking to appropriate divinity for oneself. It is a misguided longing, rooted in a deep-seated desire to overcome our inherent finitude, to delay the inevitability of death for as long as possible, or defy it altogether. Pride represents a self-elevation, a reckless ascent into the realm of the divine, in an attempt to transcend our mortal limitations.[13] In essence, the intrusion of evil has not only left us deeply anxious and separated from God, but it has also instilled within us a restless longing for power and control. This longing, manifesting as pride, seeks to fill the void created by our severed connection to the divine. It is a self-centered desire that propels us to strive against our finite nature, pursuing a false sense of superiority.

Pride is the disintegration of beauty, goodness, and truth and leads to a fractured and discordant existence, where the human spirit is left

---

12. Peters, *Sin*, 87.
13. Peters, *Sin*, 87.

longing for unity and coherence. It breeds cynicism, despair, and a sense of meaninglessness as we witness the erosion of the values that bring depth, purpose, and transcendence to our lives. We construct intricate mazes of deceptions and distortions; we fabricate a sham reality that deviates from the foundation of all being, which is God. This contrived reality is detached from the ultimate source of truth, goodness, and beauty. We fail to heed the warning of Gregory of Nyssa, that if the mind were to deviate from its alignment with the divine, if it were to stray from its mirrored reflection, it would be deprived of that inherent beauty.[14] In this self-constructed reality, the boundaries between truth and falsehood become blurred, and moral principles become subjective and malleable. This detachment from the ground of all being not only distorts our perception of reality but also severs our connection with the transcendent and the sacred. We become disoriented, lost in a labyrinth of our own making, and disconnected from the ultimate source of meaning and purpose. Our concocted reality now lacks the foundation of divine truth and becomes a fragile construct built upon shifting sands.

BETWEEN CONCUPISCENCE AND SCARCITY OF RESOURCES

For Ted Peters, the aftermath of pride is concupiscence, an insatiable craving for worldly pleasure and satisfaction.[15] Concupiscence, an archaic but evocative English term, offers us a profound understanding of the complex human condition, particularly the state of being *incurvatus in se*. At its core, concupiscence encapsulates desire—the intricate interplay of intense longings interwoven with envy, greed, avarice, and covetousness.[16]

---

14. Gregory, *On the Making of Man*, 12, 10. "Thus so long as one keeps in touch with the other, the communication of the true beauty extends proportionally through the whole series, beautifying by the superior nature that which comes next to it; but when there is any interruption of this beneficent connection, or when, on the contrary, the superior comes to follow the inferior, then is displayed the misshapen character of matter, when it is isolated from nature (for in itself matter is a thing without form or structure), and by its shapelessness is also destroyed that beauty of nature with which it is adorned through the mind; and so the transmission of the ugliness of matter reaches through the nature to the mind itself, so that the image of God is no longer seen in the figure expressed by that which was moulded according to it; for the mind, setting the idea of good like a mirror behind the back, turns off the incident rays of the effulgence of the good, and it receives into itself the impress of the shapelessness of matter."

15. Peters, *Sin*, 87.

16. See Peters, *Sin*, 123.

Peters sheds light on the intricacies of concupiscence as he locates it in our mimetic nature—a yearning for what others possess, driven by an underlying conviction that we need it more than they do. These desires, however, extend beyond mere longing; they shape and evolve into intricate schemes, even if their realization remains elusive. Concupiscence essentially signifies a distortion of love. We recognize that God, the very embodiment of love, created us, but we have strayed from his divine embrace. In our anxious state, we have redirected our love away from God, fixating it upon ourselves. This redirection of love gives birth to the perversion of its essence, intertwining it with idolatry—a pernicious force that entices and ensnares us, drawing us deeper into the abyss of self-centered desires. It arises from our detachment from God and our redirection of affection toward ourselves—a convoluted state entangled in the snares of idolatry. It unveils the profound complexity of human existence, the way our desires shape and transform us, often diverting us from the path of love and toward self-centeredness.

Regardless of how self-deluded we may become, Peters asserts that deep down, we are aware of our mortality. We recognize that concupiscence, with its misguided attempt to secure immortality, is ultimately a futile strategy. Moreover, an innate understanding exists within us that distinguishes between good and evil.[17] While we may not possess absolute certainty, a persistent suspicion lingers that goodness transcends the boundaries of time, while evil does not. Perhaps we retain a faint echo of the mind that once knew real beauty, goodness, and truth, but is now only a nagging, distant memory. However, in our desperate quest to uphold the delusion that concupiscence can secure immortality, we resort to weaving a web of lies. These fabrications serve to identify us with what is deemed good, creating a façade that masks our underlying motivations. Regrettably, these lies often extend beyond self-identification and manifest in the dehumanization of others, labeling them as evil.

BETWEEN SELF-JUSTIFICATION AND VILIFICATION OF OTHERS

In the original serpent's interaction with humans, he sowed doubt and brought confusion. The point of his interaction with Adam and Eve was to destabilize them and cause disorientation and perplexity. His sole aim

---

17. See Peters, *Sin*, 161.

was to undermine Adam and Eve's ability to interpret the words of God so that he could gain control over their thoughts, emotions, and actions. This is what we do to hide our concupiscence. The purpose of the serpent is not to hide the truth or to reveal the lie. But lies have a life of their own it would seem. Lee McIntyre explains that when we intend to deceive and we choose to hide the truth, we lie: "This is an important milestone for we have here crossed over into attempting to deceive another person, even though we know that what we are saying is untrue."[18] But this is not where it ends, if only lying were all that we were capable of doing. Beyond, and more insidious than lying, is "Bull-sh*tting," says Harry Frankfurt, one of the world's most influential moral philosophers.[19] According to Frankfurt, for the bull-sh*tter, all these bets are off: he is neither on the side of the true nor on the side of the false. His eye is not on the facts at all, as the eyes of the honest man and of the liar are, except insofar as they may be pertinent to his interest in getting away with what he says. He does not care whether the things he says describe reality correctly. He just picks them out, or makes them up, to suit his purpose. Ted Peters says, "Sometimes these lies identify others as evil, justifying the conclusion that they should die, and we should live. Identifying ourselves with good is called self-justification. Identifying others with evil is called scapegoating."[20]

These intricate webs of lies become powerful tools not only for self-justification but also for enabling the dangerous practice of scapegoating, which operates on a much broader scale. Scapegoating involves attributing blame or responsibility to others for our own wrongdoings, misfortunes, or societal problems. We deploy it to externalize our guilt or negative emotions onto individuals or groups which we perceive as different, threatening, or vulnerable. By shifting the blame onto others, self-justification and scapegoating provide a cathartic release from personal or collective guilt, allowing us to preserve our own self-image and maintain a sense of social superiority. This practice of self-justification and scapegoating extends beyond individual actions and infiltrates the very fabric of broader social structures.

In the process of scapegoating, individuals or groups convince themselves that the victims of their actions or prejudices somehow deserve

---

18. McIntyre, *Post-Truth*, 8.

19. I would prefer to abbreviate the word because I find it a bit jarring, but, I fear, it might lose its power to confront. I have chosen to use an asterisk to soften the blow. Frankfurt, "On Bullshit."

20. Peters, *Sin*, 161.

the mistreatment or negative outcomes they experience. Scapegoating involves attributing blame or responsibility to others in order to alleviate guilt or justify our own actions. This often involves dehumanizing the targeted individuals or groups and creating a narrative that justifies their mistreatment or marginalization. By scapegoating, we distance ourselves from any feelings of guilt or responsibility for their actions or the systemic issues at play. We create a false sense of justification, convincing ourselves that the victims somehow deserve the pain they suffer. This distorted thinking allows individuals to maintain a positive self-image and avoid confronting the uncomfortable reality of their own prejudices or immoral behavior. In this way, scapegoating is a harmful and destructive process that perpetuates injustice, discrimination, and the devaluation of human life. It is an expression of the distorted desire for power and control, where individuals seek to elevate themselves at the expense of others. By engaging in scapegoating, we not only harm the individuals or groups targeted but also contribute to a culture of division, animosity, and social inequality.

BETWEEN KILLING OR BEING KILLED

When we wilfully use our power over those we have turned into scapegoats, we move from pride, concupiscence, and self-justification to cruelty. "The suffering of others works like a drug; the cruel person needs increasingly larger doses to attain the same high. The ultimate fix is the death of the other."[21] As self-deception takes root, and self-justification and scapegoating intertwine, cruelty emerges, grotesque and vile, as the next, haunting manifestation of our ontological anxiety. Cruelty inflicts pain, but since none of us wants to look at pain, says Peters, in this act, we look away. What we have done, taking what is not ours, inflicting punishment on those who are undeserving, categorizing people in ways that dehumanize them, is cruel. But we look away so that the cruelty, the scapegoating, and attribution of blame can continue, to the point that it may cause irrevocable harm. We become blind to the pain and suffering we cause.

Cruelty is addictive, as Peters explains clearly. What accounts for this perverse pleasure? Perhaps the Lifton principle applies here: "killing

21. Peters, *Sin*, 194.

others relieves our own fear of being killed."[22] For example, as we face the difficulties of climate change, we have an awareness of the problem that we have created, in part, by our over-consumption, our concupiscence, for the flesh of other creatures. But we justify our behavior to consume meat far beyond what is needed, and then we inflict pain on animals in order to consume their flesh.

BETWEEN BLASPHEMY AND DEFAMING GOD

However, cruelty does not mark the culmination of our ontological anxiety; instead, blasphemy emerges as a grave, final manifestation. Blasphemy is the final attempt of evil to sever the bond between the name of God and the grace of God. It involves the manipulation of God's name, both directly and indirectly, to conceal evil behind a façade of righteousness. Blasphemy, in essence, embodies hypocrisy, presuming the goodness of God while exploiting that goodness to cloak our insidious injustices.[23] According to Peters, blasphemy poses a significant danger; it can lead observers to question the authenticity of any language pertaining to God, perceiving it as innately deceptive. Blasphemers tarnish the name of God to such an extent that people no longer feel inclined to call upon it, beseeching divine grace. Instead, we use it as a curse.

We blaspheme if we destroy the means by which someone else can experience grace. "Blasphemers," says Peters, "tarnish the name of God to the point that people no longer think to call on it to ask for divine grace."[24] Normally, we would associate blasphemy with using God's name inappropriately. While I can understand that using God's name in vain is blasphemy, it is ironic that we can be cruel and even torture people in the name of God—even claiming to do this as an act of worship. The intricate webs of lies we have constructed, whether to fortify our own self-perception or to condemn others in the name of God, has created a reality where the means of grace have been colonized and corrupted. Now, the unity of beauty, goodness, and truth becomes twisted and distorted, losing its ability to uplift, inspire, and liberate. Instead of appreciating the inherent beauty in the world and others, a lack of aesthetic harmony, ugliness, and chaos confront us. We corrupt goodness,

22. Peters, *Sin*, 194.
23. Peters, *Sin*, 217.
24. Peters, *Sin*, 17.

replacing it with selfishness, cruelty, and a disregard for the well-being of others. The pursuit of self-interest prevails over acts of compassion, justice, and selflessness. We obscure and manipulate truth and overshadow it with lies, deceit, and misinformation. The search for objective reality becomes challenging as subjective agendas and hidden motives dominate. "To a black South African," says Peters, "who has felt the eye and heel of racial injustice, the name of a gracious God may provide the only grounds of hope for deliverance. When the perpetrators of oppression claim this God as their own possession, they leave the oppressed with no symbol of hope. Nothing to hang onto."[25] It follows that blasphemy is a defamation, deforming the character of God; and it prevents others from discovering God as the covenanting other, as we live in liminality.

BETWEEN ANXIETY AND A NON-ANXIOUS PRESENCE

It is difficult to break free from this cycle of beliefs that might be blatantly untrue but keep us from falling apart. The advice to snap out of it simply will not work. Robert Kegan and Lisa Lahey's research reveals that humans resist change. Even those who know that they will die if they continue with their habits often still do not change.[26] They argue that, just as immune systems respond to foreign objects in the body, our mental and emotional systems have a similar protective mechanism. Our assumptions—the deeply held beliefs, often unconscious, that shape our understanding of ourselves, others, and the world around us—act as filters through which we perceive and interpret information that in turn influences our thoughts, emotions, and behaviors. They serve as the architecture and foundations of our mental frameworks and shape our sense of identity and how we make sense of the world. When confronted with information that contradicts or challenges our assumptions, our mental immune system can be triggered, and we may experience resistance or defensiveness. This is because our assumptions "create a disarming and deluding sense of certainty."[27] They propose that our resistance to change stems from our deep-rooted preference for comfort and familiarity. It is akin to how our brain automates thinking and decision-making

---

25. Peters, *Sin*, 17.
26. See Kegan and Lahey, *Immunity to Change*, 37–39.
27. Kegan and Lahey, "Real Reason Why People Won't Change," 91.

to reduce cognitive effort, leading to a natural aversion to engaging with new and uncomfortable ideas.

Daniel Kahneman, in *Thinking, Fast and Slow*, introduces the concept of two thinking systems, the fast and slow systems, which help illuminate how self-delusion can occur.[28] The fast system, characterized by quick, intuitive thinking, relies on biases, preconceptions, and assumptions. This system operates rapidly, allowing us to forge connections and construct mental narratives without extensive conscious deliberation. These biases and preconceptions influence our perceptions and judgments, leading to self-delusion when they distort our interpretation of reality. The slow system, on the other hand, serves as a corrective mechanism. It engages when we detect inconsistencies or discrepancies, prompting us to slow down, analyze, and reflect on the situation at hand.

If we read the creation narrative as an allegory, the serpent represents the layers of self-delusional stories Adam and Eve called on to interpret the tree of good and evil. In this allegory humans are gullible creatures who are easily misled by false stories we hear and we tell ourselves, which causes ontological anxiety. The serpent symbolizes the lies we tell ourselves and how they lead us away from God. In this way of reading the text, evil acknowledges that the human stories we call on to attend to the world can become laden with toxic cognitive artifacts, including untested assumptions, biases, and heuristics, or self-delusion, which influence how we see and experience the world. It also serves as a powerful encouragement to recognize we need critical introspection to unclog our narratives from cognitive artifacts that cause delusion.

In an age of ontological anxiety, self-delusion is an attractive option to escape the harsh realities we face. It, I believe, is our greatest temptation, as I can easily demonstrate with the rise of Donald Trump in American politics and his popularity among certain brands of Christianity. During Donald Trump's campaign for the presidency of the United States, a barrage of stories about his personal, business, and public life inundated the liberal media. Simultaneously, conservative news outlets wove alternative narratives, presenting substitute or optional facts. As if this were not enough, Trump adeptly spun tales about both himself and his opponent, employing willful ignorance, falsifications, bull-sh*tting, and outright lies, resulting in a distorted perception of reality. Trump seemed to have mastered the art of gaslighting, using stories to disorient

---

28. Daniel Kahneman, *Thinking, Fast and Slow*.

his opponent and rally his supporters. Coinciding with Trump's election as the forty-fifth president of the United States, the *Oxford Dictionary* selected "post-truth" as its word of the year, describing it as "relating to or denoting circumstances in which objective facts are less influential in shaping public opinion than appeals to emotion and personal belief."[29] It leads me to the conclusion that in the face of ontological anxiety, post-truth is our collective constructed delusion, not different to what Germans experienced before World War II and South Africans under apartheid.

It seems as if the world has lost its ability to be reasonable. We appear to be adrift on a sea of augmented reality, with no sense of where we have come from or where we are going—with deep ontological anxiety. All we seem to have are ancient stories that somehow tether us to reality—centripetal forces that establish a comprehensive sense of coherence. Without them, we are left adrift, devoid of meaning. In these stories, a memory is awakened of a time when humans could appreciate the beauty, goodness, and truth of the source of all being—God. We once again need slow thinking and careful attention to our way of being in the world to suppress our impulse to expel this memory from our immune system.

In this book, I argue that this is the task of theology: to develop practices that awaken us to the presence of God so that we can integrate our affection for and knowledge of God to live this human life wisely—free from deception and lies (yes, without bull-sh*tting)—in union with God. Theology, in this view, is a disposition or a way of being in this world—a subsidiary awareness of what we know tacitly. This vision for theology sees it not just as an intellectual pursuit or an emotional experience but as a practice that led to practical wisdom. This orientation of theology aligns it with the ultimate purpose of our existence—to know that God is with us even in our anxiety. If we view theology as the practice of integrating our affection and knowledge of God, our starting point cannot be a system. It is, instead, our senses that are ordered by the presence of beauty, goodness, and truth of God—the ground of being, our ultimate attachment figure, our covenanting other in liminality. This is what we will turn to now.

---

29. Steinmetz, "Oxford's Word of the Year."

PART B

With God in the Middle

8

Trinity

IN THE NETFLIX MOVIE *Rectify*, the protagonist, Daniel, finds himself grappling with major adjustments to live outside prison after being released from death row, where he spent nineteen agonizing years awaiting execution for a crime he did not commit. When Tawney, a young Christian woman, asked him how he survived knowing that his execution was always just hours away, Daniel's response is breathtaking. He learned, he said, to live in "the time in between the seconds." These words capture the essence of living fully in the present moment, cherishing the fleeting instances that exist between the past and the future. For Daniel, the past represents a haunting chapter of his life that he cannot alter—a period marred by the injustice of his wrongful conviction and the torment of waiting for his life to be snuffed out. On the other hand, the future was uncertain, overshadowed by the lingering possibility of his imminent execution. In this context, the only tangible reality he possessed was in the space nestled between the seconds, the moments of liminality. This concept of liminality extends far beyond Daniel's personal journey, shining a light on the universal human condition.

It serves as a reminder that our reality is lived between seconds, minutes, hours, and days. Our existence unfolds within the temporal realm of betwixt and between, where the past has slipped away, and the future is yet to unfold. Like Daniel, we find ourselves constantly dwelling in the time between the seconds, in the embrace of liminality. As we have already seen, theologians have referred to this state of liminality as a tension between the "already and not-yet." It acknowledges that believers are already part of God's kingdom, yet the kingdom's full expression will manifest itself in the future, upon Christ's return. John the apostle proclaims that Christ came "to destroy the works of the devil,"[1] and Paul believes that Christ has disarmed "the rulers and authorities."[2]

In the same epistle, Paul says that Christ liberated the world from "the dominion of darkness and brought us into the kingdom of the Son he loves."[3] He tells us that our lives are now, even as we live this human life here on earth, hidden with God in Christ.[4] For Paul, the believers in Colossae who live in their beautiful city also already live with Christ in "God in the heavenlies." That Paul says "now" is significant because it highlights the present reality of the believers' new life in Christ. Paul is emphasizing that they are no longer defined by their old way of being but by their new life in Christ. The word "hidden" is also important since in Col 3:3 it can be translated as "having been hidden" or "being hidden."[5] The action of hiding has been completed in the past and continues in its present state or condition. Therefore, the phrase "your life is now hidden with Christ in God" refers to a present reality, not just a future event.

BETWEEN LIFE AND DEATH

But how is it possible to live in union with God in this world? Our traditional view is that God and humans live in separate dimensions: "God is up there and we are down here." This is why those who watched the tragic execution of the Jewish boy, a story we recounted earlier, presumed that God was absent and uncaring. At the beginning of chapter 8 we heard imprisoned witnesses to the boy's execution ask the despairing question "Where is God now?" The question penetrated to the very core of Elie Wiesel's being. And it provoked an astonishing answer, not from those around him, but from deep within his own being. Like the small, still voice that assured Elijah of the nearness of God, Wiesel also heard a voice

---

1. 1 John 3:8 (NIV).
2. Col 2:15 (NIV).
3. Col 1:13 (NIV).

4. See Col 3:3-4, "For you died, and your life is now hidden with Christ in God. When Christ, who is your life, appears, then you also will appear with him in glory."

5. κεκρυμμένη (kekrymmene), which is the perfect participle passive form of the verb κρύπτω (krupto). The perfect participle indicates that the action of hiding has been completed in the past and continues in its present state or condition.

saying, "He is here. He is hanging there on the gallows."[6] Even in suffering and death could this little boy be in union with God. With its inherent beauty, truth, and undeniable power, this message never fails to inspire awe and stir hope within me that God is with us. This is the power of the cross. For Jürgen Moltmann, "there is no other suitable Christian response when confronted with the brutal torture inflicted on this innocent child. To speak here of a God who could not suffer would make God a demon."[7] It would also mean that we have not begun to understand the meaning of the cross. Any notion of an indifferent God would relegate God's suffering to insignificance, at the same time rendering our existence meaningless. In the face of such horrors, discussing an indifferent God would condemn us to a state of apathy.[8]

BETWEEN FRIDAY AND SUNDAY

To fully grasp the significance of Moltmann's assertion, it is worthwhile making a short detour to understand how he arrived at this profound and transformative conclusion. Moltmann's journey to faith in Christ was deeply influenced by his experiences as a prisoner of war during World War II. Born in Hamburg, Germany, in 1926, he was drafted into the German army at the age of eighteen. He was captured by British forces in 1945 and placed in a prisoner of war camp in Belgium and later in Scotland. While in captivity, he and his fellow prisoners were confronted with pictures of concentration and extermination camps at Belsen and Auschwitz. The initial disbelief among the German soldiers soon gave way to a grave realization that they were part of the war machine that enabled these horrors to occur. As Moltmann recounts in his book *The Source of Life*, "The depression over the wartime destruction and a captivity without any apparent end was exacerbated by a feeling of profound shame at having to share in this disgrace. That was undoubtedly the hardest thing, a stranglehold that choked us."[9] In the midst of this emotional turmoil, a chaplain gave Moltmann a Bible. Through reading the Bible, particularly the Psalms and the book of Job, he began to find solace and hope.

6. Moltmann, *Crucified God*, 274.
7. Moltmann, *Crucified God*, 274.
8. Moltmann, *Crucified God*, 274.
9. Moltmann, *Source of Life*, 4.

Moltmann was particularly struck by the suffering of Jesus Christ on the cross and the idea that God, too, suffered and was present in the midst of human pain. This understanding of a suffering God resonated with Moltmann's own experiences and brought him comfort, eventually leading him to embrace Christ. "I began to understand the assailed Christ because I felt that he understood me," he recalls.[10] "This was the divine brother in distress, who takes the prisoners with him on his way to resurrection. I began to summon up the courage to live again, seized by a great hope."[11] His words remind me of my own experience of being in union with God in the basement of Pitts Theological Library. Moltmann remembers: "I never 'decided for Christ' as is often demanded of us, but I am sure that then and there, in the dark pit of my soul, he found me. Christ's God-forsakenness showed me where God is, where he had been with me in my life, and where he would be in the future."[12]

The cross works against the separation, against the consequences of the break that occurred between humans and God. On the cross, we see God, in Jesus, laying down his life; God taking on the risk of death. God did not die, nor did God cease to exist. Jürgen Moltmann wants us to see that the cross is not the death *of* God but rather the death *in* God.[13] Jesus, the second person in the Godhead, is being crucified. The Father and the Spirit are therefore ontologically present in his death. Moltmann maintains that we need to think about the cross in trinitarian terms since the "Son suffers dying, the Father suffers the death of the Son. The grief of the Father here is just as important as the death of the Son . . . he also suffers the death of his Fatherhood in the death of the Son."[14]

On the cross, the trinitarian union of God is stretched to breaking point; this was the most dangerous moment in divine existence, the darkest point in human history, and the near annihilation of Being itself, the end of the unity of beauty, goodness, and truth. However, the good news is that God overcame the death spiral of nothingness as the bond of love, the Holy Spirit, overcame the *death in God*. The crucifixion and resurrection of Jesus show us the forces that have taken control away from people and kept us from God. The resurrection is as important as the cross in this understanding of the events of Easter. This is the moment when God

---

10. Moltmann, *Source of Life*, 5.
11. Moltmann, *Source of Life*, 5.
12. Moltmann, *Source of Life*, 5.
13. Moltmann, *Crucified God*, 243.
14. Moltmann, *Crucified God*, 243.

overcame the threat of non-being, and in Christ, it is available to all of humankind. This same Spirit that raised Jesus from the dead dwells in us.[15]

Therefore, the cross is God's answer to what has happened to humanity and our ontological anxiety that resulted from our separation from God. It reveals the gravity of the human condition as it unveils the seriousness of our delusion and the depths of the relational rupture that we have suffered as a consequence. H. R. Mackintosh reminds us that the "elusive greatness" of God's sacrifice is the measure of the danger that threatens humankind.[16] On the cross, God confronted the darkness into which we should have sunk and the extent to which God would go to reconcile the world to himself. The crucifixion marked a pivotal moment in history, altering the world's trajectory and initiating God's plan for the future. N. T. Wright says the cross "was the moment when something happened as a result of which the world became a different place, inaugurating God's future. The revolution began then and there; Jesus's resurrection was the first sign that it was indeed underway."[17] The apostle Paul further deepens our understanding of this transformative power by showing how God made us alive with Christ. He portrays the cross as the epicenter of forgiveness and redemption, where our sins are absolved, and our moral debts are canceled. The cross becomes the divine instrument through which God disarms "the powers and authorities," triumphantly declaring victory over them. In this grand narrative, Jesus assumes all our sins, evils, and the chasms separating us from God. Jesus suffered "all the contingencies and evils recorded in the Gospels,"[18] taking upon himself all our sins, iniquity, and ontological anxiety.

BETWEEN SATURDAY AND SUNDAY

Balthasar invites us to reflect on the Saturday before the resurrection, urging us not to rush too quickly to celebrate the resurrection without considering what happened in the intervening time, the space between two days, two moments. Balthasar believed that Jesus's suffering did not end with his death on the cross but continued with his descent into hell.[19]

---

15. See Rom 8:11.
16. Mackintosh, *Christian Experience of Forgiveness*, 159.
17. Wright, *Day the Revolution Began*, 34.
18. Jenson, *Systematic Theology*, 1:144.
19. Von Balthasar, *Mysterium Paschale*, 151.

In Christian theology, the church fathers spoke of limbo when they spoke of Jesus's descent into hell, where he is believed to have proclaimed the good news to the souls of the righteous who had died before his resurrection. While Balthasar's perspective differs from this traditional understanding of what happened on the day between Friday and Sunday, the space between death and life, his emphasis on the Saturday before the resurrection is significant because it invites us to give more focal attention to what happened on this day. His theology seems to help us locate our own experience of living in liminality with the suffering that it entails. By contemplating the Saturday before the resurrection, we are invited to enter into the mystery of Jesus's descent into hell and to reflect on its meaning and our own liminal experience.

Saturday represents the separation or distance[20] that the Trinity endured to make our union with Jesus possible. On this day, he experiences the ultimate separation from the Father in his divine nature. In Balthasar's understanding, Jesus's suffering on Saturday involves him being "made sin," which means that all the sins of humanity are transferred to him. This leads both the Father and the Son to feel as though the Trinity is destroyed.[21] When the Son suffers the ultimate separation and distance from the Father and experiences the hellish consequences of being separated from the very ground of his being, his suffering reverberates through the perichoretic union, affecting the Father and the Holy Spirit as well. The question in this dark abyss of ontological schism is also the question that echoes through chambers of the darkness that Jesus entered on that day. Where is God? The answer also comes as a whisper as it did for Elie Wiesel. The Holy Spirit—the bond of love between the Father and Son—answers he is here in death. The Holy Spirit, says Balthasar, remained unbroken despite the hellish separation that was threatening to rip the Godhead apart. This bond of love was and is so strong that it encompasses the infinite distance created by sin and ultimately encloses sin within divine love.[22]

---

20. The word here is *diastases*, διάστασις, "a parting, a separation," but Balthasar also uses the German word *abstand*, which can mean "distance" geographically or metaphorically.

21. This view is taken from the interpretation provided by Pitstick, *Light in Darkness*, 119.

22. Von Balthasar, *Theo-Drama*, 5:261–63.

BETWEEN THE LIFE, DEATH, AND RESURRECTION

So how is it possible to live in union with God in this world? Moltmann and Balthasar help us locate our own experience of living in liminality between death and life and the role that the Holy Spirit plays as we find our way through our own space between spaces. It is a life lived in the Spirit of the one who bonds us to God in liminality. God is always near. As we have seen, for Clark Pinnock it is the Spirit who "is leading us into union with God to transform our personal intimate relationship with the triune God."[23] The Holy Spirit is the change agent in the process of salvation. Salvation is not just being rescued from sin and death; it is also a process of change that leads to an intimate relationship with God. Through the Holy Spirit's work, believers not only come to a deeper understanding of the triune God but also enter into union with God. This union is not just a matter of being in God's presence but of participating in the divine life of God. Through salvation, we can share in God's perfect love and community, which is shown in the way the Father, Son, and Holy Spirit bond in love. Therefore, the goal of salvation is not just to be released from sin and death but to be transformed and united with God. This transformation involves the renewal of our minds and the reordering of our desires so that we become more like Christ. As we are changed, we are able to take part in God's divine life and have real relationships with him. And, through salvation, we receive the privilege of sharing in God's life and experiencing the perfect love and community that exists within the Trinity, even now, like the Christians in Colossae, as a present reality.

The Holy Spirit is the bond of love, who indwells and draws humans toward participation in the life of the triune God. In the words of Pinnock, "United to Christ in his participatory journey, we are on the path to share in God's life through death and resurrection. The living flame of love is preparing souls for union with love."[24] Theologically, this relationship also speaks to our existence in a state of liminality, where we inherently seek secure attachment to navigate uncertain times and spaces. God is the secure attachment humans can choose to accept or reject. The secure attachment is available for all humanity in liminality, making it possible for all of us to find meaning and hope in our journey toward the light that comes in the morning. This divine connection illustrates how God's presence, particularly through the Holy Spirit, serves as the

---

23. Pinnock, *Flame of Love*, 149.
24. Pinnock, *Flame of Love*, 152.

ultimate source of security and support as we navigate the uncertainties of life. Therefore, Paul can encourage all Christians in all eras to prefer gentleness or reasonableness ahead of anxiety.[25] It comes from a deep awareness of God's presence in our lives and an understanding of how important it is to live in union with him.

Again, this does not surprise the careful reader of the Bible; the Holy Spirit is the divine presence that animates and enlivens all things, bringing them to their fullest expression of beauty, goodness, and truth. In the creation narrative in Genesis, the Spirit of God hovers over the formless and the void, bringing beauty, goodness, and truth that we know as creation. "Everything that exists is in some way true, good, and beautiful."[26] Similarly, in the redemption story, the Holy Spirit brings the beauty of new life[27] and beauty out of the death and sin that had entered the world through disobedience. The life, death, and resurrection of Jesus Christ demonstrated this, which brings hope and restoration to humanity. In sanctification, the Holy Spirit continues to work in the lives of believers, bringing beauty out of destruction and disordered hearts.[28] This means that the Holy Spirit transforms believers from the inside out, changing their desires, affections, and attitudes, and making them more like Christ.

Jonathan Edwards believed that the process of sanctification, or the inward transformation of our affections to make us more like Jesus, is also a process of beautification accomplished by the Holy Spirit. He believed that as we become more like Jesus, we also become more beautiful, both in our inner selves and in our outward appearance. In his sermon "God's Excellencies," he makes it clear that to be sanctified is to be beautified:

---

25. Phil 4:5. See my reference to this passage in chapter 4. According to Rienecker, *Linguistic Key to the Greek New Testament*, 560, To epieikes (τὸ ἐπιεικὲς) can be translated as "reasonableness in judging." "The word signifies a humble, patient, steadfastness, which is able to submit to injustice, disgrace, and maltreatment without hatred or malice, trusting in God in spite of it all."

26. Kreeft, "Lewis's Philosophy of Truth, Goodness, and Beauty." See also Kreeft, "Goodness, Truth, Beauty, and Boredom."

27. See John 3:5–8 (NIV). "Jesus answered, 'Very truly I tell you, no one can enter the kingdom of God unless they are born of water and the Spirit. Flesh gives birth to flesh, but the Spirit gives birth to spirit. You should not be surprised at my saying, "You must be born again." The wind blows wherever it pleases. You hear its sound, but you cannot tell where it comes from or where it is going. So it is with everyone born of the Spirit.'"

28. See Rom 8:10–11 (NIV). "But if Christ is in you, then even though your body is subject to death because of sin, the Spirit gives life because of righteousness. And if the Spirit of him who raised Jesus from the dead is living in you, he who raised Christ from the dead will also give life to your mortal bodies because of his Spirit who lives in you."

"Tis the excellency of his excellencies, the beauty of his beauties, the perfection of his infinite perfections, and the glory of his attributes. What an honor, then, must it be to a creature who is infinitely below God, and less than he, to be beautified and adorned with this beauty, with that beauty which is the highest beauty of God himself, even holiness."[29]

Over the coming chapters, we will delve deeper into understanding what it means to be in union with God. This awareness of God's presence goes beyond mere intellectual acknowledgment. It entails a profound spiritual understanding of everything and recognition that God's presence permeates all of life. It invites us to find the ways in which we can deepen our connection with God and cultivate beauty, goodness, and truth as we live in union with God in liminality.

---

29. Edwards, *Sermons and Discourses*, 10:430.

9

Indwelling

As Christians, we can choose how we understand what it means to be in union with God. As we explore this idea further, we should prepare ourselves for a journey that will take us beyond contemplating the idea of closeness with God or casually interacting with concepts of God. The expedition will take us deep into questions about the essence of life, and we will explore what it means to indwell a world that encompasses both the physical and the spiritual. This journey will need to take us beyond the limitations of dualism to appreciate that this binary option is just one of many to consider. As we reflect on what it means to be human beings living in union with God, we will be called upon to reexamine our tendency to separate the spiritual from the material, and instead to see them as interconnected, mutually indwelling aspects of a greater reality. Along the way we will discover God as that bigger reality, whose Spirit permeates everything, who indwells us, and enables us to indwell God.

My proposition is not a new theological concept. However, I understand that my thesis may seem strange since we are used to seeing the world through one of two lenses, materialism and dualism. Is there room for another option in the middle? For the materialist my words would be strange because in this view everything in existence is physical, and there could be no room for views about God indwelling matter. For the dualist, the opening paragraph may also present some challenges, since this approach holds that the material and the spiritual are two fundamentally different realities, and I am arguing that the physical and the spiritual are not two separate entities but interconnected and mutually indwelling aspects of a larger reality.

BETWEEN MATERIALISM AND DUALISM

Pitirim Sorokin, in his ground-breaking four-volume masterpiece *Social and Cultural Dynamics* (1937–41), offers a thought-provoking lens through which to analyze and understand the ebb and flow of cultural systems.[1] Rather than relying on the conventional terms of materialism, idealism, and dualism, Sorokin proposed alternative labels and outlined a dynamic pattern. According to Sorokin, cultures undergo recurring cycles, shifting between two contrasting poles: the sensate and the ideational. In sensate cultures, emphasis is placed on sensory experiences and the pursuit of scientific knowledge. They are often secular and pragmatic in nature, and they emphasize the importance of things like science, technology, and economic growth. On the other hand, ideational cultures prioritize the realm of the spiritual, embracing faith, intuition, and transcendent experiences as valuable components of their worldview. Idealism holds that the physical world emerges from the spiritual, that reality is ultimately spiritual. His model also accounts for an intermediate stage known as the idealistic value system. It is important to note that this concept should not be confused with idealism in the philosophical sense. Instead, the idealistic value system seeks to strike a balance between spiritual and material values, acknowledging the significance of both. In this cultural expression, there is a conscious effort to integrate the two opposing poles, resulting in a nuanced approach. We can view Sorokin's proposal as a sociological framework that incorporates elements from idealism, materialism, and dualism. Ideational cultures align with the philosophical concept of idealism, where the spiritual realm takes precedence. Sensate cultures, on the other hand, bear resemblance to materialism, focusing on tangible experiences and factual pursuits. Finally, idealistic cultures hold that matter exists as separate and autonomous entities: one is a non-physical substance, while the other comprises corporeal substance. While dualism[2] represents various schools of thought,

---

1. Sorokin, *Social and Cultural Dynamics*.
2. See McLaughlin, "Epiphenomenalism," 277. For those who adhere to interactionist substance dualism, both non-physical and physical substances possess the capacity to causally influence one another. This mutual causality allows for a dynamic interplay between the mind and the physical realm. However, epiphenomenalism, another

none of these would take the view that materials and non-material realities could mutually indwell each other.

According to Sorokin, the timing and intensity of cultural system shifts are not constant or predictable. He acknowledges that the pace and distinctness of these transitions differ across cultures: "The tempo and the sharpness of the mutations from one type to another vary from culture to culture; some shift from one type to another within narrower limits than the others, and therefore give always a less pure type of domination of one form than the others."[3] This observation leads to an intriguing possibility: within a single generation, individuals can embody diverse cultural orientations. It is conceivable to encounter individuals who espouse materialistic beliefs alongside others who hold dualistic or idealistic views. The coexistence of varying cultural perspectives within a generation reflects the complex and vibrant nature of cultural dynamics.

However, as we study cultures, we can observe when a value system is more dominant than others. For instance, the Middle Ages was an ideational period centered around spiritual and religious values. In the renaissance transition to an idealistic age, there was a balance between religious faith and emerging humanistic values and interest in the physical world, as expressed in art, literature, and the beginnings of scientific enquiry. However, as the idealistic period waned in the seventeenth and eighteenth centuries, a new sensate culture began to take root during the enlightenment, which further solidified itself in the subsequent industrial revolution. This new cultural phase, with its emphasis on technological progress, capitalism, and material wealth, came to be known as modernity and represents a late stage in the sensate period of recent Western cultural history. Based on his model, Sorokin predicted in 1937 the rise of a new idealistic period early in the twentieth century, which we now refer to as postmodernity.

Given our current position in the shift between sensate and ideational cultural values, it is not surprising that the concept of spirituality is resurfacing in our complex age. According to Sorokin's framework, we can expect voices advocating for non-duality as a means to comprehend both materiality and spirituality. Without Sorokin's framework, it would have been challenging to understand why Bertrand Russell criticized

---

variant of dualism, contests the notion of mutual impact. It suggests that while material entities, such as the brain, can give rise to mental phenomena like consciousness, mental phenomena are incapable of causing material events or processes.

3. Sorokin, *Social and Cultural Dynamics*, 4:771.

reductionism—an approach that simplifies complex phenomena by breaking them down into more fundamental components. Russell argued that reductionism often neglects emergent properties and intricate interactions, resulting in an incomplete understanding of reality. In *An Outline of Philosophy* in 1927, he relied on the perspectives of Arthur Schopenhauer, Henri Bergson, and Alfred North Whitehead, stating, "there is not a sharp line (between mind and matter), but a difference of degree; an oyster is less mental than a man, but not wholly un-mental."[4] According to Russell, there are limits to what science can address, particularly in the domains of metaphysics, ethics, and human values.

BETWEEN MIND AND MATTER

For Joseph Levine, this outer limit of science points to an explanatory gap[5] between our subjective first-person experiences, such as sensations and perceptions, and the objective third-person descriptions the natural sciences provide. For him, the explanatory gap is an epistemological problem that arises from the fact that subjective experiences, also known as *qualia*, seem fundamentally different from the objective physical processes that occur in the brain. While science can explain the neural correlates and mechanisms associated with certain mental states, it struggles to account for the phenomenal qualities of conscious experiences—the "what it is like" to have those experiences. While the explanatory gap is an epistemological and not a metaphysical problem for Levine,[6] David Chalmers describes this conundrum as the "hard problem of science,"[7] which has metaphysical overtones. The hard problem highlights the limitations of providing a materialistic explanation for subjective experiences and the challenge of understanding how physical processes give rise to consciousness. Chalmers suggests that consciousness possesses irreducible properties that cannot be fully accounted for by physical processes alone.[8] He believes that even with the most sophisticated scientific theories, we may not be able to explain the correlations between brain activity

---

4. Russell, *Outline of Philosophy*, 209.
5. The term "explanatory gap" was coined by Levine, "Materialism and Qualia," 354–61.
6. Levine, *Purple Haze*, 10.
7. Chalmers, "Facing Up to the Problem," 200–19.
8. Chalmers, "Consciousness and Its Place in Nature," 102–42.

and conscious states. However, we still lack an explanation of why those correlations exist.

The hard problem goes beyond being solely an epistemological issue concerning knowledge and explanation and becomes a metaphysical problem concerning the nature of reality itself. This perspective challenges the prevailing assumption in science that everything in the universe, including consciousness, can ultimately be understood and explained in terms of physical causation. By framing the hard problem as a metaphysical enigma, Chalmers underscores the idea that understanding consciousness requires more than just refining our epistemological methods or gathering additional empirical data. Science requires the assistance of philosophy and other disciplines to gain a broader perspective beyond its materialistic scope. He suggests there may be fundamental entities or principles beyond the physical realm that are necessary to explain and understand consciousness fully. It implies a need to expand our understanding of reality and acknowledge the potential existence of nonphysical aspects or principles that play a crucial role in the nature and origin of consciousness.[9] Today, we commonly encounter philosophers such as Alain de Botton, Rupert Sheldrake, and Sam Harris, who attempt to account for spirituality within a materialistic culture, illustrating Sorokin's view that the transition from one type of culture to another is not a sudden and abrupt change, but a gradual evolution.

Galen Strawson's book *Real Materialism* (2008) offered micropanpsychism as a means of comprehending the relationship between consciousness and the physical world.[10] This view suggests that all fundamental particles possess some form of consciousness, providing an explanation for the pervasiveness of consciousness in the universe and recent scientific discoveries such as quantum entanglement. We can trace panpsychism back to Greek philosophers predating Socrates, who contemplated whether the mind was either an elemental and fundamental aspect of the world, existing separately from the physical realm, or if it could be reduced to more basic elements. For example, Anaximenes (sixth century BC) believed that *psyche* (or *pneuma*) was the underlying principle of the cosmos, while Heraclitus (fifth century BC) believed that all things possessed souls, and Anaxagoras (fifth century BC) envisioned

---

9. See the discussion in Chalmers, Chalmers, "Consciousness and Its Place in Nature," 102–42.

10. For a very concise and creative understanding of this view, see Strawson, "Realistic Monism," 33–65.

a mind that ordered and regulated all the substances constituting the world. However, as the Greek culture of that time moved toward sensate values, Democritus (fourth century BC) believed that everything in the universe comprised tiny, indivisible particles called atoms. These atoms, he believed, had different shapes that allowed them to fit together like puzzle pieces. He proposed that the interactions and combinations of these atoms gave rise to the emergence of more complex objects and phenomena. By interlocking and combining in various ways, atoms could form larger structures with different properties and characteristics. This view would ultimately lead to the dualism of Galileo and Descartes during the enlightenment. It would culminate in the physicalism at the height of the most recent sensate culture, where physicalism is all there is, the mind is the product of the brain, and consciousness is a physical phenomenon.

This brings us back to a contemporary of Strawson, Daniel Dennett, who describes panpsychism as "a backwater movement which has got some adherence which is pushing non-naturalist lines."[11] In *Consciousness Explained* (1991), Dennett argues that consciousness is not a separate entity or substance but rather a result of complex neural processes that give rise to our cognitive functions, including our sense of self-awareness.[12] Therefore our subjective experiences can be explained and understood by examining the processes and mechanisms of the brain. As a result, these subjective experiences do not have intrinsic, non-physical qualities. And so we continue to shift from sensate, to idealistic, to idealism, and back, repeatedly.

As we have already seen, the question of mind and matter has occupied thinkers for many centuries. In Christian theology, these questions are already present in the New Testament. The very idea of incarnation is revolutionary. In this fundamental belief, Christians confess that mind and matter interweave as a complex, mystical union that has inspired theologians like the apostolic fathers to ask similar questions to those on the lips of people like Levine, Chambers, Dennett, and Strawson. Gregory of Nyssa immediately springs to mind. Throughout this book, I have avoided long quotations from authors, but I think it is worthwhile to hear directly how this apostolic father approached the problem:

---

11. Dennett and Ward, "Mind, Consciousness and Freewill."
12. Dennett, *Consciousness Explained*.

> If, then, color is a thing intelligible, and resistance also is intelligible, and so with quantity and the rest of the like properties, while if each of these should be withdrawn from the substratum, the whole idea of the body is dissolved; it would seem to follow that we may suppose the concurrence of those things, the absence of which we found to be a cause of the dissolution of the body, to produce the material nature: for as that is not a body which has not color, and figure, and resistance, and extension, and weight, and the other properties, while each of these in its proper existence is found to be not the body but something else besides the body, so, conversely, whenever the specified attributes concur they produce bodily existence. Yet if the perception of these properties is a matter of intellect, and the Divinity is also intellectual in nature, there is no incongruity in supposing that these intellectual occasions for the genesis of bodies have their existence from the incorporeal nature, the intellectual nature on the one hand giving being to the intellectual potentialities, and the mutual concurrence of these bringing to its genesis the material nature.[13]

For this fourth century apostolic father, the discernability of intelligible qualities such as color, resistance, quantity, and others is necessary for the existence of the material nature of a body. While each quality exists separately from the body, their concurrence gives rise to bodily existence. He goes on to say that since the perception of these properties is a matter of intellect and the divine is also intellectual in nature, it is not incongruous to suppose that the intellectual causes for the creation of bodies originate from incorporeal nature. The intellectual potentialities, originating from the intellectual nature, come together to bring about the genesis of the material nature.

David Hart believes that we can take Gregory of Nyssa's theology as a "rebellion against the mechanized picture that either the dualistic or the materialists version of this picture of creation as nothing but a collection of organic machines."[14] Gregory and his brother, Basil the Great, rejected the notion that matter is something inherently dead, which is brought to life simply as a matter of functional arrangement. Rather Gregory presents a vision in which the Spirit of God permeates matter, reflecting

---

13. Gregory, *On the Making of Man*, 24:2.

14. Gospel Conversations, "David Bentley Hart in Conversation." I follow this conversation closely in this paragraph, with great appreciation for Hart's scholarship on this topic.

divine nature. The divine illuminates matter as "a coalescence of radiant forms." There is no inanimate, non-divine level of material existence, only spirit. Humans as physical beings come into existence "first and foremost as noetic beings." As such, humans possess the ability to engage in intellectual pursuits, contemplate abstract concepts, and seek spiritual truths. Gregory's vision suggests that the true essence of human existence lies in their ability to cultivate their noetic faculties and pursue spiritual growth and understanding. He challenges the reductionist view that humans are merely physical beings with no inherent spiritual dimension. And he rejects the notion of an inanimate, non-divine level of material existence and instead posits that the Spirit of God permeates everything, including matter. In this understanding, matter itself is a manifestation of divine radiance and a reflection of the divine nature.

BETWEEN UNITY AND INDWELLING

I find echoes of Gregory's thought in the work of Pierre Teilhard de Chardin who coined the term "noosphere" to describe a collective domain of human thought and consciousness.[15] He proposed that human consciousness, as it evolves and becomes more complex, contributes to the development of a global sphere of interconnected minds. The noosphere, for Teilhard, represented the culmination of human intellectual and spiritual development, where the collective consciousness transcends individuality and leads to a greater unity of human thought and purpose. In Teilhard's perspective, the noetic is the realm of collective human consciousness and its impact on the evolution of humanity as a whole. The noetic, therefore, encompassed the capacity for interconnectedness, shared knowledge, and the potential for collective transformation.[16]

For Teilhard, the development of the noosphere was a key aspect of the process he called "cosmogenesis" or the evolving complexity of the universe.[17] He believed that through the growth of the noosphere, humanity could reach a higher level of consciousness in God and contribute to the ongoing transformation of the world. He saw this process as part of a larger evolutionary movement toward a higher state of unity and divine

---

15. De Chardin, *Heart of Matter*, especially 30–39. I will follow the convention to refer to him as Teilhard.

16. De Chardin, *Heart of Matter*, 39.

17. De Chardin, *Heart of Matter*, 31.

convergence. The evolutionary movement begins with the Father, who is the source of all that exists and brings life and vitality to creation. The Father is seen as the fontal source, the wellspring from which all things flow, including the personal center of the Son and the word. The Spirit, in Teilhard's view, is the divine energy of love that unifies the Father and the Son.[18] God is dynamically present within creation, gradually guiding all things toward their full realization as reflections of the Trinity in what he called the "omega point."[19]

In this perspective, the majestic act of creation stretches across the expanse of time, weaving together a tapestry of diversity and unity. Within the intricate fabric of creation, we catch a glimpse of the harmonious dance found within the Trinity itself. Yet, the workings of this creative life often elude our grasp, operating subtly amid a symphony of causal factors, its presence pervasive yet hidden from plain sight. Like a gentle undercurrent, it shapes and influences every aspect of existence, enveloping all in its embrace. Teilhard envisioned a world where every element of creation brims with an overflowing presence, ignited by a vibrant energy that allows beings to flourish according to their inherent capacities. From the depths of each entity, the spirit animates and energizes a wellspring of emerging life and purpose.[20] It is the very essence that infuses creation with vitality, propelling it toward its truest potential. Yet, let us not mistake this animating force for being itself; for creation dances to the rhythm of its own inner dynamism, an expression of interconnectedness and love that resonates with the heartbeat of existence.

In this awe-inspiring perspective, the unfolding of evolution takes on a profound new meaning. It becomes a magnificent symphony of dynamic love orchestrating the journey of creation toward deeper levels of connection and unity. With each passing moment, the cosmic melody draws beings closer together, harmonizing their diverse melodies into a grand opus of interrelatedness. Through the ebb and flow of evolution, the invisible hand of dynamic love guides creation to embrace its destiny. Teilhard invites us to marvel at the intricate beauty of creation that we indwell for, within its vast variety, we witness the divine mind at work. Beneath the surface of the visible lies an unseen presence, infusing every

---

18. De Chardin, *Heart of Matter*, 39–52.

19. De Chardin, *Heart of Matter*, a theme developed throughout this book. See especially 19, 39–52, and 91–95.

20. He writes: "Matter is the matrix of the Spirit. Spirit is the higher state of Matter." De Chardin, *Heart of Matter*, 35.

particle with purpose and possibility. And as we contemplate the journey of evolution, he wants us to find inspiration in the symphony of energetic love, steering us to a future where unity and indwelling are the new norm.

BETWEEN INDWELLING AND PARTICIPATING

God in Christ has become man in Jesus for that very reason, to create a new reality. According to Paul's teaching, Christ "is before all things, and in him all things hold together."[21] For Paul, Jesus is the second Adam and he holds all humanity together in him. All of God's "fullness dwell in him, and through him to reconcile to himself all things, whether things on earth or things in heaven, by making peace through his blood, shed on the cross."[22] Jesus is God's dynamic love that penetrates everything, visible and invisible, by manifesting the love of God for human beings by becoming one with them in order that human beings might become one with God.

As Jesus walked alongside his disciples, he seized every precious moment to instill in them the profound truth of oneness. Sensing the weight of their final gathering for a shared meal, Jesus tenderly urged his beloved companions to abide in him, just as he would abide in them. "No branch can bear fruit by itself; it must remain in the vine," he imparted.[23] And in a prayer that echoed through the ages, he interceded for all future believers, longing for their complete unity: "I pray . . . that all of them may be one . . . I in them and you in me—so that they may be brought to complete unity."[24] Days later, when the resurrected Jesus graced his disciples with his presence, a moment of breathtaking significance unfolded. In a striking parallel to the divine act of breathing life into clay, Jesus breathed upon his followers, filling them with his very Spirit.[25] This same Holy Spirit, like a rushing, mighty wind, surged forth on the day of Pentecost, immersing thousands in its awe-inspiring power, transforming them to live their lives as believers who are full of God's Spirit. In John 14:16, Jesus promises to send the Holy Spirit as the helper who will abide with the believers, testifying about Jesus and

---

21. Col 1:17 (NIV).
22. Col 1:19–20 (NIV).
23. John 15:4 (NIV).
24. John 17:19–23 (NIV).
25. See John 20:21–22.

guiding them in truth. The Spirit, who once rested temporarily upon people for specific tasks under the old covenant, now permanently indwells believers under the new covenant since the Holy Spirit "dwells with you and will be in you."[26]

Paul echoes this theme in his writings, stating that believers are united with the Lord in Spirit[27] and are baptized into one body through the Spirit.[28] In fact, for Paul, when the Holy Spirit baptizes people into the body of Christ, the Spirit not only immerses the baptized, it saturates them as they drink deeply of the Holy Spirit.[29] This metaphorical expression reveals a profound truth; through the Spirit believers indwell the reality that is the ground of all being. Transcending individuality, we indwell God who indwells us in a reality that is spiritual and life-giving. Paul unveils a profoundly mystical vision of humans as the body of Christ—a living organism with interlocking cells that God's breath animates. But this transcendent revelation extends beyond the individual; it presents a breathtaking panorama for all of humanity. The grand body of creation God lovingly crafted pulsates with his indwelling presence, awakening every atom, every quark to his divine touch. The Holy Spirit, like a gentle mist, infuses every cell, permeating the very essence of existence.

BETWEEN PARTICIPATION AND EMBODIMENT

We are baptized into a "theo-drama" according to Hans Urs von Balthasar.[30] In his view, Jesus Christ plays the leading role in this dramatic perspective of Christian life. The divine and human exist in harmony in Christ, and his life opens a new sphere of action, or "theo-drama," that the Spirit baptizes Christians into. The drama of the New Testament involves the interplay between divine and human freedoms in Christ. Jesus only does what his heavenly Father is doing, and even when he hesitates at the cross, he ultimately accepts his Father's will. This is the entire

---

26. See John 14:17.
27. See 1 Cor 6:17.
28. See 1 Cor 12:13.
29. See 1 Cor 12:13.
30. Von Balthasar, *Theo-Drama*, 3:17. He explains that "drama, with its horizontal-temporal restriction that calls for the action to be meaningfully brought to a conclusion within it, provides a metaphor of the dimension of meaning in all human finitude, and hence it also allows us to discern a (vertical) aspect of infinity." Von Balthasar, *Theo-Drama*, 1:345.

drama of our spiritual and human existence—living this human life while united with God. It defines not just who we are but also how we live our lives every day by surrendering to divine freedom; it identifies us, claims us, and commissions us for our identity lies within fulfilling our mission within this "theo-drama." Participating in God's mission is not merely an assignment for humans; instead, it is inherent to our very essence.[31]

Christ Jesus is the best example of one who lived this life in union with God, says Paul. So he encourages the Christians in Philippi in their relationships with one another:

> have the same mindset as Christ Jesus:
> Who, being in very nature God,
> did not consider equality with God
> something to be used to his own advantage;
> rather, he made himself nothing
> by taking the very nature of a servant,
> being made in human likeness.[32]

The passage is known as the Christ Hymn, which was used in worship by the very early Christians and would have shaped the way they saw Christ and their own place in the world. In these words, we catch a glimpse of the mind of God that permeates all of creation and from which all consciousness springs, since the mind of Christ is also the mind of God.[33] This hymn illustrates a sequential narrative from Christ's divine pre-existence, followed by his self-emptying in the incarnation and crucifixion, and finally his exaltation. Any understanding of this passage hinges on whether we interpret verse 6 as "*although* he was in the form of God, he emptied himself"[34] or "*because* he was in the form of God, he emptied himself."[35] If *because* is the best translation, it implies that Christ's self-emptying was not contrary to his divine nature but rather demonstrative of it. This interpretation highlights God's humility and

---

31. Balthasar, *Theo-Drama* 3:263–82.

32. Phil 2:5–7 (NIV).

33. See Gorman, *Inhabiting the Cruciform God*, 9–39, for a detailed discussion of how he has come to this view and who shares this interpretation. I will follow Gorman closely here.

34. See English Standard Version.

35. What we find in this passage is a counterintuitive understanding of the mind of Christ, which, according to Michael Gorman, is shared by notable scholars such as N. T. Wright, Stephen Fowl, and Markus Bockmuehl.

vulnerability to indwell humans and his creation, allowing humans to participate in God's life.

This interpretation challenges any view suggesting that the physical and the spiritual are fundamentally distinct and separate realities. The idea of Christ's incarnation and crucifixion as portrayed in Phil 2 challenges this. Christ is depicted as embodying both divinity (spiritual) and humanity (physical) in a manner that demonstrates the fullness of God's mind. This challenges a dualistic worldview by indicating that the physical and spiritual are not inherently separate or opposed but can coexist within one entity: Jesus Christ. In other words, the spiritual is not superior to the physical; rather, they both have their places in the fullness of reality. Materialism would also struggle to accommodate the concept of a God who becomes incarnate, or the idea of a divine consciousness permeating and influencing human life. The Christological hymn in the Epistle to Philippians, on the other hand, speaks to the spiritual dimension of existence, suggesting a deeper purpose and meaning to life that transcends mere physical existence. So, it comes as no surprise that Christ, "*because* he was in the form of God," was willing to empty himself:

> God exalted him to the highest place
> and gave him the name that is above every name,
> that at the name of Jesus every knee should bow,
> in heaven and on earth and under the earth,
> and every tongue acknowledge that Jesus Christ is Lord,
> to the glory of God the Father.[36]

Paul's vision of humanity draws heavily on what it means to be image bearers of God who are now conforming to Christ. He sees the potential for humans to embody not only the Spirit of God but also to share the mind of Christ. This hymn unveils a profound connection between divine and human consciousness, highlighting our ability to express the divine in our earthly existence. Just as Jesus took on human form while being in the form of God, humans too, created in his image, have the capacity to bear divinity within us, just as Mary did.

Just as the spiritual and the physical are indistinguishable in Jesus, so too do the spiritual and the physical intertwine in humans through God's Spirit that indwells us. Humans are not mere physical organisms driven by selfish genetic imperatives or economic units who consume

---

36. Phil 2:9–11 (NIV).

and are consumed. Instead, as image bearers, we are physical and spiritual beings with God as the ground of our being. As we begin to grasp this new understanding of who we are, we begin to imagine "what it is like" to live in the embrace of the interconnectedness of life that originated with God. This is what we will turn to next.

10

Belonging

We have seen that consciousness is the subjective interpretation of the world from an individual's viewpoint, essentially exploring "what it is like" to indwell the world that God created. It offers us a significant starting point for our discourse on what it means to be with God. However, to broaden and deepen this conversation, we need to articulate what has been subtly suggested throughout: being with God is not an individual endeavor but a communal one. The concept of "being with God" transcends our personal experiences and perceptions, enveloping us in a more encompassing reality of shared existence. It signifies our spiritual interconnectedness, placing us within a broader tapestry of divine purpose and shared belonging. It is not merely a description of our personal relationship with God; it expresses how we as humans embody and express that divine connection. Hence, the importance of "belonging" becomes crucial in our spiritual journey—it emphasizes that our spiritual existence with God is not in isolation but intrinsically connected to others. Our communion with God, therefore, is shared, highlighting the significance of community and belonging in our spiritual lives.

BETWEEN VULNERABILITY AND IDENTITY

As we engage with the intangible aspects of human life, the significance of social belonging becomes ever more evident. We have already referred to the important work of the prominent anthropologist Victor Turner and psychologist John Bowlby, who introduced us to the concept of liminality

(Turner), highlighting the significance of attachment and emphasizing our innate need for belonging (Bowlby). According to Turner, during transformative rituals and liminal experiences, individuals enter a state of liminality itself. Here, they exist between their previous social identities and other, elevated states they hope or sense may follow, opening up new realms of grace and divine connection. In this threshold state, characterized by ambiguity and openness to change, *communitas* emerges as an intense community spirit and solidarity.[1] Rituals such as rites of passage, pilgrimages, or festivals often trigger this liminal phase.

During this transitional period *communitas* arises, suspending social norms and fostering collective equality, or at least engagement or a sense of shared equilibrium. *Communitas* goes beyond the structured roles and hierarchies of everyday life, blurring boundaries and transcending divisions of rank, status, and hierarchy. This state of *communitas* engenders a deep sense of togetherness and shared emotional intensity among participants. It forms a cohesive kinship where individuals come together as equals, united by a shared purpose or collective experience. Kathleen Ashley explains what happens in *communitas*: "the individual (1) entering into a liminal state marked by nakedness, ignorance, or symbolic death, (2) seemingly gaining a sense of his essential humanity (communitas) during or as a consequence of his stay in this condition, and (3) developing through various adventures a new identity which serves as a model of what has been determined to be appropriate behavior."[2]

One of the remarkable aspects of *communitas*, as Turner conceptualized it, is its alternative nature. It is a "social anti-structure,"[3] a positive alternative to the rigidities of traditional social order. It embodies a bond that brings people together on a deeper level, fostering a shared understanding and connection that surpass formal hierarchies and divisions. He explains that "the bonds of *communitas* are anti-structural in that they are undifferentiated, equalitarian, direct, nonrational (though not irrational), I-Thou or Essential We relationships, in Martin Buber's sense."[4] *Communitas* represents a departure from the structured and hierarchical social order of everyday life, offering an alternative way of being and relating to one another. In *communitas*, the usual divisions of rank, status,

---

1. See Turner, *Ritual Process*, 131–65. Here I will follow Turner, *Dramas*, especially 45ff.
2. Ashley, *Victor Turner and the Construction*, 33.
3. Turner, *Dramas*, 45.
4. Turner, *Dramas*, 46–47.

and power are abolished, giving rise to a sense of collective equality. This is best seen in liminal transitions.[5] This alternative form of community challenges established norms and social boundaries, allowing for a more inclusive and egalitarian space to emerge. It provides a temporary respite from the constraints of societal roles and expectations, fostering an environment where individuals can connect on a deeper level and experience a different mode of social interaction. Within *communitas*, there is an opportunity for individuals to experience a profound sense of togetherness and solidarity. It encourages a shared emotional intensity that transcends individual differences and fosters a deep bond among participants. This alternative nature of *communitas* allows for the exploration of new possibilities, the expansion of personal horizons, and the formation of transformative social connections. By offering an alternative way of being and relating, *communitas* challenges the dominant structures and norms of society. It highlights the potential for alternative social orders based on cooperation, empathy, and shared experiences. *Communitas* invites us to envision and experience different ways of being a community, where the emphasis is on collective well-being, mutual support, and authentic human connection.

BETWEEN LOSS AND ATTACHMENT

In the opening chapter of this book, we discussed John Bowlby's attachment theory in the light of liminality. There we argued that a newborn baby experiences liminality with great intensity and immediately craves human connection. Bowlby's seminal work, *Attachment and Loss*, underscores the inherent human need for social belonging.[6] Bowlby posited that humans, from infancy, are biologically predisposed to form attachments with caregivers, a process crucial to emotional and psychological development. That the infant is alarmed when the caregiver is absent, prompting them to cry, emphasizes this need for close, protective relationships. This crying triggers a response in adults to care for the child, evidencing an evolutionary adaptation aimed at the survival and well-being of our young. His research—starting with maternal care in the 1950s—reveals that from the earliest stages of our lives, we are biologically inclined to form attachments with caregivers, a process that plays a pivotal role in

---

5. Turner, *Dramas*, 47.
6. Bowlby, *Attachment and Loss*.

our emotional and psychological development. The quality of our early attachments profoundly shapes our growth, mental well-being, and capacity to forge meaningful relationships. This reinforces the crucial role that social belonging plays in human life.

Matthew Lieberman includes John Bowlby's research among the work of many other researchers to make the point in *Social: Why Our Brains Are Wired to Connect*, that social connection is a fundamental human need deeply ingrained in our biological and neurological processes.[7] He presents compelling evidence from neuroscience, psychology, and associated social sciences to support the idea that our brains are engineered for social interaction and that social connection has a profound impact on our well-being and overall functioning. According to Lieberman our brain's social wiring has evolved over millions of years to prioritize social interactions and relationships. Our preoccupation with belonging is so deeply inbuilt that the default network of our brains is social thinking.

Gordon Shulman found that, when we do not have to focus on any task, when our brains enter default mode, we do not think about nothing, we think about others and our relationships with them.[8] This may involve reflecting on past social interactions, anticipating future social scenarios, trying to understand the viewpoints and emotions of others, or contemplating our own social standing and relationships. This constant "buzz" of social cognitive activity in our downtime suggests that our brains are fundamentally geared for social interaction and a sense of belonging. It is painful not to belong.[9]

Lieberman's own research discovered that social pain, such as rejection or isolation, activates the same neural pathways in the brain as physical pain. This demonstrates that our brains interpret social rebuffs or exclusion as a threat to our well-being or even survival. This understanding underscores the significance of fulfilling our need for belonging. When we feel socially connected and accepted, we sense a positive impact on our mental, emotional, and even physical health. It promotes feelings of happiness, contentment, and overall well-being. Conversely, experiencing social rejection or isolation can have detrimental effects on our psychological and emotional state. It can lead to feelings of loneliness, sadness, and even depression. Our brains register social pain in

---

7. Lieberman, *Social*.

8. Lieberman, *Social*, 16–19, discusses Gordon Shulman and his colleagues in 1997.

9. Lieberman, *Social*, 19–23. "To examine this, we had people lie in a scanner." Falk et al., "Creating Buzz."

a way that reflects the severity of physical harm, emphasizing the deep impact that social marginalization can have on our lives.

But this pain can be avoided with the help of our mirror neurons, since they help us understand the thinking and behaviors of others.[10] As children, we develop a sense of self through continuous interaction and mirroring with caregivers, learning to interpret and respond to social cues. This interaction is not just behavior; it is underpinned by a set of specialized neurons. These neurons create a replica of observed actions in our brains, enabling us to empathize and connect with others on a profound level. When we conform to group consensus, even against clear evidence, it is partly because these same neural mechanisms push us to harmonize with our social surroundings for acceptance and belonging. This need is so powerful it can compel us to override rational judgment to maintain social cohesion, demonstrating how our social nature deeply influences our perceptions and behaviors. It gives us a kind of superpower, the ability to read the minds of others.[11]

Vittorio Gallese, one of the first researchers to identify mirror neurons, posits that these neurons are specialized brain cells that activate both when we perform an action and when we observe someone else performing the same action. This phenomenon, known as motor resonance or mirroring, suggests that our brains simulate the neural state of others when we observe their actions. When we see someone reaching for an object, for example, our own "reaching-for" neurons become active, mirroring the neural state of the person we are observing. This motor resonance allows us to understand the other person's intentions and mental state related to their action. It provides us with an automatic way of empathetically connecting with others and intuitively grasping their experiences. In the context of belonging, mirror neurons play a crucial role. They enable us to establish a shared understanding with others, as our brains simulate and reflect their mental states. This neural mirroring facilitates a sense of connection and empathy, enhancing our ability to relate to others and comprehend their perspectives. This capacity for empathetic resonance deepens our sense of belonging, as we can more readily connect with and comprehend the minds of others.

---

10. Lieberman, *Social*, 137.
11. Lieberman, *Social*, 137.

BETWEEN I AND YOU

Archbishop Desmond Tutu famously explained that for Africans *ubuntu* is word for collective identity and mutual belonging, since "a person is only a person through other persons."[12] Many languages across sub-Saharan Africa have a word that captures the essence of *ubuntu* and the belief that its truths apply to everyone. According to Jordan Ngubane, "The Zulu, the Xhosa and the Swazi are committed as powerfully to *ubuntu* as the Bapedi, Batswana and the Basotho are to *botho*, their version of *ubuntu*."[13] In this way of thinking, we believe we are not inherently complete human beings from birth. Instead, our journey toward full humanity is through other persons, and in relationship with them. But it is not a mere superficial acquaintance that we mean here; relationship is the mutually agreed and shared participation that determines whether or not persons become fully human. For African theologian Vincent Mulago, participation is the element of connection which unites different beings as beings, as substances, without confusing them. It is the pivot of relationships between members of the same community, the link which binds together individuals and groups.[14] It is through interpersonal participation that these connections form and people bind together in a mutual sense of belonging to each other as groups. But more than that, it is an overarching unity within the multiplicity of all of creation.[15]

The Malawian concept of *moyo*, which translates to "life," encompasses both the physical and spiritual dimensions of existence. It signifies the belief that divine life, referred to as *moyo*, serves as the origin and bedrock of all life forms, illustrating the profound interconnectedness between living beings and the divine. This divine life is shared among all living entities, acting as a unifying force that binds them together. The African worldview has a strong emphasis on preserving the natural rhythms and harmonious patterns of *moyo*, allowing life to flow in a balanced manner.[16] This perspective recognizes the intricate interweaving of nature and humanity within the fabric of divine life. The understanding is that God is synonymous with life, and, as life dwells within all living things, the essence of divine life is also present in the Bemba people

---

12. Tutu, *Rainbow People of God*, 125.
13. Ngubane, *Ushaba*, 251.
14. Mulago, "Vital Participation," 145.
15. See also Ngubane, *Conflict*, 141.
16. See a full discussion in Sindima, "Community of Life."

of Zambia as well. The Bemba people refer to this principle as *umweo*, which is the *mweo*, or divine principle in all existence.[17] The worldview recognizes that the need for belonging extends beyond human beings and encompasses nonhuman nature as well. The idea that nonhuman nature is perceived as part of the family with equal values implies that humans seek connection not only with other humans but also with the broader natural world. This underscores the inherent inclination for humans to form relationships and find belonging in various aspects of existence.

Reflecting on my experiences in South Africa as an Afrikaner, I vividly recall politicians, preachers, and teachers emphasizing the importance of belonging, but for them it was to build the Afrikaner nation. This sense of collective identity was deeply rooted in every Afrikaner—man, woman, and child. The idea came into sharp relief in Afrikaner consciousness in the 1930s, amid the global strife of the Great Depression, when Nicholas Diederichs introduced the idea of the "*Volksbond*," or "nation or people's bond."[18] In Afrikaans, this word also has an alliterative connection with *Verbondsvolk*, which means a covenant nation or people, giving it strong theological and spiritual significance. This concept became the cornerstone of Afrikaner Christian nationalism[19] and subsequently gave birth to the political party that instituted the segregation and subjugation of races as its policy. For Diederichs, there was no concept of an "individual" human being; it was an abstract notion that held no grounding in reality. He asserted, "Outside of the community . . . the human being is not really human."[20] What most Afrikaners did not realize then was that this seemingly inclusive notion of collective identity was well known to

---

17. Kaunda, *Theological Education for Social Transformation*.

18. Diederichs, *Volkebond*. The idea of the bond of the nations became nationalism by the time of his third publication. See also Diederichs, *Nasionalisme as lewensbeskouing*.

19. "But more than that. The human being is not just a social being; he is also a national being. The human being is not only destined to be a member of a community, but he is destined to be a member of a nation. And without the elevating, the ennobling and the enriching influence of this most comprehensive community, which we call the nation, the human being can never develop the full potential of his being-human." Marx, "Ubu and Ubuntu," 57.

20. "The individual or single human being as such is an abstraction that does not exist in reality. Outside of the community and the communication with other human beings the human being is not really human. Because he is a social being by nature he is and becomes truly human only within human community." Marx, "Ubu and Ubuntu," 56–57.

those who would later suffer under apartheid policies of racial segregation and subjugation.

The best way to comprehend the African understanding of community through the lens of *ubuntu* is to visualize it as a single person, says Augustine Shutte. Each individual within the community is not considered as merely a part of a larger whole, but rather as a distinct person in their own right. However, the key aspect is that each individual sees themselves as intimately connected to the community and views every other member of the community as an extension of themselves. "Each individual sees every other individual member as another self."[21] This perspective fosters a sense of empathy, shared identity, and a deep sense of belonging. By perceiving every other individual as "another self," we recognize that the well-being and flourishing of one person are intimately tied to the well-being and flourishing of others. Therefore, we should not view the community as a collection of separate and isolated units, but as an integrated and cohesive whole. This perspective rejects the notion of organizing society solely based on productivity and efficiency of individuals, instead emphasizing the organic and dynamic nature of communal existence. It recognizes that the actions and choices of each person affect the broader community, and the health of the community, in turn, contributes to the well-being of every individual within it.

However, *ubuntu* is not impervious to manipulation and distortion by power-hungry leaders or individuals with ulterior motives. As Thabo Mbeki held the presidency in South Africa, Christoph Marx foresaw the rise of a dangerous cultural nationalism centered around the concept of *ubuntu*, which laid the foundation for the resurgence of malevolence in the country.[22] Regrettably, this prophecy came to pass under the three-decades-long dictatorial presidency of Robert Mugabe in Zimbabwe and Jacob Zuma's rule in South Africa, leaving behind lingering legacies of their version of cultural nationalism. These despotic leaders, like leaders of Afrikaner nationalists, skillfully exploited the narrative of unity and shared identity to garner unwavering support from the community, unquestioning of their hidden agendas. Recognizing this peril, in 1990 Desmond Tutu voiced his concerns, lamenting "with a deep chagrin that the only change experienced [in Africa] by many ordinary people is in the complexion of their oppressors."[23] Whenever Tutu noticed signs

21. Shutte, *Ubuntu*, 27.
22. Marx, "Ubu and Ubuntu," 50.
23. Tutu, *Alternatives to Apartheid*, 15.

of this danger, he fearlessly spoke out, acting as a prophetic voice that challenged both presidents Thabo Mbeki and Jacob Zuma. Mbeki, an aspiring leader at the time, sardonically remarked that Tutu was "full of a dark, foreboding about a future without President Mandela, the defender of national reconciliation, tolerance and liberty, all of which are thought to be in grave danger now that the tyrants-in-waiting are poised to take over."[24] In one of the final confrontations with Zuma, Tutu boldly declared, "Mr. Zuma, you and your government do not represent me. You represent your own interests, and I am warning you. I am genuinely warning you out of love. I am cautioning you, just as I cautioned the Nationalists. I am warning you. One day, we will pray for the defeat of the ANC government."[25]

While the term *ubuntu* originates from sub-Saharan languages, Tutu viewed *ubuntu* as more than just a cultural concept. For him, *ubuntu* theology had profound theological roots, tracing back to the universal human narrative of Adam and Eve. Rather than focusing on tribal or national divisions, Tutu saw the essence of *ubuntu* in the belief that all humans are created in the image of God. The New Testament concept of *koinonia*, which came from another cultural context in a different part of the world, carried the same meaning for him. He observes that we can be "human only in fellowship, in community, in *koinonia*."[26] His vision was that South Africa would be that kind of *koinonia*, a "rainbow nation." It was beyond dispute that we belong together in one body because Jesus has broken down the wall of partition, since he is our peace. In this *koinonia* there is neither Greek nor Jew, male nor female, free nor slave, but we are all one in him. We have a new identity which transcends our ethnic, racial, and cultural identity.[27]

BETWEEN CHILD AND PARENT

As we have seen for the apostolic fathers, for someone like Gregory of Nyssa, we do not start as ethnic, racial, or cultural identities, but as "the human" created in the image and likeness of God. "This was nothing less

---

24. Tabane, "Tutu Did Not Spare," §8.

25. Tabane, "Tutu Did Not Spare." Desmond Tutu was never a member of the African National Congress.

26. Tutu, *Rainbow People of God*, 94.

27. See Battle, *Reconciliation*, 109.

than the totality of all human beings throughout time united in a single body," says David Hart.[28] These external labels do not simply define us. Rather "the human" does—a remarkable embodiment of the divine image within us. It is an extraordinary concept that unifies the entirety of humanity across time, weaving us together in a web of interconnectedness. We are not isolated beings, but integral parts of a sacred whole. Our uniqueness and individuality are cherished within the larger context of a single, divine body. It is a vision that requires that we once again ask, What does it mean to be created in the image and likeness of God?

As we know, "image and likeness" traditionally refers to the physical human form without implying deeper spiritual or existential similarities. This view is unsatisfactory, since it emphasizes a physicalist understanding of humans and limits human nature to ethnic, racial, and cultural characteristics we can mistakenly and harmfully separate into discriminatory categories.[29] Further, the alternative view that the phrase "image and likeness" extends beyond a mere physical resemblance heads in the right direction since it highlights the unique personal relationship between God and humans. Yet, it still seems vague since the nature of this relationship is unclear.[30] For that reason, Carly Crouch's proposal that image and likeness point to a parental relationship intrigues me. Her view proposes that we can derive a deeper understanding of the phrase "image and likeness" in the context of humanity's creation by examining the relationship between Adam and Seth in Gen 5:3. The passage suggests a connection between Seth's image and likeness and his father, Adam. This implies that the same parallel can be drawn between humanity and God. The emphasis on physicality in terms such as "image" and "likeness" looks like a symbolic device to evoke the parent-child relationship rather than implying a literal physical resemblance. This interpretation suggests that the image and likeness of God signifies a profound relational connection between God and humanity, akin to the familial bond between parent and child.

The biblical texts of Genesis and Isaiah provide intriguing insights into the origin of human beings, highlighting the use of two distinct

---

28. Gospel Conversations, "David Bentley Hart in Conversation."

29. Carly L. Crouch says that "image and likeness become empty terms, lacking any particular content and requiring further definition to obtain meaning." See Crouch, "Genesis 1:26–7 as a Statement," 5. I will follow her closely in this paragraph but will add my perspective.

30. Crouch, "Genesis 1:26–7 as a Statement," 8. According to Crouch, "many theologians have been drawn to the Barthian argument that the image is lodged in the personal relationship unique to God and humans."

Hebrew words: *bara*, "to create or form," and *yasar*, "to form." These two terms introduce us to two distinct nuances of human origin. It is well known that *bara* used in Gen 1 points to human creation *ex nihilo*, out of nothing. Conversely, Gen 2 employs *yasar* when God shaped humanity from soil ready to be tilled. We should not lose sight of the implied fertility of this image: *yasar* is a feminine noun. It reminds me of the Spirit of God, watching over a motherly figure. She in turn hovers lovingly but nervously over the act of imminent creation to which she is so intimately and intricately bound.[31] It suggests the dramatic theater of a mother bird with her eggs about to hatch or with fledglings in her nest.

In Gen 2:7 the use of *yasar* is imbued with profound theological and anthropological implications. After this account, the woman's womb is where human life is formed. In Isaiah, we read that God created Jacob and formed Israel,[32] but the paternal power of these words come to full strength when the prophet exclaims, "But now listen, Jacob, my servant, Israel, whom I have chosen. This is what the Lord says—he who made you, who formed you in the womb, and who will help you."[33] Israel was formed in God's womb; there is no reference to an early mother. It is in the womb of God that Israel is created, the nation that is called to be a blessing to the nations;[34] it is in God's womb that all humanity is created. I agree with Carly Crouch, who explains, "God's creative powers are continually applied *in utero*; the verse aptly combines God's role as creator with highly organic language of generation and biological parenthood."[35]

The concept of belonging to God as a child to a parent carries weighty suggestions, resonating with our innate longing for a secure attachment figure. A fragile newborn seeks to be seen, soothed, safe, and secure with its caregiver,[36] and when a secure attachment is established, the groundwork for healthy emotional and relational growth is done, enabling the child to explore the world with confidence and resilience. Likewise, perceiving our belonging to God as a secure attachment figure

---

31. "Now the earth was formless and empty, darkness was over the surface of the deep, and the Spirit of God was hovering over the waters" (Gen 1:2). *Rāhap* in it primitive root means "to brood."

32. See Isa 43:1.

33. Isa 44:1–2 (NIV).

34. See Gen 12:1–3b: "I will make you a great nation; I will bless you and make your name great ... And in you all the families of the earth shall be blessed" (NIV).

35. Crouch, "Genesis 1:26–7 as a Statement," 13.

36. Thompson and Fujimura, *Soul of Desire*, use these four words to describe secure attachment. We discussed this view in chapter 1.

fulfills our primal need to be seen, comforted, and protected. During infancy the attachment becomes a secure foundation from which we can navigate life's challenges, discover solace amid turmoil, and bask in a profound sense of love and belonging.

This interpretation that image and likeness are a symbolic device to evoke the parent-child relationship suggests that humans share a similar yearning for a connection with God. Furthermore, this understanding assures us of our intrinsic worth and value, constantly reminding us that God profoundly loves, fully knows, and cherishes us. We often conceptualize belonging in the context of human relationships, communities, or cultures. However, it is not confined to the temporal and tangible; it extends into the spiritual, unfolding into a profound way of being with God. As we release the illusion of separateness, we awaken to the realization that we are not merely individuals in pursuit of personal growth, but that we are part of a greater reality. Belonging, in this context, is a profound spiritual connection that goes beyond our individual selves. It involves recognizing that we are part of something much larger and more meaningful—a grand, divine reality that encompasses our existence and purpose. So, it is not merely "you" or "me"; it is "us" in a cosmic sense, deeply intertwined in a divine truth.

BETWEEN RESTORATION AND REINTEGRATION

Humans belong to God, but, perhaps even more correctly, we belong with God. This is true for all humankind; we are all from God's womb; we are all looking for a caregiver who will help us find our way in liminality. Because this search is fraught with danger the biblical narrative reveals that God has provided means of grace to establish ways to find our way back to him that always involve communities to which we can belong. In the story of Abraham, God raises up a people that would be a blessing to the nations. The blessings that he would bestow on them were to flow through them to the nations. They were not supposed to have a king; they were called to be priests who mediate the grace of God to the nations. Israel was supposed to be a *communitas*, a "social anti-structure,"[37] a positive alternative to the kingdoms around them. They were called to become a bond that brings people together on a deeper level, fostering a shared understanding and connection with God, that introduces God to the world as a covenanting

37. Turner, *Dramas*, 45.

other. But when nationalism captured their imagination, they appointed their kings and the rest is a sad tale of pride, fall, and exile.

But all was not lost, because the man Jesus, who was formed in the womb of a young girl, Mary, would come to introduce the world to the possibility of knowing God as parent, and a mother and a father. Throughout his teachings, Jesus portrayed God as a compassionate and loving parent who desires the well-being of his children. He taught his disciples to address God as *Abba*, an Aramaic term of endearment similar to "daddy," expressing a sense of closeness, trust, and affection in their relationship with God. In his parables and teachings, Jesus often employed parental imagery to convey the depth of God's love and concern. He spoke of God's tender care for sparrows and the lilies of the field. And he emphasized that if earthly parents, flawed as they may be, knew how to give good gifts to their children, how much more would our heavenly Father provide for us? By invoking the image of a heavenly parent, Jesus sought to deepen our understanding of God's character and foster a sense of intimate connection and belonging. He prayed, as we have already seen, "I pray also for those who will believe in me through their message, that all of them may be one, Father, just as you are in me and I am in you. May they also be in us so that the world may believe that you have sent me."[38] But then God's desire to gather his children "as a hen gathers her chicks under her wings"[39] was rejected, and Jesus was crucified by his own brothers and sisters.

The disciples who followed Jesus around the countryside of Palestine and those who came after his death formed a *communitas* to continue the work of Israel as a "social anti-structure," a positive alternative to the kingdoms that divide people. Jesus prayed for his disciples, because they would need it, then and now.[40] His prayer that we might be one reminds me of Gregory's understanding of Gen 1, where all were one. Is Jesus praying for this reunification that was known to "the human" that was created when God breathed into a lump of clay that became a living soul, animated by the breath of God? Jesus's prayer for his disciples, both present and future, to be completely one reflects a profound understanding rooted in the unity that Gregory of Nyssa identified in the first creation account. For Gregory, as we have seen, humanity in Gen 1:27 was united;

---

38. John 17:20–21 (NIV). See our discussion in the previous chapter.

39. See Matt 23:37 and Luke 13:34.

40. "My prayer is not for them alone. I pray also for those who will believe in me through their message" (John 17:20 NIV).

there was inherent oneness before any division or separation occurred. Jesus's prayer seems to echo the creation narrative; indeed, we can interpret it as a plea for the restoration of that original unity, the reunification of all humanity with itself and with God. It echoes the moment when God breathed life into a handful of clay, animating the archetypal human. In Jesus's prayer, we can discern an aspiration for the reconciliation of humanity with its true essence and purpose, its source and origin. It conveys a longing for the restoration of the intimate relationship between God and his creation, a unity that transcends all divisions and differences. By praying for oneness among his disciples, Jesus expresses his desire for them to experience the same divine communion and interconnectedness that characterized the primordial state of creation.

However, this prayer also carries implications for the wider human family, encompassing all people throughout history. Jesus's words extend beyond his immediate followers to include those who would come after, highlighting his yearning for the unity and wholeness of all humanity. It speaks to the intrinsic value and dignity of each individual, underscoring the significance of their participation in this grand reunification. Ultimately, Jesus's prayer invokes a vision of the restoration of unity among all people, the reintegration of the human family with God, and the realization of humans as God's image bearers in creation. It emphasizes the divine longing for humanity to rediscover its original unity, where the breath of God fills every soul and unites them in a profound oneness, just as Jesus is in the Father and the Father in him. Jesus prays that he will be in us as the Father is in him, and all of this is possible because he has given us the glory, or the Glory, the indwelling of the Holy Spirit.[41]

It is the Holy Spirit who unites believers into one body, who is the same Spirit who is the bond of love between the Father and the Son in a trinitarian understanding of God.[42] Clark Pinnock says, "Being love, God seeks to share being and communicate presence with creation. As a bond of love, as One who fosters fellowship, the Spirit opens up the relationship between God and the world."[43] He also observes, the "Spirit is leading us into union—to transforming, personal, intimate relationship with the Triune God."[44] Paul says to the church in Corinth that they "were all baptized by one Spirit so as to form one body—whether Jews or Gentiles,

41. See John 17:20–23.
42. Pinnock, *Flame of Love*, 37.
43. Pinnock, *Flame of Love*, 56.
44. Pinnock, *Flame of Love*, 149.

slave or free—and we were all given the one Spirit to drink."⁴⁵ Paul is confident that the believers, irrespective of race, gender, or social standing, have become one with each other through the Spirit, who continues to baptize them into the body of Christ and from whom they drank. But it is more than just taking a sip from a cup; it conveys the idea of being filled or saturated.⁴⁶ It implies a full immersion or absorption in the Holy Spirit, rather than just a simple act of sharing. By filling us with his Spirit and immersing us into the trinitarian life, God transforms us into his temples, the places he indwells, where we belong.

---

45. 1 Cor 12:13 (NIV).

46. The Greek verb for "made to drink" used in 1 Cor 12:13 is ἐποτίσθημεν (*epotisthemen*), which is a passive aorist tense form of the verb ποτίζω (*potizo*). The aorist tense suggests a completed action in the past, while the passive voice indicates that the action was done to the subject. The word ἐποτίσθημεν implies that the Holy Spirit has completely filled and saturated the believers, providing them with spiritual refreshment and a source of spiritual life. This word suggests a full immersion in or absorption of the Holy Spirit's presence and power, rather than simply a symbol of unity or shared experience.

11

Conversing

THE IMPORTANCE OF COMMUNICATION becomes increasingly significant as we attempt to understand what it means to live in union with God. Building any relationship, including our relationship with God, hinges on good communication. When it comes to our communion with God, communication takes on a unique and critical role, since no other relationship holds greater weight or carries more profound consequences for how we navigate our lives. Just as regular conversations and interactions strengthen human relationships, maintaining open communication with God deepens our spiritual bond and widens our understanding of what it means to be human. It is in communion and communication with God that we are able to delve into the depths of our being and explore the mysteries of our existence. In this exchange, we open ourselves to divine guidance, wisdom, and comfort, paving the way for a more purposeful and meaningful life. Communication leads to community, says Rollo May.[1]

BETWEEN SENDER AND RECEIVER

At its core, communication is the process of exchanging information, ideas, and emotions between individuals or groups. However, effective communication is not a one-way street; it involves a reciprocal exchange of information between sender and receiver. This mutuality allows understanding, clarification, and adjustment of conveyed messages. Whether in personal relationships, professional settings, or social

---

1. May, *Power and Innocence*, 247.

intercourse, communication thrives on this back-and-forth interaction. It encompasses not only the act of conveying information but also active listening, interpreting, and responding to shared information. Engaging in a feedback loop, where the receiver provides input, asks questions, seeks clarification, or expresses thoughts and feelings, communication becomes a dynamic process. This interactive exchange enables the refinement of messages, reduces misunderstandings, and fosters mutual understanding.

This dynamic interplay of communication is also evident at the cellular level of life, where various forms of communication allow organisms to function and maintain balance. Cells communicate with each other to coordinate essential processes, respond to stimuli, and carry out specialized functions within the body. In biology, we learn that the DNA molecule lies at the heart of this intricate web of communication, symbolizing communication at the cellular level of life. Within its elegant structure lies the blueprint, the fundamental instructions necessary for constructing and nurturing living organisms. As we recognize communication as a foundational element of life, we find the marvels of signaling mechanisms at the molecular level. In the complex realm of cells, a symphony of molecules, such as hormones, neurotransmitters, and chemical messengers orchestrates the transmission of information and enables communication between different cellular components. These particles engage in a dynamic exchange, seamlessly traversing intricate pathways between cells, initiating cascades of events that ensure the smooth flow of information.[2] This intricate dance of molecular communication aligns physiological functions, harmonizes responses to external stimuli, and maintains the delicate equilibrium of homeostasis, allowing life to flourish.

---

2. Since I have used "information" to define "communication," it will be helpful to remind ourselves of the etymology of the word, which derives from the Latin roots *in* (meaning "into" or "within") and *forma* (meaning "form" or "shape"). This etymological reflection underscores a significant revelation: information is not merely the transfer of data; it possesses an inherent agency and potency that molds and shapes both the giver and the receiver. When information is shared, a bond forms between the disseminator and the recipient. The act of imparting information breathes new life into the recipient's understanding, expanding their perception and potentially catalyzing transformative shifts in their perspective. Simultaneously, the act of sharing information enriches the giver, for in articulating and conveying knowledge, they bestow clarity and deeper insights on their own understanding. In this mutual exchange, they weave a vibrant network of ideas and perspectives.

As scientists explore the flow of information within the inner-communication networks of our world, spanning from the infinitesimal landscapes of quantum mechanics to the majestic expanses of astrophysics, communication has become a subject that ignites intellectual fires across philosophical and theological circles. For instance, John Wheeler, a renowned physicist, explored and discussed the relationship between information and the nature of reality. He made significant contributions to quantum physics and general relativity and coined the phrase "it from bit" to express his ideas about the fundamental nature of the universe.[3] According to Wheeler, information is not just an abstract concept but an intrinsic component of the fabric of reality. He suggested that the fundamental building blocks of the universe, such as particles and forces, arise from the interplay of information. In his view, the universe can be thought of as a self-excited circuit, where information plays a central role in shaping and determining the physical phenomena we observe. In a parallel vein, Max Tegmark, a Swedish-American physicist, delves into the mysterious relationship between matter and information, asserting that "human consciousness is how information feels when being processed in certain complex ways."[4] In his view matter and energy are simply different manifestations of information, and that consciousness is a form of information the brain processes in a complex way.

BETWEEN EMANATION AND REVELATION

To grasp the philosophical perspective on communication, we must explore the cultural backdrop of ancient Greece and Rome, which exerted a profound influence on the Christian concept of God. Prior to the advent of Christianity, the gods held a sacred and transcendent status in ancient Greece. Their knowledge was thought to surpass mortal understanding, holding the key to cosmic order, human destiny, and the inner workings of the universe. Humans sought to catch glimpses of this divine wisdom through divination practices and the interpretation of signs and omens. A significant turning point in Greco-Roman thought concerning the gods emerged with Plotinus, a Roman philosopher from the third century and the founder of Neoplatonism.

---

3. Wheeler, "Information, Physics, Quantum," 311.
4. Tegmark, *Our Mathematical Universe*, 289.

At the core of his philosophy lies "the One," the ultimate reality and the wellspring of all existence. The One is pure unity, beyond the limitations of all categories encompassing both being and non-being.[5] From the One emanates a hierarchical progression of substances, each representing a distinct facet of reality. Within this cosmological framework, observers regard the material world, including physical bodies and individual entities, as the lowest level of reality. Multiplicity, change, and imperfection characterize reality, fragmenting its unity within the material realm. Every emanation from the One yearns to return to its source, seeking reunion with the one. This process of return encompasses a spiritual journey, involving the pursuit of unity, wisdom, and the realization of one's true nature. He explains, "The emanation, then, must be less good, that is to say, less self-sufficing: now what must that be which is less self-sufficing than The One? Obviously the Not-One, that is to say, multiplicity, but a multiplicity striving towards unity; that is to say, a One-that-is-many."[6]

Emanation "reveals" the one in lower forms of existence. Everything originates from a divine source and flows as an automatic process in which beings or realities simply emerge or emanate from a higher source without a personal intention or purpose. It is helpful to remember that this is not creation in the traditional sense, like God creating the universe in Christian thought. Instead, the emanation is a necessary and eternal process that is inherent to the One. Just as a light cannot help but shine in contrast to darkness, or water cannot be other than wet, the One emanates hierarchical substances that represent different aspects of reality.

First, the One emanates the intellect, or divine mind, which contemplates the One and generates forms or ideas, the eternal and unchangeable archetypes of all things. Following this, the soul, world-soul, or psyche emanates from the intellect, which is the principle of life in the universe and is responsible for ordering the material cosmos according to the forms. It acts as a bridge between the intelligible and sensible world. In this view a kind of dualism does exist, but it is not between two independent and coequal realms, but between the One—the source of all existence—and the many, the multiplicity of beings that emanates from the One. However, it is important to note that all levels of reality are interconnected and have their source in the One, which tempers the sense of opposition

---

5. Plotinus, *Enneads*, First Ennead, Tractate 3, 20. See also Third Ennead, Tractate 8: "The nature of Contemplation and the One." Ennead 5 provides a detailed discussion of the One.

6. Plotinus, *Enneads*, Fifth Ennead, Tractate 3, 304.

found in many other forms of dualism. As such, Plotinus's view is a kind of "qualified monism" or "emanative monism," rather than classical dualism, because while there is a clear distinction between different levels of reality, all are ultimately grounded in, and are emanations of, the One.

Communication requires back-and-forth interaction and is more than the act of conveying information. It also involves active listening, interpreting, and responding to shared messages. It is therefore hard to see how the one who does not receive or respond to anything can communicate in the traditional sense of the word. Plotinus did not explicitly say whether or not the One communicates, but he did suggest that it was possible to have a mystical experience of the One, which could be seen as a form of communication. The lower levels of reality, the intellect, the soul, and the material world can "know" the one through a process of contemplation and realization. In this philosophy, the goal of human life is to strive for a return to the One by recognizing the divine within us, a process known as "anamnesis" or recollection of our true divine nature.[7] This return or reintegration is achieved through ascetic practices and philosophical contemplation.

The biblical narrative offers a striking contrast to the concept of emanation found in Greco-Roman thought. Instead of emanating from the divine, God's communication is portrayed through acts of creation, incarnation, and inspiration. In this communication, the very act of God speaking creation into being is intricately tied to the notion of God's breath or Spirit becoming the substance of all existence.

BETWEEN REVELATION AND CONVERSATION

As we have seen in a previous chapter, when we consider human speech, we can observe that it involves the vibration of our vocal cords and the exhalation of breath. This breath carries sound vibrations that travel to the ears of the listener, allowing communication to materialize. Similarly,

---

7. See Plotinus, *Enneads*, Fourth Ennead, Tractate 4, 224. Here he explains, for instance, "The total scheme may be summarized in the illustration of The Good as a center, the Intellectual-Principle as an unmoving circle, the Soul as a circle in motion, its moving being its aspiration: the Intellectual-Principle possesses and has ever embraced that which is beyond being; the soul must seek it still: the sphere of the universe, by its possession of the soul thus aspirant, is moved to the aspiration which falls within its own nature; this is no more than such power as body may have, the mode of pursuit possible where the object pursued is debarred from entrance; it is the motion of coiling about, with ceaseless return upon the same path—in other words, it is circuit."

the narrator of the creation narrative in Genesis wants us to recognize that when God speaks, his words contain ideas, knowledge, and information which materialize as physical phenomena. In this creative act God structures quantities of divine data that contain his ideas in a meaningful way to convey his knowledge and prepare the way for communication and comprehension. In this view, the act of speaking and breathing life into existence is a deliberate and intentional act of God. It expresses the idea that creation is not a random or accidental event, but rather a purposeful act that divine communication initiates and sustains. It means that God's breath is an essential component of various phenomena, including cognition, language, consciousness, and the laws of nature. It is necessary for the organization and functioning of complex systems, and it can have causal efficacy in the world. From this perspective, God's breath is the ideas, knowledge, and information that manifests in all aspects of reality and is not a by-product of physical processes. It is not contingent; rather, it possesses the power to bring about material existence as God speaks, and as such it has its own distinct ontological status.

When God declares, "Let there be light," radiance emerges instantaneously. These words contain God's ideas, knowledge, and the necessary information for the formation of light out of nothingness. This pattern persists as God continues to speak, bringing forth various elements of the natural world such as the sky, land, vegetation, animals, and ultimately human beings. While it is not necessary to interpret these accounts as literal events, the creation narrative employs anthropomorphic language to depict the creative infusion of God's breath into all aspects of creation as they are spoken into existence. This portrayal emphasizes the intimate connection between the divine and the physical realm, highlighting God's continuing communication and involvement in the unfolding of the world. Here God is not a distant or impersonal force, but rather an active and involved participant in the unfolding of the universe. By speaking creation into existence, God establishes a direct connection between him and the created order. His communicative role in creation sets the stage for ongoing conversation and relationship between him and humanity. In this narrative tradition, the belief in a God who communicates through speech lays the foundation for the concept of revelation—whereby God makes known divine intentions, purposes, and guidance to humanity through various means such as prophets, Scripture, and personal experience with God in Christ through the Holy Spirit.

This view challenges dualism, which necessitates emanations from a divine source or a purely physicalist view that explains all existence solely through material processes. Instead, this understanding acknowledges the existence of a spiritual reality that precedes and underlies the physical world. The act of God speaking and breathing life into creation implies that reality encompasses more than we can observe or measure solely in physical terms. The materialization of matter from God's breath and spoken words implies a metaphysical aspect to creation that surpasses the mere interaction of physical particles. It suggests that the material world finds its foundation and sustenance in a transcendent spiritual reality, which provides a framework for comprehending the origin and nature of existence.

BETWEEN *AD INTRA* AND *AD EXTRA* DIALOGUE

By affirming that God is a communicative being, we assert that divine communication takes place within the inner dynamics of the Godhead, *ad intra*, or considered from within. This ontological understanding serves as the foundation for comprehending the existence of creation. Communication is not an incidental trait of God, but an inherent and essential aspect of God's being. Unlike Neoplatonism, which, as we have seen, believes in automatic emanation from the one, Christian theology maintains that God engages in communication *ad extra* or viewed externally, precisely because of the divine communication *ad intra*. Creation is not merely the result of an automatic internal process of God; rather, it is God actively communicating.

This implies that God is transcendently immanent or immanently transcendent; that the duality between immanence and transcendence, the physical and the spiritual, is overcome, since God's breath and his words animate all reality. In this view, God's communication is inherent in the very fabric of existence, expressing itself through the ongoing creative and evolving processes of the universe. It is possible to see God's ongoing communication as essential for maintaining a dynamic and evolving relationship with the world. God's communication is an expression of divine love, guidance, and involvement in the continuing development of the universe. We view the universe as dynamic and evolving, with new forms and expressions emerging over time. Creation, in this sense, is not a one-time event but a rolling unfolding of the divine within the world.

Because God is transcendently immanent, he is actively present in the world and intentionally involved in its constant development. From this perspective, creation is not static or fixed but continuously evolving, with new possibilities and manifestations emerging. After all, the biblical narrative starts with God creating the heavens and the earth and concludes with him making a new heaven and earth.

This dialogue between the inner divine dynamics and the external realm of creation creates a reciprocal relationship, a continuous exchange of communication. The *ad intra* communication informs and shapes the *ad extra* communication, while the *ad extra* communication provides a space for the expression and manifestation of the *ad intra* communication. This is a never-ending communication loop. All of reality originates from this communication, and nothing in creation can exist apart from its connection to the Trinity, since the entirety of creation is encompassed within the divine conversation. Everything that is revealed to us through divine revelation we can trace back to the eternal communication that takes place among the persons of the Godhead. Within God exists a perfect and eternal exchange of communication between the Father, Son, and Holy Spirit. This divine communion expresses and shares the fullness of God's being, attributes, and purposes.

In this theological framework, creation is not merely a passive product of God's creative speech, but rather an active participant in divine communication. Humans, as sentient beings within creation, have a crucial place in this conversation. God creates us in his image and endows us with the capacity for communication and relationship. Humans have the capacity to engage God in dialogue, to commune with God in the inner dynamics of the divine life, and also participate in the outward expression and reception of God's communication in the created world. When God communicates with humanity, whether through Scripture, prophetic revelation, or personal encounters, he offers a sharing of himself, an invitation to partake in the divine life. Divine revelation unveils glimpses of the eternal communication that occurs within the Godhead, allowing us to participate in the knowledge and understanding of God's nature, character, and divine purpose. Therefore, the content of divine communication is rooted in the eternal dialogue between the persons of the Godhead, that is marked by beauty, goodness, and truth.

God calls humans to absorb his communication and listen attentively to the divine voice speaking within and through creation. Through prayer, worship, obedience, and acts of love and justice, humans become active participants and co-communicators, providing a dynamic interplay between the divine and the created, where God's communication finds expression, reception, and response.

BETWEEN INCARNATION, INSPIRATION, AND ILLUMINATION

Christians consider Jesus Christ as God's ultimate form of self-communication to humanity, embodying the essential knowledge required to "live, move, and have our being" in God.[8] While God's word has come to creation in various ways, through different media, and over the expanse of time and space, the incarnation marks a significant moment in the communication loop between God and creation. In this moment Christ, God's Word spoken through his Spirit, is the special revelation of God. God is immanently transcendent in Christ. Jesus brings divinity into the material being. God, like humans, becomes what he loves. As such, the incarnation is an act of love in which God gives himself and humanity receives God's love as the ultimate declaration of love. But since communication is reciprocal, Jesus, the Nazarene, a man scarred by human violence, ascends to be one with God, bringing with him intimate knowledge of the human experience of life in liminality.

The incarnation of the Word unites people—with themselves, with each other, and most crucially, with God's constant creative communication. This, as we have seen, is what Jesus prayed would happen: "That they may all be one, just as you, Father, are in me, and I in you, that they also may be in us."[9] This oneness has the goal to communicate, "so that the world will believe you sent me."[10] Following Jesus's crucifixion and ascension, the divine communication did not cease; instead, it continues through the Holy Spirit. As we have already seen, the Holy Spirit baptizes people of faith into the body of Christ. Through the Holy Spirit, humans can become vessels through which God's presence manifests in the world and his self-communication continues. It is the Spirit who was

---

8. See Acts 17:28. "'For in him we live and move and have our being.' As some of your own poets have said, 'We are his offspring'" (NIV).

9. John 17:21a (NIV).

10. John 17:21b (NIV).

instrumental in the incarnation who, now, continues to inspire and illuminates God's words.[11]

BETWEEN THE ORDINARY AND THE EXTRAORDINARY

The church is intended to be a tangible expression of this divine communication and communal belonging. Within the church, believers come together in unity, drawn by their shared love for God and their openness to the transformative power of the Holy Spirit. As a *communitas*,[12] the church provides a sacred space where individuals can belong in liminality—a state of being betwixt and between the ordinary and the extraordinary. In this liminal space, the Holy Spirit works through the collective body of believers, fostering a deep sense of connectedness and enabling personal and intimate communication with God. Through the church, the Holy Spirit empowers individuals, equipping them with spiritual gifts and guiding them in their journeys of faith. These gifts are not meant for personal gain or achievement but are bestowed for the edification and service of the entire community.

It should not go unnoticed that many of the gifts of the Spirit enable communication and connection within the church.[13] The gift of prophecy allows individuals to speak forth messages inspired by God, offering guidance, encouragement, and correction to the community. Prophetic words can illuminate divine truths and provide direction for the collective body of believers. Similarly, the gift of tongues, or glossolalia, enables believers to communicate with God through a language unknown to them, transcending the limitations of human understanding. This gift, often accompanied by the gift of interpretation, fosters a deeper connection with the divine and enhances communal worship experiences.

Moreover, the gift of wisdom allows individuals to discern and understand the mysteries of God's will, offering profound insights and guidance to the community. With the gift of knowledge, believers can receive divine insights and understanding about spiritual matters, contributing to the collective understanding and growth of the church. These gifts of communication and revelation create an atmosphere of divine interaction within the congregation, facilitating the flow of divine messages,

---

11. Enns, *Inspiration and Incarnation*.
12. See our discussion of Victor Turner's work in the previous chapter.
13. See 1 Cor 12.

wisdom, and understanding among believers. Also, the gift of teaching empowers individuals to effectively convey and explain the truths of the faith, nurturing spiritual growth and understanding within the community. Through skilful communication, teachers can help believers grasp complex concepts, deepen their faith, and help them to live wisely. Similarly, the gift of exhortation enables individuals to encourage, comfort, and motivate others through their words, fostering unity, resilience, and perseverance in the face of challenges.

The church exists to bring the world into communion with God and, in doing so, embodies the communication between God and his creation. One of the primary ways for the church to fulfill this role is by speaking on God's behalf. In Christian communities, people gather around the Bible to hear the word of God preached and explained. The authority of the Bible lies in the fact that God personally speaks through it, and it cannot be separated from God himself. Thus, the proper approach to Scripture is to listen to God speaking through it and recognize his presence in the word. When God speaks, his word is intimately connected to his person. Just as a person's breath or voice is connected to their presence, the word of God carries the essence of God himself. When the word is spoken, it brings the presence of God to the listener. The ultimate proof of the truth of Scripture is the fact that God himself speaks through it. However, the concept of the word of God extends beyond the written text of Scripture. It represents God's continuing communication with humanity, signifying that he has spoken in the past and continues to speak in the present. Through the spoken word, God enters into a relationship with humanity, communicates his thoughts and intentions, and invites people to participate in his divine life of beauty, goodness, and truth.

BETWEEN THE BIBLICAL STORIES AND HUMAN EXPERIENCES

Before we explore the importance of narrative in communication, we have to take a step back to understand the classical concept of myth. In classical Greek a myth was an idea in the mind of a maker to create a reality that did not yet exist.[14] In this ancient understanding, the biblical creation narrative qualifies as a myth, possessing a truly cosmogonic

---

14 ."Myth" is an idea that has "an inner urge to express," according to Stählin, "μῦθος," 766–67.

and sacred essence as it both shaped and continues to shape the world in which Christians reside. The creation narrative commences with God's conception of creation and ultimately culminates in the formation of humans in his image. As Moltmann elucidates, God fashions the world out of his eternal love for the Son. He eloquently says, "In his heart, God has this passionate longing, not just for any, random 'other,' but for 'his' other—that is, for the one who is the 'other' for him himself. And that is humanity, his 'image.'"[15]

Moltmann argues that love not only serves as the impetus behind creation but also functions as the sustaining force that perpetually nourishes and upholds it. Eugene Peterson's translation of Paul's words beautifully captures this concept: "Long before He laid down the foundations of the earth, He had us in mind, and we were the focus of His love, intended to be made whole and holy through His love."[16]

Despite the shortcomings or flaws of the church, the theological reality remains that its institutional duty is to act as a medium of communication for God within the world. In this way the church is called to not only communicate with God *ad intra*, but also partner with God in his communication *ad extra*. God continues to communicate with creation in diverse ways that surpass our understanding, and require faith. And while God's way of communicating extends beyond the church's ability and responsibility, God still called people to embody his communication in the world. The church has the duty of entering and maintaining a dialogue with God and the world. But as we have seen, the Holy Spirit empowers the church to speak. The same Spirit that breathed over creation and brought forth the spoken word now resides in those who have placed their faith in Christ, the Word who became flesh.

For centuries Christians have immersed themselves in a compelling narrative, one interwoven with the very fabric of existence itself—an original idea born from the notion that creation is God's masterpiece. This majestic concept reveals a God of love who not only breathes life into humanity as objects of his affection but, akin to how parents love their offspring, engages in an eternal conversation with all of creation. This age-old conversation, spanning millennia, has been carefully chronicled, narrating a tender tale of how God's image bearers embark on a heartfelt odyssey to rediscover their way back to God. This enchanting narrative

---

15. Moltmann, *Trinity and the Kingdom*, 45. I edited the translation to read "humanity" instead of "man."

16. Eph 1:4 (MSG).

reaches its climax in God's triumph over sin, death, and the formidable forces of darkness—an awe-inspiring amalgamation of the cross, resurrection, and ascension.

The plot of the narrative unveils the plight of humanity, snared in sin's clutches and trapped by the machinations of evil, seeking liberation and redemption through the extraordinary act of Jesus's sacrificial offering. It is a tale where God willingly places his own life in mortal jeopardy, boldly venturing to rescue humanity from the precipice of ultimate destruction. When Christians read the sacred narratives of the Old Testament, they uncover a divine promise that the offspring of a woman will one day crush the head of the serpent—a clarion call heralding the ultimate defeat of Satan's dominion. Within the poetic verses of Isaiah, a vibrant tableau emerges, portraying a suffering servant whose selfless sacrifice serves as a fount of healing and redemption. This tapestry—woven with intricate threads of prophecy—anticipates with fervor the ultimate triumph of Christ over the depths of sin and malevolence. It infuses the Christian narrative with an elegance and allure that enraptures both heart and mind.

By engaging with the biblical story, believers can construct coherent narratives that align with their experiences of God and help them make sense of their situation. We live in and through narratives; they are not like monuments we can observe from a distance. They more closely resemble our dwelling places.[17] Narratives exercise a profound power. They act as memory connectors, stitching together the diverse events and experiences that constitute our personal histories. They provide us with a meaningful framework, allowing us to make sense of the twists and turns, and joys and sorrows that color our lives. In this context, the words of Paul ring true, asserting that "Scripture is God-breathed and is useful for teaching, rebuking, correcting, and training in righteousness, so that the servant of God may be thoroughly equipped for every good work."[18]

The biblical chronicle, handed down through generations, offers believers a vast reservoir of wisdom and insight that people gained as they lived in union with God. Within its pages lie stories of triumph and failure, love and hatred, trust and betrayal, evil and redemption, and offense and forgiveness—universal themes that resonate across time and

---

17. See Crites, "Narrative Quality of Experience," 295. This idea is taken from Stephen Crites's famous observation: "Stories, and the symbolic worlds they project, are not like monuments that men behold, but like dwelling-places. People live in them."

18. 1 Tim 3:16–17.

cultures. As believers delve into these accounts, we discover a profound interconnectedness between the stories of biblical figures and our own experiences. Through this engagement, the Scriptures come alive, breathing wisdom into our lives and providing a lens through which they can navigate the complexities of existence.

Rather than offering an abstract or distant concept of God, the biblical story presents a God who converses with humanity and plays a crucial role in shaping life and history. This understanding invites believers to trust in God's regenerative story and actively participate in it. While theories and explanations can help us understand the world, the biblical stories offer a unique way of living in the world and transforming it through personal and collective change. By engaging with the biblical narrative, believers find guidance, wisdom, and meaning in their pursuit of understanding life's complexities.[19] But these narratives do more than just tell a story that we may find interesting. They let us communicate in real time. The legends are alive and dynamic, still recited, read, heard, and remembered, enlivening us even as we interpret them.[20]

As we live this human life in union with God, we enter a story that God tells us, that we indwell, not only to understand the realm we occupy, but also to have the vocabulary, the reference points, the grasp of events and a sense of the narrative arc to communicate with God wisely. When we see ourselves as part of God's story, we recognize that our lives have a purpose and meaning beyond what we imagine. We become aware of the bigger picture and how our autobiographies can slot into the grand narrative God unfolds through history and the future.

BETWEEN INTERPRETATION AND UNDERSTANDING

This understanding grants us a coherent framework for interpreting our experiences and life around us. It helps us make sense of the complexities of our days and equips us with a language to engage with God in dialogue, comprehension, worship, and prayer. By immersing ourselves in the story that God unerringly tells us, we gain a deeper understanding of his character, purposes, and influences in our domain, along with how others responded to him. This appreciation enables us to communicate with God in our own way.

---

19. See Goldberg, *Theology and Narrative*, ch. 5.
20. Hauerwas, *Vision and Virtue*, 71.

We live at the intersection where our personal stories and God-breathed testimony culminate in the person and ministry of Jesus the Nazarene. There we find the beauty, goodness, and truth that permeate all reality and make it possible to enter and remain in an open conversation with God.

12

Loving

IN A MEMORABLE ADDRESS to Kenyon College's class of 2005, David Foster Wallace remarked, "There is no such thing as not worshipping. Everybody worships. The only choice we get is what to worship."[1] Consider die-hard sports enthusiasts; they might not view their passion as worship in conventional terms. Yet their commitment and the importance they attach to games suggest a kind of veneration. Similarly, a business leader who elevates her career above all else, spending endless hours in pursuit of success and valuing herself by her accomplishments and assets, also shows a kind of reverence. So in this sense everyone worships something, consciously or subconsciously. The question is whether we elevate things beyond ourselves—a spiritual figure, an ethereal presence, scientific ideals, or moral values—or lean into gratifying personal ambitions or mere materialistic aims.

While the choice is ours as we live this life, we should not take it lightly, says Wallace, since the consequences are very real. The problem with desires and material goals is that we never acquire enough; they will consume us in the end. "Worship your own body and beauty and sexual allure," Wallace said, "and you will always feel ugly, and when time and age start showing, you will die a million deaths before they finally grieve you."[2] For him, this is common knowledge, but the "trick is keeping the truth up front in daily consciousness. Worship power—you will feel weak and afraid, and you will need ever more power over others to keep the

---

1. Wallace, "This Is Water."
2. Wallace, "This Is Water."

fear at bay. Worship your intellect, being seen as smart—you will end up feeling stupid, a fraud, always on the verge of being found out."[3]

BETWEEN LOVE AND WORSHIP

We should add that our worship reveals what and who we love. Love and worship are intertwined expressions of the heart, guiding us toward the objects of our greatest devotion. According to James K. A. Smith, saying "'you are what you love' is synonymous with saying 'you are what you worship.'"[4] From this perspective, our innate capacity for love inevitably gravitates toward the worship of something or someone, whether it be God or any other object of devotion. Our ability to love is an intrinsic and unchanging aspect of human nature, yet sin distorts the object of our affection, leading us to prioritize and pursue unworthy expressions of love and worship.

We yearn to love and be loved, especially because we are liminal creatures, feeling our way through the world. We long for an attachment figure, a covenanting one who sees and soothes us, with whom we sense that we are safe and secure. This one is none other than God himself. As Augustine writes in his *Confessions*, "The thought of you stirs us so deeply that we cannot be content unless we praise you because you made us for yourself and our hearts find no peace until they rest in you."[5] For Augustine, there is no other devotion, no deeper affection, than love for God. He is the ultimate focus of our love, and only in him do we find rest. What we love ultimately is what we worship, and worship, which brings an end to our restlessness, is love for God ultimately. When we love God, we find our deepest fulfillment and contentment. We are at peace, knowing that the one who created us and whose breath permeates every part of us loves and accepts us.

Marriage was also intended to be the place where humans found their deepest fulfillment and contentment, a refuge in a restless world. In the Genesis account, we see a man leave his birth family to unite with his wife. This departure is not merely physical; it is an emotional,

---

3. Wallace, "This Is Water."

4. Smith, *You Are What You Love*, 23.

5. This quote is from Saint Augustine's *Confessions*, 1.1.5 I have changed the singular pronoun to make the statement more inclusive. I did not ask for permission, but I ask for forgiveness. I enjoy this old translation: Augustine, *Confessions*, trans. R. S. Pine-Coffin, 21.

psychological, and spiritual transition. Drawn by his deep love, he leaves everything and everyone he has loved before to devote his entire being to his wife. Together, they "cleave," a biblical term that encapsulates the feeling of being seen, soothed, safe, and secure. Their bodies join as they become "one flesh," weaving a new identity. What is so beautiful in this simple account is that this couple becomes something else through leaving, cleaving, and weaving: they become the other. They become what they love.

Ilia Delio's summary of Clare of Assisi's teachings becomes particularly relevant at this point. According to Delio, at the heart of Clare's theology is this truth: "We become what we love, and who we love shapes what we become."[6] Our love, whether directed toward God or a mortal human being, shapes our identities and personal growth. But more than that, if love leads to worship, then our worship of God or mortals molds us in the image of the beloved. Just as a spouse's identity evolves through their deep love and commitment to their partner, our love for and devotion to God shapes our relationship with him. Our deepest affections transform us, gradually molding us into a reflection of what or who we hold dear.

BETWEEN WORSHIP AND FORMATION

This leads us to ask, How are we transformed by what we love and therefore worship? This important question is at the heart of James K. A. Smith's theological project, where he finds the answer lies in understanding liturgies. For Smith, liturgy, in this broad application, is a particularly powerful form of ritual designed to shape our desires in alignment with our vision of the good life.[7] In this view, humans are more than just believing creatures; we are fundamentally liturgical animals, "*homo liturgicus*; embodied, practicing creatures whose love/desire is aimed at something ultimate."[8] These practices can be found in various aspects of our lives, such as cultural customs, social behaviors, and personal habits. Each of these liturgies influences us, affecting our values, priorities, and the ultimate goals we pursue. For instance, the daily ritual of scrolling

---

6. Examining the works of Clare of Assisi, Ilia Delio reaches this poignant conclusion. This quote has been mistakenly attributed to Clare of Assisi. See Delio, "Clare of Assisi," 54.
7. Smith, *You Are What You Love*, 53.
8. Smith, *Desiring the Kingdom*, 40.

through social media, a seemingly mundane act, might not appear to have any profound impact on our beliefs. In reality, it becomes a practice when it shapes and directs our desires and affections toward an ultimate love. Through the content we consume, we form preferences, longings, and aspirations. This means that our actions, embodied in practices, play a significant role in shaping our beliefs and desires, ultimately pointing our love toward something we ought to consider as worthy of our devotion as it promises a good life.

As we live this human life in liminality, in the spaces between spaces, we live it as worshipers, people who want to love and be loved; to worship what we love ultimately. At the heart of our being is a kind of "love pump"[9] that can never be turned off, not even by sin or the fall. Instead, the effect of sin on our love pump "is to knock it off-kilter, misdirecting it and getting it aimed at the wrong things."[10] Even with hearts that are misaligned, we are searching to attach ourselves to someone or something that can imbue us with the comfort of being seen, soothed, safe, and secure. This vision of the good life captures our hearts and imaginations, as it paints a picture of what it looks like for us to flourish and live well.[11]

It is perhaps helpful to think about this in terms of the well-known parable of the so-called prodigal son that Jesus told. The prodigal son was born into a traditional Jewish home, and as the younger son, he was loved and appreciated, but he would always be second to his older brother. In this culture, the good life for him would be to know his place and to follow the rules that guide the life of a son who is not the eldest. But his desire was for a life where he would be free from these practices, routines that shaped his identity and formed his loves. However, slowly over time he began to embody the practices of the distant son, he developed routines and rituals that became a liturgy that grabbed "hold of his heart"[12] through his imagination of living in a distant land, free and without constraint. While he was not there yet, even while he was doing the chores of the youngest son, he could taste and smell what it would be like to be

---

9. Smith, *Desiring the Kingdom*, 52.

10. Smith, *Desiring the Kingdom*, 52.

11. For Smith, this is the kingdom. See Smith, *Desiring the Kingdom*, 52. "Human persons are intentional creatures whose fundamental way of 'intending' the world is love or desire. This love or desire—which is unconscious or noncognitive—is always aimed at some vision of the good life, some particular articulation of the kingdom."

12. Smith, *Desiring the Kingdom*, 62.

free; it was a visceral experience.[13] "This sort of ultimate love," says Smith, "could also be described as that to which we ultimately pledge allegiance; or, to evoke language that is both religious and ancient, our ultimate love is what we worship."[14]

The prodigal son represents all of us; we are all embedded in cultural practices that operate as transformative rituals, shaping our affections and focusing our love on what is culturally worthy of devotion. The pervasive influence of the dominant culture in most Western countries deftly molds our desires toward material possessions, social standing, and personal gratification. In a world inundated with ceaseless marketing and persuasive advertising, our longings for specific products, services, lifestyles, and benefits cultivate us to become what we love and worship. Jesus faced his own cultural pressures, and as we consider his life, we can find clues to how we live this human life in union with God through worship.

BETWEEN FORMATION AND VISION

One of the best places to turn to is at the very beginning of Jesus's ministry as the Spirit leads him into the desert to face his test. As I reflect on this very important account of Jesus's ministry, it is clear that worship lies at the heart of the temptations. In Matthew's account, which was aimed at a Jewish audience, he concludes the temptation of Jesus with Christ saying, "The Lord, your God, shall you worship, and him alone shall you serve."[15] One way to read the temptations is to see them as three visions of the good life. Each one of these is strong enough to awaken our desires and become the genesis of a liturgy of ultimate concern. They represent distinct portrayals of what we might desire and aspire to achieve.

First is the enticement of material possessions and financial independence. Satan tempts Jesus to transform stones into bread, tantalizing him to fulfill his physical needs effortlessly, without reliance on God. This portrayal of the good life revolves around an abundance of material possessions and generational wealth, surrounded by all the comforts we feel entitled to enjoy.

Second, the allure of social standing comes into play. Satan tempts Jesus to prove his divine identity by performing a daring act from the

---

13. See Smith, *Desiring the Kingdom*, 52.
14. Smith, *Desiring the Kingdom*, 51.
15. Matt 4:11 (NIV).

temple's pinnacle, thereby gaining immense influence over how people see him and what he represents. Such a display would instantly elevate him to a position of fame and adoration, appealing to the masses eagerly anticipating the arrival of their long-awaited messiah. In our contemporary world, this vision resonates with the desire for stardom, fame, and success, yearning to become a beloved, admired, or envied celebrity in others' eyes.

Finally, the temptation of personal gratification emerges. Satan offers Jesus authority over all the kingdoms of the world. This opportunity extends far beyond a status as the sole messiah of Israel; it presents the chance of assuming supreme leadership and the potential to govern the entire earth, with all his desires immediately gratified. Although most of us may not envision such grand authority, we nonetheless harbor aspirations of influence and control over others to advance the causes we hold dear.

The ensuing exchange between Jesus and Satan is not just a narrative of resisting temptation; it also provides a window into Jesus's foundational practices that shape his worship—practices deeply woven into his daily routines and rituals, effectively his liturgy that shaped his ultimate love—his love for God. The lure to turn stones into bread reveals Jesus's practice of personal dependence on God. By responding with "man shall not live by bread alone, but by every word that comes from the mouth of God," Jesus highlights his profound reliance on God. This is a dependency akin to a fledgling bird drawing sustenance from a parent. Jesus's dependence on God his Father is also a sign of his deep humility, a mark of his entire life. The early church sang about it, and the apostle Paul records an old Christological hymn in Phil 2:6–8, affirming this humility and painting a picture of Jesus forgoing his divine privilege to assume the role of a servant, even unto death. Personal humility, then, forms a cornerstone of Jesus's worship, a worship that places God as the source of all life and sustenance.

Satan's challenge to Jesus—to survive a leap from the temple pinnacle and gain recognition as the long-awaited messiah—would exaggerate the allure of social standing and the urge we sometimes have for external validation. However, Jesus's reaction to this temptation reveals his strong sense of identity as the fruit of the practice of internal validation. His divine identity and his mission do not rely on public spectacle or endorsement. This understanding was apparent in his exchanges with his disciples and even during his trial before Pilate. His identity was secure in God's revelation, not the whims of human approval. This internal self-confidence came from his unwaveringly secure attachment to God as the one who sees and soothes him, and with whom he is safe and secure.

The third temptation, where Satan offers Jesus all the kingdoms of the world if he will bow down to him, could indeed be seen as a temptation toward personal gratification and power. Satan was essentially offering Jesus a shortcut to rule the world, bypassing the suffering and sacrifice that awaited him. However, Jesus demonstrates his loving devotion to God the Father. His fidelity is not simply in word but in action, as seen in his refusal to succumb to Satan's inducement. Jesus's life is replete with examples of this fidelity. In the Garden of Gethsemane, he surrendered his desires to God's will, and Paul commends this obedience in Rom 5:19. Implicit in Jesus's response is the spiritual practice of self-denial. He puts God's will above his own, even when offered all the kingdoms of the world. This reflects the call to self-denial that Jesus later extends to his disciples when he said: "If anyone would come after me, let him deny himself and take up his cross and follow me."[16]

Jesus's practices of personal humility, internal validation, and loving fidelity were not only responses to temptation. They were also the practices that Jesus embodied. They were ritualized in thought and behavior to become a liturgy that directed his love away from distracting visions of the good life that excluded love for God. His "habits or dispositions that formed in [him] through affective, bodily means, especially bodily practices, routines, or rituals grabbed hold of [his] heart through [his] imagination" and aimed his love or desire that was also always aimed at his ultimate love.[17] So for those who knew Jesus, he became what he loved, but in reality, he was that even before they recognized that the man from Galilee was Emmanuel, God with us. Thus, the life and worship of Jesus provide the blueprint for their, and our, lives of worship, beckoning us to become what we love ultimately.

BETWEEN RITUALS AND SACRAMENTS

The liturgical practices that Jesus embodied and ritualized while he was with them also directed the love of the early Christians to order their affections as people of the way. They gathered together to remember and celebrate the life, death, and resurrection of Jesus through the breaking

---

16. Matt 16:24 (NIV).
17. See Smith, *Desiring the Kingdom*, 62.

of bread and sharing of the cup, following the example Jesus set at the last supper. They prayed, read scriptures, taught each other, sang hymns and psalms, and exercised spiritual gifts. They devoted themselves to fellowship, the sharing of resources, and caring for one another.[18] Through these liturgical practices, they became who they loved, and they worshiped who they loved. The apostle Paul says it beautifully, that as they "with unveiled faces contemplate the Lord's glory, [they] are being transformed into his image with ever-increasing glory, which comes from the Lord, who is the Spirit."[19] And like Jesus, the Christ, "they were being transformed to become vessels of God's compassionate love for others."[20]

Since the inception of Christianity, Jesus Christ has held an unequivocal and profound place within the sacred customs of the church. As believers congregated, drawn together by his name, an unmistakable sense of his presence pervaded their gatherings. At the core of their worship stood the Lord's table, where the simple elements of bread and wine took on a profound significance, representing the very essence of Jesus's body and sacrificial offering. Jesus's role in worship extended far beyond that of a mere mouthpiece for God, a rabbi, or a prophet. Rather, Jesus became the wellspring of adoration, devotion, and intimate spiritual connection with God as Father through the Holy Spirit, embodying the very reality of God's boundless love and redemptive presence. In the preaching of the early churches, Jesus Christ embodied the good news, through the act of baptism. New believers confessed their faith in his name, thus underscoring the depth of their dedication to him as Lord.

The New Testament consistently connects the resurrection of Jesus with his lordship. As Paul boldly proclaims, acknowledging Jesus as Lord is inseparable from believing in his triumphant resurrection.[21] Jesus was called upon as Lord and venerated in preparation for the day when every knee would bow to him.[22] This understanding has its origin in the fourth Gospel, when Thomas declared Jesus as "My Lord and my God," infusing the title "Lord" with divine implications associated with Jesus. The fourth century marked a crucial turning point when Athanasius contested the distortions of Arianism, "We do not worship a creature. Far be the thought. For such an error belongs to heathens and Arians. But we

18. See Acts 2:42–47.
19. 2 Cor 3:18 (NIV).
20. Delio, "Clare of Assisi," 54.
21. See Rom 10:9.
22. See Phil 2:5–11.

worship the Lord of Creation, Incarnate, the Word of God."[23] The ultimate triumph of Nicene orthodoxy firmly entrenched the practice of lifting prayers and praises toward the Son, embracing him as a focal point of devotion. Church history wove the Son into the very fabric of orthodox liturgy, and Jesus was honored as the Christ, the Son of God and the savior of the world. The definite article, calling Jesus "the Christ," gives the name and status of Jesus an extra historical and theological significance, since he is seen as the fulfillment of what it means to be the anointed. The adoration of the human figure on the cross, the open tomb, and the ascension of Jesus as human to be with God has captured the imagination of worshipers for two thousand years and shaped liturgical practices to direct our love or desire to God, our ultimate love.

In that way, Jesus functions as a liturgy, or as Augustine puts it, a mystery or sacrament. For him, "There is no other sacrament of God, but Christ."[24] He is a kind of *Ursakrament*. Karl Rahner explains, "Christ is the primal sacramental word of God, spoken within the shared history of humanity, through which God revealed an unshakable mercy that transcends any power to revoke, be it divine or human. This revelation found its expression in Christ, effecting an unwavering proclamation of God's mercy, thereby making it known to all."[25]

Jesus as the Christ is the original, personal embodiment of the meeting between God and humanity, a sacrament. In Christian practice, sacraments are outward and visible signs of inward and spiritual divine grace. As Elaine Graham says, God is present in these practices for Christians.[26] As I have already observed, this understanding has inspired Christians to live out their faith by participating in religious practices and rituals. But now, Christ is God's sacrament, a sign and reality of his grace. Christ is the sacrament of God since he enables us to live a life in the reality and grace of God's presence, even in liminality. As God's original sacrament,

---

23. Athanasius, "Letter LX. To Adelphius," §3.

24. "*Non est enim aliud Dei mysterium, nisi Christus.*" ("There is no other *mysterium* of God, but Christ.") Augustine, *Epistulae*, 187, 11.34, in Goldbacher, *Corpus Scriptorum Ecclesiasticorum Latinorum*, 113. Augustine uses *sacramenta* in *On Genesis*, 2.17, as "any sacred or hidden truth or reality signified by some other thing mentioned in scripture" (*On Genesis*, 1:83n29). In his explanation it is clear that Augustine does not distinguish between *mysterium* and *sacramentum*, and it can be concluded that *sacramentum* is a sign that contains and presents a *mysterium*.

25. I have edited the translation of W. J. O'Hara to be more gender-inclusive. Rahner, *Church and the Sacraments*, 18.

26. Graham, "On Becoming a Practical Theologian," 4.

Christ is the conduit through which God's presence permeates human existence. Jesus, in his life, death, and resurrection, becomes the primordial meeting point between God and humans. The incarnation of Christ is hence the ultimate sacramental event, with all other sacraments of the church deriving their significance and efficacy from it.

BETWEEN PRESENCE AND BECOMING

Therefore, Christian worship is not so much that we worship God as an object, but that we enter into eternal worship within God. Jesus the Christ is our worship leader since he "comes to be Priest of Creation, to do for men what man fails to do, to offer to God the worship and the praise that we have failed to offer."[27] That would make sense, since our affections are disordered, but now, in Christ we become like the one we love. In his humanity, now ascended, he is the conduit and the embodiment of our worship. In this sense, Jesus's love for his Father directs our love for God. Our "love pump" that has been knocked out of kilter, causing havoc as we loved and love wrongly, is no longer misaligned in Christ. We who were searching to attach ourselves to someone or something that can imbue us with the comfort of being seen, soothed, safe, and secure have entered into a loving relationship with the Trinity. This vision of the good life captures our hearts and imaginations, as it introduces us to a model of what it is like to flourish and live well as people who live in union with God.

Through the Holy Spirit, we can enter into the holiest place—the very presence of God. Our union with Christ makes this access possible through the work of the Holy Spirit.[28] Through his incarnation, life, death, and resurrection, Christ tore down the barrier that separated humanity from God. Now, the Spirit unites us with Christ, granting us the privilege of approaching God with a simultaneous boldness and intimacy in worship. As believers, says Torrance, "The Holy Spirit enables us to enter through the veil of the flesh of Christ into the holiest and connects us with Christ as He dwells in the immediate presence of God in unbroken communion."[29] But since, as we have argued in the previous chapter, the dialogue with God is a continuous loop, Christ's worship echoes within

---

27. Torrance, "Place of Jesus Christ in Worship," 348.

28. 1 Cor 12:13. We have discussed this passage at length at various points, and I shall not repeat it here again.

29. Torrance, *Theology in Reconciliation*, 140.

us, and our own worship becomes an outflow of his worship. The Spirit enables us to express our adoration, praise, and prayers to the Father in a manner intimately connected to the worship of Christ himself. It is difficult to say it better than Torrance: "to worship God, therefore, is to worship with Christ who worships with us and for us, and to worship with Him is to present His worship, the worship of His life which He offered in our place and on our behalf, and in which, though with Christ in the one Spirit, we are continually participant."[30]

If we view Christ as the *Ursakrament*, it follows that we can perceive all aspects of life sacramentally, providing a liturgical understanding of life since it is Christ, the Word, who called creation into existence. Creation materialized through Christ, the primal sacramental Word of God. The reality and grace of God's presence imbues all creation, not just grand, communal liturgical celebrations, even in liminality.

If Christ as God's original sacrament is the conduit through which God's presence permeates human existence, then creation was intended to embody the reality of God's beauty, goodness, and truth. All of creation is sacred; all life is sacred since there can be no creation without the original sacrament, the Word of God. As such, the sacred infiltrates the ordinary, making all of life a potential theophany, or visible manifestation of God.

To see life in this way would mean that every interaction on every level at every moment is a chance to encounter God, to partake in the sacramentality of existence. It softens the contradiction between sacred and secular. It shows us that if we live mindfully, every facet of life can transform into an act of worship, a spiritual tryst with the divine. In this way, life becomes a perpetual liturgy, where the mundane morphs into sacred rituals, echoing divine love and beckoning us to become what we love ultimately.

---

30. Torrance, *Theology in Reconciliation*, 209.

13

Serving

BEFORE THE DAWN OF time, in the silence of nothingness, God began a great work. An artist at the easel, a poet before the empty page, God spoke the cosmos into existence as he made space for life. In the pages of Genesis, the creative narrative reveals God the creator, not distant or idle, but actively engaged in the work of creation. Then, in a divine flourish, he formed humanity from the dust in the image of himself, commissioned to continue this great work. From the verdant expanses of Eden to the farthest reaches of the cosmos, he entrusted us with a sacred responsibility: to act as his hands and feet on Earth, to engage with creation as God does: creating, tending, nurturing. Yet, this is not simply to do with laboring for survival or subsistence. Rather, our work is intimately bound up with our worship. When we engage in the sacred act of work, we echo the divine activities of our creator. Each task, each moment of effort, is an opportunity to reflect God's creative love and care. We are, in essence, worshiping through our work and service. As we think about what it means to live in union with God through acts of service, this foundational insight from Genesis will guide us: our work and service were intended to be worship.

BETWEEN WORK AND WORSHIP

Even after the break that occurred in Eden, amid the thorns and thistles of post-Eden work, the sacred link between work and worship persists in the liminality that we indwell. When we work and serve—in our homes, in our communities, in the wider world, we are not simply performing tasks—we are invited to join in God's ongoing creative work, reflecting his beauty, goodness, and truth in all that we do. Service, in all its forms, has the potential to be a living prayer, a tangible act of devotion, and a vibrant expression of our love for God and his creation. It stands as a testament to the divine image within us, echoing the work of the creator and drawing us closer to the heart of what it means to be human.

As we have seen, what it means to be human has been a vexing question for centuries. In the context of our discussion here, we will need to return to our concept of *imago Dei*. If we are created in God's image from the earth's clay as God's image bearers, what significance does this hold for our understanding of our God-given life's purpose? The answer might seem quite obvious initially, as God instructed humans to "be fruitful and increase in number; fill the earth and subdue it. Rule over the fish in the sea and the birds in the sky and over every living creature that moves on the ground."[1] Before God assigns human Adam a gender in Gen 2, he gives the instruction "to work it and take care of it."[2] For those who find the first set of instructions harsh, these latter commands might reveal a more compassionate stance toward creation. So, humans are to use their lives to fill, subdue, rule, reign, work, and care for God's creation.

This list of instructions has occupied the minds of theologians for centuries. Among the many commentators on these verses, some justify exploiting the earth to extract whatever humans need to survive and thrive. Others cringe at the thought that God would instruct humans to subdue, as if the earth were a foe to be conquered. Is this what God has called us to be as his image bearers—to vanquish his creation? Why should we overpower creation if God has already declared it good and blessed it, expressing satisfaction with his work? After all, the creation narratives do not depict us as bearers of a conqueror's image; instead, we bear the image of a creator. Whatever these words mean, they do not imply conquest. Instead, we should understand them in light of God's desire to create a world reflecting his own beauty, goodness, and truth.

Human creativity bears the marks of God's creativity. As image bearers, we, like God, have creative ideas, energy, and power, says Dorothy Sayers. Her explanations have provided a way to understand creativity since *The Mind of the Maker* was first published in 1941:

---

1. Gen 1:28 (NIV).
2. Gen 2:15 (NIV).

> First, [not in time, but merely in the order of enumeration] there is the Creative Idea, passionless, timeless, beholding the whole work complete at once, the end in the beginning: and this is the image of the Father. Second, there is the Creative Energy [or Activity] begotten of that idea, working in time from the beginning to the end, with sweat and passion, being incarnate in the bonds of matter: and this is the image of the Word. Third, there is the Creative Power, the meaning of the work and its response in the lively soul: and this is the image of the indwelling Spirit. And these three are one, each equally in itself the whole work, whereof none can exist without the other: and this is the image of the Trinity.[3]

In our daily lives, we are called upon to undertake creative work. This involves generating ideas and investing energy to bring these ideas into existence—a process that is akin to incarnation, where the intangible thought becomes a tangible reality. As Sayers explains, through this incarnation, the creator effectively declares, "See! This is what my eternal idea looks like in terms of my creation . . ."[4] In the course of creation, the incarnation of the idea must be communicated effectively, and the original idea needs to resonate before the creative process can be deemed complete. This resonance is the creative power that needed to conclude the work of creation. Consider a young philosophy student absorbing the insights of a great thinker, or a new mother holding her baby for the first time. In these moments, when an idea—now tangible—resonates as beautiful, good, and true, we can declare the creative work fulfilled.

BETWEEN IDEA AND REALIZATION

But it all starts with the creative idea, the all-encompassing vision of the intended creation, which exists before any physical realization. It is the timeless, passionless prototype of the work that captures its wholeness even before it comes into being. While this seems straightforward, the creative idea is actually the most complex and challenging aspect of the creative process because it is internal, subjective, and potentially prone to misinterpretation. Unlike the creative energy, which we can see through the effort expended in creation, and the creative power, observed in the

---

3. Sayers, *Mind of the Maker*, 37–38.
4. Sayers, *Mind of the Maker*, 90.

reaction of the audience to the completed work, the creative idea is often invisible and intangible. It is a concept that resides in the creator's mind, elusive and hard to define or measure. Its intangible nature makes it difficult to communicate, translate into action, or even to fully understand oneself. Moreover, we must face the challenge of ensuring that we preserve the original idea and accurately reflect it throughout the entire creative process, from the initial spark to the final outcome.

Perhaps the best way to understand a creative idea is to define it as a fresh thought that will produce something novel, and perhaps—after the fall—that will make something new, to be reconciled to God, each other, and creation. "We spend our lives putting matter together in new patterns and so 'creating' forms that were not there before. This is so intimate and universal a function of nature that we scarcely ever think about it. In a sense, even this kind of creation is 'creation out of nothing.' Though we cannot create matter, we continually, by rearrangement, create new and unique entities."[5]

In the words of Barry Liesch, the process of creating something new involves several key requirements. First, it should be an irreducible phenomenon to the already known or easily explained. This uniqueness sets it apart from existing concepts and ideas. Second, it should possess an element of surprise, introducing unexpected or innovative elements that captivate and intrigue. Third, a truly new creation often showcases an elegant solution: it is simple, efficient, and aesthetically pleasing in its design, execution, and function. Moreover, a transformative element is essential in the creation of something new; the creation has the power to change or evolve over time, adapting to different contexts and challenges. Finally, the freshness and novelty of the creation should endure, and it ought not lose its originality or appeal as time goes on.[6] It is not so much that creation loses its original appeal, but rather that it carries within itself the seed for constant renewal and reinvention.

BETWEEN IMAGINATION AND INNOVATION

Whatever newness is, it does not occur without imagination, and humans have been gifted with the power of imagination. Very early in the

---

5. Sayers, *Mind of the Maker*, 90.
6. Liesch, "Creativity in the Bible."

creation narrative, God invites humans to name the animals[7] and to join him in his creative work. The act of naming in the Bible goes beyond just the classification of animals; it extends to people and carries profound theological implications. God often renames individuals to signify their destiny and purpose. For instance, Abram becomes Abraham to symbolize his new identity and mission as the father of a multitude of nations. This act of renaming highlights the transformative power of names in the biblical context, reflecting God's authority to shape our lives and destinies of individuals. It emphasizes that names are not merely labels but expressions of identity and purpose, and that God is intimately involved in the unfolding of human history. From this perspective, Adam's categorizing of the animals becomes even more significant. God's invitation to Adam to participate in the creative process through naming reflects the divine intention to grant humanity a share in the stewardship of creation. By giving Adam this responsibility, God dignifies human beings and elevates us to co-creators, allowing us to exercise our imagination as part of our innovative destiny.

Human imagination represents a remarkable cognitive gift that allows us to invent mental images, concepts, and ideas surpassing our immediate sensory experiences. It serves as a gateway to innovation, progress, and the betterment of society. Imagination fuels creativity, and throughout history, its impact has been profound in many ways, leading to significant advancements and improvements in the world. From Leonardo da Vinci's imaginative sketches of flying machines to Albert Einstein's thought experiments that led to the theory of relativity, human ingenuity has driven scientific inquiry and expanded our understanding of the universe. Medical researchers imagine new treatments and methods to combat diseases, resulting in the development of vaccines, antibiotics, and advanced surgical techniques that have drastically improved human health and longevity. Painters, writers, musicians, and other artists use their creative faculties to inspire emotions, provoke thought, and foster empathy, helping to bridge gaps between people and cultures. Visionaries like Mahatma Gandhi, Martin Luther King Jr., and Nelson Mandela imagined a world free from racial discrimination, and their dreams spurred social movements that continue to bring about positive change today. The concept of a more equitable and just society arises from the power of imagination to envision a better world for all.

---

7. See Gen 1:19.

BETWEEN MYTH AND SOCIAL IMAGINARY

Perhaps a great example of human imagination is found in our ability to make cultures in which we live. Theologians often refer to Gen 1:28 and Gen 2:15 as cultural mandates. Charles Taylor is perhaps the best known for the direct line he draws between imagination and culture. According to Taylor, humans "imagine their social existence, how they fit together with others, how things go on between them and their fellows, the expectations that are normally met, and the deeper normative notions and images that underlie these expectations."[8] This is what he calls a "social imaginary."[9] "Imaginary" seems a peculiar word, and certainly not as easy on the ear as a theory. It would be easier to say we share a common hypothesis on the kind of society we want to create. But how could this work? Theories often emerge from and thrive on abstraction; and the educated and the elite regularly claim them as their exclusive preserve. A social imaginary, on the other hand, penetrates deeper than a theoretical understanding; we could say it engages our affections as we imagine our social existence through "images, stories, and legends."[10] Taylor explains that the social imaginary is "much broader and deeper than the intellectual schemes people may entertain when they think about social reality in a disengaged mode."[11] Instead, social imaginaries are embodied in the work and artifacts of a culture.

No society or culture on earth lacks a creation myth or myths possessing cosmogonic and sacred essence(s) that shaped and continue to shape the world people inhabit. Carl Jung argued that before individual cultures arose, universal archetypes ranged across broader cultures—recurring themes or characters that appear in myths, legends, and stories woven through different cultures and eras. These archetypal motifs, such as the hero, the wise old man, or the shadow, are deeply ingrained in our psyche and profoundly impact the stories humans have been telling themselves over millennia.

Joseph Campbell, in his seminal work, *The Hero with a Thousand Faces*, explores the recurring patterns and archetypal motifs in mythological narratives. We follow the hero through the call to adventure, crossing the threshold into the unknown, facing challenges and tests,

---

8. See Taylor, "What Is a 'Social Imaginary'?," 23.
9. Taylor, "What Is a 'Social Imaginary'?," 23.
10. Taylor, "What Is a 'Social Imaginary'?," 23.
11. Taylor, "What Is a 'Social Imaginary'?," 23.

encountering mentors and allies, undergoing a transformation, and ultimately returning with newfound wisdom. J. R. R. Tolkien's Middle-earth, in *The Lord of the Rings*, is a richly detailed and immersive realm populated by various races, cultures, and landscapes. Middle-earth reflects his belief in the existence of a collective consciousness, where shared symbols, archetypes, and themes resonate across cultures and time periods. C. S. Lewis, Tolkien's friend, infused the *Chronicles of Narnia* with archetypal characters, metaphors, and allegories, revealing universal themes and desires threaded through the fabric of human existence, transcending cultural and individual boundaries. Through his stories, Lewis tapped into these shared elements of the collective consciousness, inviting readers to investigate fundamental questions about the nature of reality, morality, and the human condition.

In *Sapiens*, Yuval Harari argues that *homo sapiens* conquered this planet because of our unique ability to create and spread stories. What sets us apart from other mammals is our capability to cooperate with strangers by creating, telling, and spreading stories about what we imagine. In this way can convince millions of others to believe our stories and to act accordingly. Humans band together and collaborate because everyone believes in the same stories and derives the same meaning.[12] According to Jonah Sachs, "Our culture is pulled forward or changed through stories and the myths embedded in them. Myths are not lies; they hold us together around a set of common beliefs and values. When myths are functioning properly, they bring us together and get us to act by using a specific formula that appears to be universal across all cultures."[13]

The premise of Sachs's argument is that the best ideas survive, from campfire to campfire, from table to table, from blog post to blog post. We are social imaginaries, not only because we like a good story but also because we want to promote, convey, and share ideas that will make our lives better. We convey our imaginative ideas about the world as stories because we experience the world, liminal as it is, as narrative. Memory retains individual experiences as stories; we weave and connect stories to give us a sense of coherence, creating networks of ideas to communicate meaning. It explains why, as we have seen, Stephen Crites claims that narrative is the quality of human experience.[14] Narrators lace such stories into inventive tales and "are not like monuments that men behold," says

---

12. See Harari, *Sapiens*, 27.
13. Sachs, *Story Wars*, 59.
14. Crites, "Narrative Quality of Experience," 291–311.

Crites, "but like dwelling-places. People live in them."[15] We indwell these stories, but the ideas they contain also live in and through us. While we create these stories, the stories also create us.

BETWEEN HOSTILITY AND RECONCILIATION

As we have already discussed, Cornelius Plantinga, the Christian story starts when everything "in the universe is all jumbled together. So, God begins to do some creative separating: he separates light from darkness, day from night, water from land, the sea creatures from the land cruisers."[16] But this creative sorting was a means to an end; it was not separation as a final state. It was partition to create a new state of being. He explains, "At the same time God binds things together: he binds humans to the rest of creation as stewards and caretakers of it, to himself as bearers of his image, and to each other as perfect complements."[17] When evil enters the human story, it also separates, but this time separation is not a means *to* an end, it is *the* end. Humans live in separation from God, others, themselves, and creation. In this state of division, we are drawn into ourselves, as Augustine graphically depicted with the phrase *incurvatus in se*—turning inwardly.[18]

We are introduced to evil, with its many different faces. The Judeo-Christian story has much to say about evil, revealing its determination to separate what should be bound together. As we have seen, it makes sense that *diabolos*, the Greek word for "evil," is often associated with tearing things apart. The image here is of God and humans who were once joined together now having been wrenched from each other. *Diabolos*, at its simplest, means slanderous, false accusation—so the devil as *diablo* is the accuser of humankind. His malicious, fabricated allegations intend driving a wedge between God and creation, starkly illustrated in the story of Job. This idea of someone whispering slanders to cause a split also brings to mind Wormtongue murmuring into the ear of the King of Rohan in Tolkien's trilogy. What was designed to be united has been broken up.

---

15. Crites, "Narrative Quality of Experience," 295.
16. Plantinga, *Not the Way It's Supposed to Be*, 29.
17. Plantinga, *Not the Way It's Supposed to Be*, 29.
18. See Jenson, *Gravity of Sin*, for a discussion of the development of the concept through theological history. He discusses Luther's expansion of the concept beyond original sin to religious "man," as well as Karl Barth's broadening of the concept for *homo religiosus* beyond pride and hubris.

That which belonged together is now opposed. The sadness we see in the biblical narrative is that we are not only separated but strive to gain power over each other, to be served by others.

From this point onward, the Old and New Testaments, up to the crucifixion, tell the story of this hostility, this fight, this struggle to gain the upper hand. Now we have moved into the second act of our drama, from union to disunion, from orientation to disorientation. In this stage, we have rupture, but more than that, we compete with God, others, and creation in this frantic struggle to overpower our perceived opponents. This struggle culminates as a Galilean is crucified on a hill outside Jerusalem. Those close to him called him the Christ, the Son of the living God.

For N. T. Wright, who believes that humans handed their authority over to the powers of this world when we turned from worshiping the true God, we surrendered the authority God has given us to the powers and principalities of darkness, the idols of this world.

After Adam, God called Abram to become the father of a priestly state which would be the conduit of God's blessings to the nations. But sadly, Israel became obsessed with having a king and became a kingdom. Instead of conducting God's blessings to all nations, it dammed the flow of God's blessings, filling its storehouses in the name of nation-building. As just another self-serving kingdom, it became an enemy and competitor and was soon overpowered and exiled. It is the Garden of Eden all over again. On return from its exile, Israel longed for a messiah who would remove their foreign oppressors, reinstate Jerusalem to its former glory, and restore the temple. But Jesus had a more urgent agenda, to remove the power of evil in the world, to end the thirst to overpower. According to Wright, the cross is the solution, the victory over the power of evil. He explains that the cross "was the moment when something happened as a result of which the world became a different place, inaugurating God's future plan. The revolution began then and there; Jesus's resurrection was the first sign that it was indeed underway."[19] On the cross, Jesus says, God made us alive with Christ. "He forgave us all our sins, having canceled the charge of our legal indebtedness, which stood against us and condemned us; he has taken it away, nailing it to the cross. And having disarmed the powers and authorities, he made a public spectacle of them, triumphing over them by the cross."[20]

---

19. Wright, *Day the Revolution Began*, 34.

20. Col 2:14–15 (NIV). It is interesting to note that "having canceled" is εξαλειψας meaning "blot out," the εξ prefix implying completeness. Aristotle used the word for

A third part to this story remains, a third act of the theo-drama. This section is still unfolding; it is not yet a complete revolution. With the death of Christ, God regenerates, renews, restores, and reconciles the world to himself again.[21] In Ephesians chapter 2, Paul describes what God achieved on the cross as having broken down the wall of hostility between Jew and gentile. The cross works against the separation, against the consequences of the break that occurred. On the cross, we see God, in Jesus, laying down his life; God taking on the risk of apparent death. As we have seen, God did not die. It is not that God ceased to exist. Jürgen Moltmann wants us to see that the cross is not the death *of* God but rather the death *in* God.[22] Moltmann maintains that we need to think about the cross in trinitarian terms since the "Son suffers dying, the Father suffers the death of the Son. The grief of the Father here is just as important as the death of the Son . . . he also suffers the death of his Fatherhood in the death of the Son."[23]

Jesus took upon himself all our sin, all our evil, and all that separates us from God. The cross reveals the weight of sin, the seriousness of the break between God, humans, and the rest of creation. H. R. Mackintosh reminds us that the "elusive greatness" of God's sacrifice is the inverse measure of the danger that threatened humankind.[24] Through the cross, we come face to face with the darkness in which we should have sunk but for the dearly paid mercy of God. In this act of death on a cross, God himself stood toe to toe with death and overcame it in Jesus through the power of the Holy Spirit. The whole Trinity is involved because the life of God is at stake. For Robert Jenson, "God the Spirit is the sphere of the triumph. And 'triumph' is the precise word: the Father and the Spirit take the suffering of the creature who the Son is into the triune life and bring from it the final good of that creature, all other creatures, and of God. So

---

striking persons' names from the rolls in Athens. It is also used with νομος to mean the canceling of the effect of a law. "Legal indebtedness" is χειρογραφον, handwritten testimony, or written report, the meaning being the personally ascribed record of our offenses has been expunged—like a youthful offender whose record is cleared when a stipulated measure of time has passed without further offense. "Stood against us" is υπεναντιον, "oppose" or "set against," used of enemies on the battlefield, but also sometimes used as "oppose secretly or thwart."

21. A beautiful account of this is to be found in 2 Cor 5.
22. Moltmann, *Crucified God*, 243.
23. Moltmann, *Crucified God*, 243.
24. Mackintosh, *Christian Experience of Forgiveness*, 159.

and not otherwise the true God transcends suffering."[25] Consequently, the wall of hostility between Jew and gentile, male and female, and other clashing groups has been broken down. Instead of separation or subjugation, we have a model of what it means to serve selflessly.

BETWEEN D-DAY AND V-DAY

While there is much to celebrate, we know that, while there are signs of God's triumph over evil, the world remains in a state of war, physically and spiritually. To explain this confusing state of affairs, we need to return to the work of Oscar Cullmann, who introduced the illustration of the Decisive Day and Victory Day of the Second World War. He explains, "Just as the 'Victory Day' does, in fact, present something new in contrast to the decisive battle already fought at some point or other of the war, just so the end which is still to come also brings something new. To be sure, this new thing that the 'Victory Day' brings is based entirely upon that decisive battle and would be absolutely impossible without it."[26] While the consummation of redemption awaits Christ's return, Christians are not left without a foretaste of the future. Cullmann points out that, even now, believers are allowed to "taste the powers of the future world" and experience God's anticipatory work within themselves through the Holy Spirit (Heb 6:5).[27] We could say that the Spirit awakens within believers a social imaginary, providing us with glimpses of the new world that is to come. The author of Hebrews speaks of how this imaginary helps us to see a different future, even though at present, we do not see the world reconciled to God. "But we do see Jesus, who was made lower than the angels for a little while, now crowned with glory and honor because he suffered death so that by the grace of God he might taste death for everyone."[28]

Christians have been living with this social imaginary of God's kingdom that is coming, even when there is scant evidence of God's new world. Between a theological D-Day and V-Day, there is still much to be done; much remains at risk, and much suffering and many deaths will still occur. While the kingdom of God has been inaugurated, it is not a

---

25. Jenson, *Systematic Theology*, 1:144.
26. Cullmann, *Christ and Time*, 114.
27. Cullmann, *Christ and Time*, 79.
28. Heb 2:9 (NIV).

distant, abstract concept but an active, transformative force that beckons Christians to be engaged in all walks of life. As Bosch compellingly articulates, the divine mission is not merely about awaiting salvation or a distant eschatological vision. Instead, Christians are called to be "agitators for God's coming reign; they must erect, in the here and now and in the teeth of those structures, signs of God's new world."[29] When Paul speaks of believers as "God's handiwork," they embody the artist's vision, not as passive entities like paintings or sculptures. What Paul envisions seems more akin to the performance art of Joseph Beuys, as these works of art will "do good works, which God prepared in advance"[30] for them to perform. As works of art, we are servants of change, equipped for acts that illuminate God's desire to end separation and subjugation and to establish peace. As Christ is "our peace, who has made the two groups one and has destroyed the barrier, the dividing wall of hostility, by setting aside in his flesh the law with its commands and regulations. His purpose was to create in himself one new humanity out of the two, thus making peace, and in one body to reconcile both of them to God through the cross, by which he put to death their hostility."[31] This implies that the kingdom of God is not just a future reality to be hoped for but a continual mission to be lived out. Christians are not merely spectators of a divine drama but active participants, tasked with the sacred duty to act as agents of reconciliation, justice, and love in a fragmented world.

God calls every Christian to respond to his work in the world. And therefore, the church, made up of everyday people who live their lives in the tension between the "already and the not-yet," listens for the call of God to join him in a ministry of reconciliation. Paul explains that "if anyone is in Christ, the new creation has come: The old has gone, the new is here! All this is from God, who reconciled us to himself through Christ and gave us the ministry of reconciliation."[32] Many voices call us, demanding our attention, desiring to set the agenda for the rest of our lives, but Frederick Buechner says there is a way to tell if it is God's voice. "The kind of work God usually calls you to do is work (a) that you need most to do and (b) that the world needs most to have done. The place

---

29. Bosch, *Transforming Mission*, 276.
30. Eph 2:10 (NIV).
31. Eph 2:14–16 (NIV).
32. 2 Cor 5:17–18 (NIV).

God calls you to is the place where your deep gladness and the world's deep hunger meet."[33]

Jesus was very clear about the world's deep hunger when he opened the scroll and he read from the book of Isaiah. He felt called to proclaim the "year of the Lord" to the poor, the imprisoned, the oppressed, and the blind. The year of the Lord refers to the "year of jubilee" mentioned in the Old Testament, specifically in Exod 25. Traditionally, every fiftieth year, all debts were to be canceled, slaves and prisoners were to be freed, and the mercies of God would be particularly manifest. The proclamation of the "year of the Lord" was a declaration of God's favor, a time of restoration, freedom, and divine grace. When Jesus read from Isaiah and spoke of proclaiming the "year of the Lord," he was essentially announcing that, in him, the time of God's favor and the promises of the jubilee had come.[34] It did not concern economic or social justice only, but spiritual restoration. Through Jesus, those spiritually impoverished would find richness in faith; the imprisoned would find freedom from sin; the oppressed would experience God's liberation; and the blind would gain spiritual sight. This proclamation underscored Jesus's mission on earth and the transformative power of his message.

The jubilee was a blessing, when people were restored, families reunited, and debts struck off. The theme of blessings is also the central theme of his Sermon on the Mount. In words that recall how God blessed creation and the Sabbath—and as a reminder that Abraham and Israel were called to be a blessing to the nations—the demographics Jesus addressed in the first four Beatitudes were emblematic of societal oppression. These were the not-so-blessed. Among them were those plunged into penury, those who grieved in enduring sorrow, and the meek. Contrary to current popular perception, the meek—referred to as the *anawin*—were the downtrodden and faithful underclass: the enslaved, the widowed, the orphaned, the foreigner, and all those marginalized individuals battling for sheer survival. Then there were those starving for justice and righteousness, yet they remained deprived, lacking the political or judicial means to gain them. In four parallel blessings, Jesus

---

33. Buechner, *Wishful Thinking*, 95.

34. The Bible introduces the concept of the jubilee year in Exod 25, detailing its laws and significance. However, the Old Testament does not provide clear evidence that Israel ever fully practiced the year of jubilee as described. This has led to debate among scholars, theologians, and historians about whether or how the jubilee year was observed in ancient Israel.

declares that mercy will come to the poor through those who are merciful. The pure in heart, whom God's own heart moved, would comfort the mourners, while the *anawin* would inherit what was theirs through the peacemakers, who were literally workers of servants of good will. Finally, those who have been deprived of righteousness and justice would be fulfilled and satisfied, for the righteous—who were willing to risk persecution in the name of decency—would champion their cause. The blessings were not simply passive affirmations but calls to action. For every marginalized group, another was present, endowed with the resources, empathy, and commitment to respond to their plight and serve.

Thus, the Sermon on the Mount not only recognized the struggles of the downtrodden but called to the disciples of Jesus to act as his hands and his feet and the conduits of his blessing. This is what he was doing and what he calls us to do with him now. This is the social imaginary that sparks every act of service, each gesture of kindness, and all displays of courage. It gives us faith that every heartbreak has a healer, every injustice an advocate, and every person, no matter how beleaguered, can know the touch of grace. Therefore, just as the jubilee was a time of restoration and blessing, Jesus provides the blueprint of the kingdom in which oppression is dismantled, walls of hostility razed, and every individual, regardless of their societal status, is seen, soothed, safe, and secure—making everything new.

14

Growing

IN MY EXPLORATION OF theology, the early church often offers intriguing perspectives on modern questions that we face. Their ideas prove as valuable insights into the complexities of human development, enriching our understanding of these important theological topics. For instance, Irenaeus, as we have already seen, provides promising insights on the meaning of image and likeness.[1] This is significant as we explore human development in this last chapter of the current work. For him, image is like an unchanging foundation, pointing to our inborn potential to live in union with God. According to Geoffrey Wainwright, Irenaeus proposes that image is the "ontological or structural possibility of human communion with God."[2] Likeness, on the other hand, is more dynamic, describing the moral resemblance we can develop with God over time. It "stands for the existential or moral similarity with God into which humanity is to grow as it actually lives in union with God."[3] It blossoms in relationship with God. Picture it like a seed containing the blueprint—the ontology and structure—of a tree. But that seed has to go through a transformative process, growing into a mature tree that stands as a true reflection of its innate nature. Only then can we recognize it for what it truly is: a living embodiment of its original image, now realized in likeness.

What comes clearly into view here is the concept of individuation—the process of becoming a whole and complete individual—that permeates

1. Irenaeus, *Against Heresies*, bk. 5.
2. Wainwright, *Doxology*, 17.
3. Wainwright, *Doxology*, 17.

the works of Carl Jung. Jolande Jacobi, a Jungian psychoanalyst, beautifully describes this journey in a way that resonates deeply with me. It is like "a seed growing into a tree, life unfolds stage by stage."[4] But this phrase especially captures my attention every time I read it, that the human journey toward becoming a whole and complete individual, is, she says, the "labyrinthine windings from birth to death in hope and longing."[5] In her book *The Way of Individuation*, she identifies two paths to individuation. One is unconscious personal growth, a natural physical, cognitive, and psychological maturation, while the other is a conscious engagement with our own complexities. If we return to our analogy of the seed and the tree, the first is like rain nurturing a seed. Nature provides the basics, the elemental forces. However, the young tree initially may need a gardener to guide its growth and keep it free from disease and pests, helping the tree to become the living embodiment of its original design.

According to Jacobi, Jung sees two developmental stages along the way to individuation. In the first phase—our first four decades—people need to form a distinct identity. This ego-phase is the crucible that forges the first pieces of identity, or the scaffolding that gets us ready for the deeper work of self-discovery. In the second stage—the last three decades—we enter a more mystical, inward journey. In the words of Arthur Schopenhauer: "The first forty years of life furnish the text, while the remaining thirty supply the commentary; without the commentary we are unable to understand aright the true sense and coherence of the text, together with the moral it contains."[6] That is why I think Richard Rohr gets it right describing the second phase of life as "falling upward and onward, into a broader and deeper world, where the soul has found its fullness, is finally connected to the whole, and lives inside the Big Picture."[7] It is not just to do with "getting old, dealing with health issues, and letting go of our physical life,"[8] it is exactly the opposite. Even though individuation promises a richer life, it does not proceed without its struggles. It is our return when we throw ourselves into life, fearing no struggle or hard work or experience.[9] Only then will we grow into our nascent potential. In short, individuation is *to become fully what we are in seed form.*

4. Jacobi, *Way of Individuation*, 16.
5. Jacobi, *Way of Individuation*, 16.
6. Quoted in Jacobi, *Way of Individuation*, 16.
7. Rohr, *Falling Upward*, 153.
8. Rohr, *Falling Upward*, 153.
9. Jacobi, *Individuation*, 16. "Only if he treads the path bravely and flings himself

BETWEEN STAGES AND PROGRESS

So far, we have used the idea of stages in this understanding of growth. The concept of life stages is not foreign to us; it is the metaphor through which we often categorize our evolving experiences and shifting perspectives over time. It also shows up in religion, philosophy, and psychology as people try to make order out of human chaos. Religiously, the notion of life stages is often tied up with stories of moral and spiritual progress—or decline. Christianity has an order of salvation, *ordo salutis*, or stages of spiritual growth from initial conversion to sanctification and glorification. Islam designates three stages of climbing the spiritual mountain.[10] The Hindu idea of *asramas*, or structured living, is aimed at spiritual and ethical growth.[11] Many religions lay out roadmaps for the journey, describing the virtues to value or venerate and vices to avoid at each stage—seen as milestones on the path to fully uniting with God. Philosophically, the whole concept of life stages gives us much to ponder existentially. The philosopher Søren Kierkegaard divided life into three stages: the aesthetic, ethical, and religious. In the field of psychology, many theoretical frameworks offer perspectives on growth with the help of stages as the key metaphor. For instance, Sigmund Freud's psychosexual and Jean Piaget's cognitive development stages have laid a foundation for further theories. Erik Erikson's psychosocial development stages provide insights into the crises we encounter as we mature. At the same time, Lawrence Kohlberg's moral development theory explores the progression from external moral guidance to internalized societal norms and laws. In the final stage of moral development we are even able to transcend established moral frameworks and social conventions. While these theories have their limitations and critics, they all contribute insights into aspects of human development. These theoretical frameworks shed light on how we navigate through stages to confront life's challenges or grapple with dilemmas that shape our sense of identity.

---

into life, fearing no struggle and no exertion and fighting shy of no experience, will he mature his personality more fully than the man who is ever trying to keep to the safe side of the road."

10. "The pinnacle is excellence (*al-iḥsān*), its middle is faith (*al-īmān*), and its base is Islam. Thus, every good-doer (*muḥsin*) is a believer and every believer is Muslim, but not every believer is a good-doer and not every Muslim is a believer." Parrott, "Islām, Īmān, Iḥsān."

11. The four *asramas* are: Brahmacharya (student), Gṛhastha (householder), Vanaprastha (forest walker/forest dweller), and Sannyasa (renunciant).

Jean Piaget, in a fictional conversation with James Fowler, describes his understanding of a stage as "an integrated set of operational structures that constitute the thought processes of a person at a given time."[12] But a stage can be more than thought processes; it can manifest as psychosocial ability, moral judgment capacity, or a combination of both. A faith stage could approximate a clearing in a forest from which a person could make sense of the world in which they are temporarily lost. The development of stages involves refining these overall mental structures so that they become more intricate, complex, adaptable, and stable over time. This happens as we move from balance to imbalance to balance again, says Piaget.

Imagine a stage as a well-balanced connection between ourselves and our surroundings. With this balance, we absorb information from our environment and fit it seamlessly into life—a process known as assimilation. However, if something new emerges to defy or confound our current understanding of the world, we might develop fresh perspectives to make sense of it. We call this accommodation. If we find it challenging to assimilate or accommodate the new experience, we face discomfort and confusion. This unease could trigger a learning and developmental process; it might push us to actively seek new information, alter our viewpoint, or forge new thought patterns to comprehend this unfamiliar territory.

BETWEEN CRISIS AND RESOLUTION

In *Identity and the Life Cycle*, Erik Erikson also uses the stage concept of human development. While he exhibits similarities with Piaget, he provides an expanded view of Freud's psychosexual development theory.[13] His stages go beyond the family unit that Freud focused on, or the cognitive development of Piaget, to include broader societal influences. Physical and psychological changes mark each stage, leading to new relationships and roles within societal institutions. A defining characteristic of each stage is a crisis, stemming from the tension between embracing new capabilities and failing to integrate them. These stages interconnect as each builds upon the outcomes of previous crises. In this view it is therefore important that we resolve the crisis we face in each stage of our development.

---

12. Fowler, *Stages of Faith*, 46.
13. The well-known oral, anal, phallic, latency, and genital stages of development.

Erikson claims that "each new stage is initiated by a crisis; a struggle between the optimal possibilities presented by one's emerging new capacities, on the one hand, and the failure to integrate them into one's being and well-being on the other."[14] In the first eighteen years of our lives, we learn to skillfully navigate the conflicting forces of trust and mistrust, autonomy and shame, initiative and guilt, industry and inferiority. We may have to confront a watershed between identity and role confusion during the tumultuous years of physical metamorphosis of our pubescent years. Unlike childhood and adolescence, biological changes do not as closely anchor adult stages. Instead, they are a continual negotiation between individual capabilities and the societal structures that accommodate or challenge them. In young adulthood we face the perplexity of intimacy and isolation. Next we confront the tension between generativity and stagnation in mid-life, leading to the final showdown between integrity and despair in our later years. In these years, we will either look back at our lives with satisfaction and a sense of meaning or regret our choices, leaving us with a sense of despair.

James Fowler is one of the earliest theologians to integrate developmental psychology and theology in a faith-stage approach to understanding human development across the lifespan.[15] His theory outlines a sequential, hierarchical progression through seven stages of faith. Each subsequent stage enriches and refines the preceding one, but the developmental journey is not guaranteed to advance without hindrance. At any point, personal growth can stagnate, causing an individual to plateau at a particular stage of faith, making it their final stage of faith development. To be clear, these are not stages of belief, they are stages of faith, since faith and belief are distinct concepts in this theory. Following Cantwell Smith, faith is "an orientation of the personality, to oneself, to one's neighbor, to the universe; a total response; a way of seeing whatever one sees and of handling whatever one handles; a capacity to live at more

---

14. Taken from the fictional conversation that Fowler had with Erik Erikson in Fowler, *Stages*, 48.

15. See the fictitious conversation between Erikson, Piaget, and Kohlberg, in Fowler, *Stages of Faith*, 41–50. With the help of the theories of Erik Erikson, Jean Piaget, and Lawrence Kohlberg, James Fowler was able to build a comprehensive and systematic account of the development of faith across the lifespan. Fowler discussed these stages in various publications. The most comprehensive exploration can be found in the already cited *Stages of Faith*. However, he provides a very helpful truncated version in *Faith Development and Pastoral Care*.

than a mundane level; to see, to feel, to act in terms of, a transcendent dimension."[16] It is therefore a universal phenomenon, something that we all share as humans. We can universally benefit from our shared advantage as image bearers of God'

BETWEEN FAITH AND BELIEF

Because Fowler's concept of faith as *a way of knowing and interpreting our experience*[17] is a universal phenomenon, it is different from Augustine's *fides qua creditur*—a personal act of faith, the faith with which I believe. For Fowler, before we talk about a personal faith, we should consider the phenomenon of faith that marks all humankind. He believes that faith, rather than personal beliefs "is the most fundamental category in the human quest for relation to transcendence."[18] This might be closer to Augustine's idea of *fides quae creditur*, which proceeds from a single truth that "is impressed from one doctrine upon the heart of each person who believes the same thing."[19] While it is not clear from this passage what doctrine has been etched in the hearts of believers, it might well be the human quest for relation to transcendence that Fowler speaks about. This view gains strength if we consider that we are image bearers of God and this truth is etched in our hearts, irrespective of which personal faith, culture, or religion we belong to. This universal human capacity to interpret experience in the light of the transcendence seems to resonate with Augustine's belief that faith "does not belong to that sense of the body which is called hearing, since it is not a sound; nor to the eyes of this our flesh, since it is neither color nor bodily form; nor to that which is called touch, since it has nothing of bulk; nor to any sense of the body at all, since it is a thing of the heart, not of the body; nor is it without apart from us, but deeply seated within us; nor does any man see it in another, but each one in himself."[20] As a theologian and a social scientist, Fowler is keen to understand this "*form* or *structural characteristics* of faith-knowing, rather than to its *contents*."[21]

16. Quoted in Fowler, *Stages of Faith*, 11.
17. This is one of Fowler's earliest definitions of faith. Fowler, "Toward a Developmental Perspective," 207.
18. Fowler, *Stages of Faith*, 14.
19. Augustine, *On the Trinity*, bk 13, 2.5.
20. Augustine, *On the Trinity*, bk 13, 2.5.
21. Fowler, "Toward a Developmental Perspective," 211.

But this does not mean that faith as knowing is without content. For Augustine, as we have seen, the personal act of faith, the faith that I believe, proceeds from the faith that has been etched on our hearts. In terms of our discussion here, faith as believing proceeds from faith as knowing. In other words, the human capacity for faith as knowing makes faith as believing possible. In contrast to faith as knowing, faith as believing is very personal, says Augustine; it "is in the mind of the believer, and is visible to him only whose it is; although not indeed itself but a faith like it, is also in others."[22] It should be clear by now we are not talking about two separate forms of faith, as if they can exist independent of each other; rather they are interconnected, mutually indwelling and enabling aspects of what we mean when we talk about faith. So as we mature as humans through the natural processes of "growing up," our capacity to know and interpret life also develops, enabling more nuanced, complex, and integrated ways of faith-knowing.[23] It is as if faith as knowing that emerges from our biological, psychological, and cognitive development secures us. This growing capacity to know and interpret makes new demands of the faith we believe, and may over time lead to significant changes in what and how we believe. With time, it becomes important to clarify a personal faith, a faith that we hold, by which we believe, that grows as "we throw ourselves into life, fearing no struggle or hard work or experience."[24] When this fails, we encounter an entropic or weakened believer described as one who still lives on milk, because they are "not acquainted with the teaching about righteousness. But solid food is for the mature, who by constant use have trained themselves to distinguish good from evil."[25]

From a developmental perspective, the "faith that holds us" is what we rely on during the first half of our lives, providing the essential improvement scaffolding we need to know and interpret life's opportunities

---

22. Augustine, *On the Trinity*, bk 13, 2.5.

23. In later works, Fowler refers to faith as "constitutive-knowing." While I think this is a comprehensive and very useful description, we will continue to use faith-knowing as short hand for this expanded view. The full definition of faith is "the process of constitutive-knowing underlying a person's composition and maintenance of a comprehensive frame of meaning generated from a person's attachments or commitments to centers of supraordinate value which have power to unify his or her experiences of the world, thereby endowing the relationships, contexts, and patterns of everyday life with significance." Fowler, "Faith and the Structuring of Meaning," 175.

24. Jacobi, *Individuation*, 16.

25. Heb 5:13 (NIV).

and complexities. Like Arthur Schopenhauer, I envision this as the backdrop or subtext against which the unfolding drama of our existence plays out. And I am reminded of Augustine's eloquent description that faith is "written on our hearts." It is so elemental that it transcends the boundaries of culture, religion, and individuality. But as we mature in all the various aspects of human growth, a shift gradually occurs, a "faith that we hold" begins to emerge with greater prominence.

The faith that our families and communities hold becomes the faith that we hold, until we reach the point in our development where we are able to believe for ourselves as young adults. From this point on we have a choice to continue to be held by the faith that we have inherited, or to take hold of faith. This transition is no mere rite of passage; it marks the dawn of our spiritual consciousness. This is the faith textured by the unique weft and weave of our life experiences and choices and nurtured through our love for a God who makes sense of it all. We are empowered to make our faith our own, to refine it, question it, and, ultimately, grow in it. In the process, we do not merely inherit a spiritual legacy; we actively shape our own. In the words of Richard Rohr, we are "falling upward and onward, into a broader and deeper world."[26]

From Fowler's vantage point, faith emerges not merely as a belief system but as a "way of knowing, construing, or interpreting experience,"[27] as we have already seen. It evolves at different stages of our lives, synthesizing the myriad aspects of our experience into an integrated "pattern of meaning-making."[28] The divine-like nature of the center of faith is seen in the fact that it provides the very logic by which we interpret our experiences.[29] It molds our perspectives on life, informs our moral judg-

---

26. Rohr, *Falling Upward*, 153.
27. Fowler, "Faith and the Structuring of Meaning," 175.
28. Moseley et al., *Manual for Faith Development*, 1.

29. These are the seven areas of human growth according to Fowler, and they represent the seven dimension of each stage of faith: (1) form of logic, (2) way of selecting a perspective on life, (3) form of moral judgment, (4) boundaries of social awareness, (5) locus of authority, (6) means of finding coherence in the world, and (7) way of relating to symbols. Dimensions of faith that according to Moseley et al., *Manual*, 55, "The interconnection between these aspects creates a composite lens through which we make sense of the world. They are part of the whole, that 'constitute a pattern of meaning making.' The connections between these aspects of faith become more complex and rich as the person grows toward adulthood and beyond. Each stage of faith builds on the previous stage, follows a developmental path that is sequential and invariant, but at any point the forward movement the person's development may be halted, and one of seven stages of faith may become the final stage of development."

ments, and delineates the boundaries of our social awareness. It identifies the authorities we acknowledge, provides frameworks for understanding the world, and influences our relationships with symbolic elements—be they cultural artifacts or religious icons. Essentially, the center of faith is a dynamic, centrifugal force sculpting our intellectual, ethical, social, and spiritual life. It acts as a navigational compass aiding us to navigate the "labyrinthine windings from birth to death in hope and longing."[30]

BETWEEN GOD AND GODS

Fowler's work taps into our collective desire, capturing that profound yearning we all have for something much larger than mere human interactions. He notes that we seek something or someone to devote ourselves to—an entity that holds worth for us and the promise to enrich our lives with meaning. As he eloquently states, the crux of faith is an "intensely personal relationship."[31] This pull we feel is not rooted in fear or a mindless loyalty to tradition. Quite the contrary, allegiance springs from a deeply ingrained, primal, human urge to uncover purpose and a sense of belonging amid the vagaries of life. Traditionally, this was the realm of the gods, divine figures who rise above us, guiding us toward some cosmic truth. But let us think for a moment: Do not the gods come in various forms? While some might find their "god" in the heavens, others discover theirs in earthly pursuits—be it the seduction of nationalism, the intoxicating allure of power, or the often insatiable thirst for wealth, fame, and knowledge. These are human "gods," taking shape as ideals, ideas, or even technological achievements. They might not be omnipotent beings "watching from above," but they share the core function of giving our lives a sense of grounding, serving as pillars that anchor our existence with purpose and meaning. So, these ancient gods, our modern versions of deities, or the biblical God of the Christian faith, illuminate a fundamental truth: the dynamic relationship between humans and what we hold sacred is a complex interplay that pivots around our need for

---

30. Jacobi, *Individuation*, 16.

31. Fowler, *Stages of Faith*, 18. The complete quote is: "When I speak of commitment to centers of value and power I use a highly formal language to speak about intensely personal relationships. We do not commit ourselves—'rest our heart upon'—persons, causes, institutions or 'gods' because we 'ought to.' We invest or devote ourselves because the other to which we commit has, for us, an intrinsic excellence or worth and because it promises to confer value on us. We value that which seems of transcendent worth and in relation to which our lives have worth."

attachment to one who will help us make sense in life, an attachment figure, or a covenanting other. As Fowler asserts, we do not pledge ourselves to these centers of faith merely out of a sense of duty or "because we 'ought to.'"[32] Rather, we invest in them because they promise to uplift us, adding a layer of richness to our lives that would otherwise elude us. We naturally approach what we perceive to have "intrinsic excellence or worth," and our connections to these entities give our own lives meaning.[33]

BETWEEN ENTROPY AND GROWTH

I recently came across news of Adriaan Vlok's death while working on this chapter about how we grow as humans. Vlok, South Africa's one-time Minister of Law and Order and Correctional Services, was associated with one of the darkest periods in the apartheid era. Under his political leadership, many people were detained, tortured, killed, or targeted for assassination. It did not surprise me that there was an outpouring of anger and animosity toward this "irredeemable man"[34] on media platforms like Twitter. Reflecting on my Afrikaner heritage, and that of Adriaan Vlok, I find the lines between nationalism and faith often blurred into a single, impassioned allegiance. Our collective devotion to perpetuating the control wielded by the government starkly reveals the depth of our idolization of the nation as the focal point of our faith. This, I believe, is a plain and present danger for many Christians where nationalism is on the rise around the world. Such steadfast loyalty was not innocent—it never is—in South Africa. It was grounded in an ideology marred by prejudice and systemic injustice. In this emotionally charged environment, it was not just the Christian God we worshiped. Nationhood, linguistic purity, and racial integrity became deified concepts—powerful idols in their own right. These took shape in virtually every pillar of society: culture, education, ideology, warfare, and—yes—even our understanding of God. It remains a sobering realization: the idols we place at the center of our lives can remold not only individual faith trajectories but also the destiny of entire nations. We are not exempt from entropy; a fundamental law of physics that applies to all kinetic systems also applies to us. We see the tendency to move from order to disorder in many aspects of our lives. For

---

32. Fowler, *Stages of Faith*, 18.
33. Fowler, *Stages of Faith*, 18.
34. This was a view commonly expressed on Twitter at this time.

example, our bodies age and become less efficient; our relationships wane and become less fulfilling; or our careers stagnate and their challenges decline. Perhaps worst, our dreams begin to fade. Vlok's story serves as a reminder of what happens if we are blind to the reality of spiritual entropy, a kind of negative faith development that can occur.

Intriguingly the phenomenon appears in the biblical narrative. There, too, humans who have every opportunity to grow in moral and existential resemblance to God fall short. With the insights theologians like Ted Peters provide, we have traced the stages of entropy, what he calls, "unfaith" to blasphemy.[35] We have seen how we suffer from structural and ontological anxiety after this break with God, so we take matters into our own hands. In our unfaith, we embark on a journey that takes us further from our existential and moral similarity with God. We still develop, but with a sad twist: we grow inward. And with that, we return to Augustine's wise observation that human nature is to turn inward, which he summed up as *incurvatus in se*.[36] It is the same inborn tendency that Martin Luther vividly described as a corruption that makes us focus on ourselves, even using God to attain our desires.[37] Sadly, it remains oblivious to the fact that in coveting everything, including God, it relentlessly seeks possessions for its selfish purposes.

BETWEEN GOOD AND EVIL

God initiates and enables the faith by which we believe, in order that we may come to a faith that we believe, because his love formed it.[38] The God of Abraham, Isaac, and Jacob, whom we came to know through Jesus, warned against this idolatry from the start. For Christians, this God is the center of faith and thus surpasses all other gods and worldly possessions—even nationhood, gender, or race.[39] In our quest for meaning

---

35. Peters, *Sin*, ch. 8.
36. See ch. 8 for a more detail.
37. Luther, *Luther's Works*, 291.

38. According to Lombard, faith moves from *fides assensus*, the assent to the truth, but this kind of faith is incomplete; it is *fides informis*. In order for faith to be complete, it needs to be formed by love, *fides formata caritate*. See Lombard, *Sententiarum libri quatuor*, 3:23:4–5.

39. Reminiscent of Niebuhr, in *Radical Monotheism and Western Culture*. Fowler holds that for Christians God is the "inclusive center of value and power—in relation to which all tribal gods and finite goods must be seen for what they are." Fowler, *Stages of Faith*, 23.

and purpose, we often engage in idolatry, attaching ourselves to finite and limiting centers of faith.[40] These centers, often intertwined with the structures of power in society, are not just seen as ensuring survival but also are attempting to guarantee certainty in the face of insecurity. Some will regard them as providing meaning to and quality of life as we try to make sense of why we live in liminality. They will fail us in the end.

By positioning the apartheid ideology as the core of our identity and source of authority, Christians committed a grievous error. We anchored our sense of worth and meaning in a fundamentally flawed *cultural* construct, an action that inevitably led us down a path of isolation so intense it became self-absorption. What we failed to see was how this focus distorted not only our individual lives but the very fabric of our society, obscuring any possibility for justice or genuine spiritual growth—to develop in existential or moral similarity with God regardless of all humanly imposed conditions and filters. For Vlok, and Afrikaners like me, the development of unfaith began with an unbridled pride in his nation, an aspiration to elevate the Afrikaner nation above all else, which led to concupiscence—in this case the urge or the drive to grab power and resources from the original inhabitants of South Africa.

Volk's journey then veered into the treacherous terrain of self-justification, a systematic and fastidious strategy to brand political opponents such as Frank Chikane as wrongdoers and conduits of evil, all the while feigning a façade of virtuosity. He employed what we now call gaslighting tactics to insinuate that the very victims enduring injustice deserved their punishment. His descent deepened into cruelty, a chilling enjoyment derived from inflicting pain upon others. Finally, he reached his deepest and darkest abyss—blasphemy, the audacious assumption of a god-like dominion over fellow human beings. We recognize this tendency in Adriaan Vlok's life, because it is also deeply rooted in each of us too.

As Paul said, "we all fall short of God's glory."[41] Or as Aleksandr Solzhenitsyn realized as he languished in the Soviet *gulag* political prison system, "the line separating good and evil passes not through states, nor between classes, nor between political parties either—but right through every human heart—and through all human hearts. This line shifts, inside us, it oscillates with the years. And even within hearts overwhelmed

---

40. Fowler, *Stages of Faith*, 11.
41. Rom 3:23 (NIV).

by evil, one small bridgehead of good is retained."[42] Perhaps what endures as the image of God post-fall is a mere bridgehead. Our moral and existential likeness to God has been shattered. The result is a propensity for evil that bends us toward self-absorption and spiritual laziness and stagnation. This is a universal phenomenon, since the line between good and evil runs through every human heart; we are all on a spiritual journey that requires vigilance to resist the forces of entropy at work within us.

BETWEEN BEING HELD AND HOLDING

As I reflect on my own faith development—I do not claim this is as it should be for everyone else—I see we are all on our own paths. Yet human development also unfolds in a way that is common to us all. In essence, we live our lives in two parts. Perhaps Schopenhauer is right that, on average, we receive the text in our first four decades and seek to interpret the script in the final three decades left to us. Or, as I suggest, in the first three to four decades, our faith holds us; a way of making sense of life. But even within faith's embrace, we are growing in a faith that we can call our own, that once again will hold us in a continuous, mysterious loop, reminiscent of the Möbius strip. It is a faith I hold to be similar to the process of individuation in psychology. Jolande Jacobi says the journey we embark on in life is like "a seed growing into a tree, life unfolds stage by stage. Triumphant ascent, collapse, crises, failures, and new beginnings strew the way. It is the path trodden by the great majority of mankind, as a rule unreflectingly, unconsciously, unsuspectingly, following its labyrinthine windings from birth to death in hope and longing."[43]

We do not have any influence over which families, communities, or nations, we are born into—a concept beautifully conveyed by Martin Heidegger with his idea of "*dasein*," which characterizes our existence as being thrown into life without choice or control.[44] This insight emphasizes that we cannot choose the circumstances of our birth: race, gender, ethnicity, nationality, social class, or family. It challenges those of us who

---

42. Solzhenitsyn, *Gulag Archipelago*, 615.
43. Jacobi, *Individuation*, 16.
44. Heidegger, *Being and Time*, 174. "This characteristic of Dasein's Being—this 'that it is'—is veiled in its 'whence' and 'whither,' yet disclosed in itself all the more unveiledly; we call it the 'thrownness'! of this entity into its 'there'; indeed, it is thrown in such a way that, as Being-in-the-world, it is the 'there.' The expression 'thrownness' is meant to suggest the facticity of its being delivered over."

see ourselves as the creators of our stories and firmly believe in autonomy and self-determination. Yet Heidegger posits that a particular context invariably anchors our existence and shapes our choices and horizons. We find ourselves within an effective history, according to Hans-Georg Gadamer, in historical contexts that provide interpretive frameworks peculiar to our time.[45] We recognize that we exist perpetually within a distinct historical context which leads us to acknowledge its pivotal role in shaping our social imaginary. We are thrown into the faith that holds us.[46] This means that faith is never a solitary experience, unconnected from those around us. Instead, faith is deeply interconnected with the faith of our figures of attachment, from the earliest stages of our lives. Our caregivers not only impart their love and attention, but we also inherit a faith, a way of being in the world, from them. As if, through their very being, they confer upon us a legacy of trust and wisdom. We inherit faith from them as naturally as we learn to walk or speak, and, in doing so, we gain a sense of continuity, security, and grounding within these early liminal experiences of life.

At first this faith that holds us is visceral, something felt more in the heart and gut than understood in the mind.[47] It is primal and intuitive, nestling deep within our being as an almost instinctive sensation. It is the churning we suffer in our stomachs before an exam or a public performance; the yearning we have for a loved one, especially in their absence. It is a whispering deep within that tells us there is something greater beyond what we can hear, taste, or see, or even sense. This, it seems to me, is faith in its purest, rudimentary form. We experience within our minds and bodies the raw, vulnerable nature of inherited faith. In the tender beginnings of life, the simple sensation of touch overrides hearing a caregiver's voice. We find the divine in the most ordinary acts of kindness, in the immediacy and intimacy of a mundane gesture. What resonates within our bodies, whether through a comforting embrace or a soothing hand, captures our imagination? Here, perhaps, lies one of the most authentic experiences of the *mysterium tremendum et fascinans*,[48] a profound and awe-inspiring encounter with someone who is wholly other yet attuned as one with us, embodying beauty, goodness, and truth. Yet,

---

45. Gadamer, *Truth and Method*, xx.
46. Westerhoff, *Will Our Children Have Faith?*
47. I am thinking here of Sam Keen's early description of visceral theology. See Keen, *To a Dancing God*. The final chapter is on "The Importance of Being Carnal."
48. See Otto, *Idea of the Holy*, chs. 4–6.

faith is also experienced as the feeling of emptiness and sadness when the body becomes cold or detached, and the touch that once soothed seems unendurably remote.

These contrasting experiences sowed the rich, deep markers of our inherited faith—a faith that is not static but a living entity that grows, evolves, and changes along with us. But I need to make it clear that the faith that we hold is also present in these early stages. In fact, once the umbilical cord between a mother and child is severed, our journey toward individuation begins. I fondly recall seeing my baby girl staring with wonder at her fingertips, as if she was pondering the boundary separating her body from the outside world. At first, we must physically and emotionally separate from our mothers and, as we mature, the emotions, thoughts, and behaviors once shared with her become echoes of a former conjoined life. Simultaneously, new people enter our lives, like another caregiver, sibling, or loving grandparent. They contribute to our individuality. We are held and soothed by unfamiliar hands and voices, noticing the growing communion of our own bodies and those of others. As we grow up, our faith—what holds us and which we hold—becomes more embodied, just as we become aware of our larger and more complex communities, especially during our early childhood and teenage years. Our initial gut-level faith starts to change into a communal faith. At first, faith is just a raw feeling. But it grows into something we begin to live in every day: the stories we are told and tell, our daily routines, the joyful and tumultuous events we share, and grasping the values of those central to our lives. With the passing of time and the accumulation of experiences, we do not just learn the doctrines of our faith, we absorb faith through our affections and the habits we commit to perform every day. We attune to how those close to us actually live out their faith. Their practices become part of our own habits, choices, and interactions. Their faith is our faith, and faith is no longer only visceral; it is deeply communal.

BETWEEN PROGRESS AND REGRESSION AND HOPE

Looking back on my early years, I went to an elementary school named for one of the founders of Afrikaner nationalism. Our days were full of reciting Totius's poems and stories about historical figures like Rachel de Beer, the story I recalled earlier in this book. These were not merely classroom lessons—they were *volk* rituals that connected us to a grander narrative of who we were. I have strong memories as a little boy of my heart-swelling pride to be a member of the junior Voortrekkers, a movement that was established for young Afrikaners like me. I felt jubilation at being one of thousands of other boys who marched as young cadets and saluted Hendrik Verwoerd, the symbolic father of apartheid. After all, we were called "Verwoerd's children," showing we were born just as South Africa became a republic, under his leadership. Back then, my sense of community and identity was deeply tied up in those beliefs and practices. They were more than traditions. They shaped how I understood the world and my place in it. They embodied the faith and values of my community.

The church our family attended was part of a Pentecostal denomination, so I found the content of my beliefs diverged from my Dutch Reformed Church friends, but this did not deter me. I was devoted to my Afrikaner heritage, and I nurtured a deep loyalty to my nation and God, as if they were one. My childhood memories are dominated by my deep devotion to the Afrikaner nation and inextinguishable memories of religious Pentecostal experiences—the pastor's hand on my head is seared into my consciousness as he prayed for me. I seemed to need prayer more than most people. Olive oil and tissues were never far away—the oil to anoint, and tissues for the inevitable, lachrymose aftermath of the Spirit's work.

Soon after I turned eight years old, two baptisms fundamentally shaped my young faith and spirituality: one an immersion in water and the other in the Spirit. There is not enough time here to describe the theological differences between the two forms in the Pentecostal tradition but suffice it to say that with these baptisms I exclaimed an emphatic "Yes!" to God, to my community, and how and what we believed. Adding complexity to my spiritual journey was the inescapable fact that the community that nurtured my faith, the church I grew up in, aligned itself with the apartheid nationalist government of the day.

My communal faith was a blend of national ideology and the expectation of a second coming of Christ that would usher in the kingdom of God. A central theme in Pentecostal spirituality is a millennial reign when God's peace would flood the earth, writes Veli-Matti Kärkkäinen.[49] Growing up, I was taught to expect that God was present in every part of my life. We believed that when people spoke in tongues it was a message from God which we could interpret accordingly. However, in

---

49. Kärkkäinen, "Spirit, Reconciliation and Healing," 44.

retrospect, it saddens me that God did not address the suffering caused by our actions. The emphasis on transformation within Pentecostalism was evident to me, but I did not experience the same anticipation for a social transformation where every human, regardless of race, would be treated as an image bearer of God. According to Kärkkäinen, if we claim to be filled with God's Spirit, then we should feel "impelled by that same Spirit to cooperate with God in the work of evangelism and social action in the anticipation of the new creation,"[50] but that was not the case for me. Rather than focusing on maintaining personal purity before God, our church maintained the status quo of political power. For instance, many years later I would learn about Frank Chikane, the same person whom Volk persecuted, the African Pentecostal minister who was a vocal critic of the system, who endured imprisonment and torture. During one of these periods of incarceration a fellow Pentecostal supervised his interrogation and torture. These beatings were severe; on one occasion, David Goodman writes that when Chikane, after a night of interrogation, "stepped into the serene white courtroom, he was a mess. His head hung down limply, his eyes were swollen shut. Blood was still oozing from where his hair had been pulled out. His pajamas protruded from beneath his pants. He looked like a vagrant who'd fallen asleep in the road and been run over by a truck."[51]

During my university years, I was on a quest to serve both my faith community and nation through theological study. I was not yet fully aware of the darker elements intertwined with certain religious movements—namely, the pernicious forms of Pentecostalism and the corrosive effects of Christian nationalism. Immersed in the academic world, my understanding of faith deepened, and my commitment to the Afrikaner nation soared. It was a time when scholars dissected and reconstituted apartheid theories with biblical interpretations. The political uprisings were framed as a confrontation against communism and its perceived godlessness. Naively, I believed the suffering wrought by apartheid was necessary to ensure that we were faithful to the covenant we had with God, which included racial purity and national security. I was convinced that apartheid had divine approval. The doctrines of apartheid were presented so persuasively, it felt as if our very existence hinged on them. This belief gripped me, gaining momentum each day, and started molding the

---

50. Kärkkäinen, "Spirit, Reconciliation and Healing," 45.
51. Goodman, *Fault Lines*, 39.

very fabric of my evolving identity as an Afrikaner Christian, in that order. Looking back, the university years were not just an academic journey for me; they were also an odyssey through the labyrinth of moral and ethical complexity, and a crucible that eventually forced me to reckon with the communal faith I had inherited.

That reckoning came as I listened to Bishop Desmond Tutu speak about the atrocities of apartheid.[52] In that lecture hall at the Afrikaner university where my communal faith was seeded and soared, I heard a voice of one crying in the wilderness. I sensed an initial shift, but it would take another three years for before my racism was exposed while I was in seminary in the United States. As I have written in this book and elsewhere, during a clinical placement as a chaplain at Egleston Children's Hospital in Atlanta, I met a little black boy who displayed the classic symptoms of acquired fetal alcohol syndrome. His face and head were severely malformed, and he suffered from mental retardation. James, as I have said, was the Quasimodo of the ward, and I had to care for him. As much as his physical and mental defects disgusted me, the color of his skin made matters worse. Deep down in my twisted mind, I concluded that this little boy was suffering like this because black people were all the same: they needed a superior race to take care of them. My disgust for the little boy and for all that he represented came bubbling to the surface. Here I was, a man of faith, a trainee minister of God ostensibly reborn by the Spirit, yet unable to offer compassion to a suffering child due to the color of his skin and his deformities. This boy, who needed a human to hold him and love him, found in me only loathing and abhorrence. I came to a realization, perhaps not consciously. The faith that *held* me could no longer *hold* me. In the words of Esther Meek, it was time to attend *to* the faith that I had been attending *from*.[53]

While I would love to report that self-awareness comes swiftly, the opposite is true. Even today, when my students inquire about me, I admit that I am still a recovering racist, living in a Möbius strip of progress and regression. Though the influence and presence of my communal faith wane daily, I know I will always need vigilance to prevent spiritual entropy. Doing theology is how I stay sober. This realization marked my transition from envelopment in and by a communal faith to possession of a personal faith that I clutch closely. Rather than relying on a communal

---

52. I give a fuller account in chs. 2 and 5.
53. Meek, *Little Manual for Knowing*, 55.

faith, I learned that faith must be as intimate as my own conscience unique to me and uninfluenced by another.

BETWEEN INSIDE OUT, BOTTOM UP, AND TOP DOWN

These early years of grappling for a faith to call my own were among the most challenging I have known. On our return to a South Africa locked in turmoil, rocked by political violence and brutal responses from the security forces, Marian and I heeded a call. I became the director of a small Bible institute for the so-called colored people of Cape Town. With our six-month-old girl, we joined a community victimized by apartheid. We left our extended family in Johannesburg to stand beside those we felt God had called us to serve. As an act of protest, we switched our home language from Afrikaans to English and I became an ordained minister in the "colored" department of the church. This was radical, but I needed to loosen the state's grip on my psyche. I pledged myself as a non-combatant during my compulsory national military service in the South African Defense Force. But after I accepted the appointment to teach theology on the Cape Flats, I refused to go to war against the very people I felt called to serve. The decision could have led to my incarceration, and it probably had deleterious consequences for my extended family. This is a story for another day.

As a young faculty member, I initially searched for better, more rational answers than those our opponents thrust upon us. I then believed my task was to equip students with perfect, systematized theological answers. Clinging to modernist ideals, I assumed that knowledge would empower them to transform their communities. But gradually, a shift occurred. I came to see the folly in obsessing over abstract truths, divorced from the suffering of the Cape Flats community. Apartheid's "perfect answers" had silenced their questions with bullets and imprisonment. Influenced by the likes of Desmond Tutu, James Cone, Gustavo Gutiérrez, and Rosemary Radford Ruether, I realized that the lived experiences of my students mattered more than any theological system. Lesslie Newbigin illuminated for me that theological knowledge was not a system but a service, a realm where questions often replaced answers.

Bonnie J. Miller-McLemore eloquently referred to "daily life as a site where knowledge accrues."[54] In this uncertain space, I found that Lloyd

---

54. Miller-McLemore, "Contribution of Practical Theology," 2.

Alexander is right, "We learn more by looking for an answer to a question and not finding it than we do from learning the answer itself."[55] It was here that I realized theology begins with a profound love for God and our "unwanted" neighbor. Only with hearts realigned can we dare to ask questions before offering answers or crafting doctrines. My colleagues and students taught me to practice theology from the inside out, bottom up, rather than from the top down.

BETWEEN WONDER AND WISDOM

As I transition into the autumn of my life, another transformation is taking shape, defying the dichotomies of top-down or bottom-up approaches to faith. I find myself embracing what I shall tentatively call a mystical faith, a faith where the Möbius strip of spiritual endeavor suddenly flips, leaving me marveling at the new dimensions unfolding before me. It is as if the faith I once held is now holding me. Not every day, but increasingly, experiences of beauty, goodness, and truth awaken awe within me, shaping not just my thoughts but also my actions, and not necessarily in that order. This nuanced faith is not preoccupied with seeking definitive knowledge or perfecting practices, although these are significant pursuits. Instead, it thrives on wonder—a wonder grounded in the realization that we can live this liminal life in union with God. The focus is no longer on organizing doctrines into a coherent whole or methodically sequencing actions toward an objective. Rather, my quest is to order my affections, to put my heart in order.

In this orientation, the aim is not to accumulate more knowledge or to change particular behaviors. My goal is to gain the practical wisdom that allows for a well-lived life. We yearn not merely for the intellectual comfort of knowing we are made in God's image but for the moral and spiritual growth that makes us more like God. To quote Peter Abelard, faith is "perfected by love." It transcends personal convictions and intellectual paradigms, becoming an all-encompassing love—a love for the divine, for humanity, and for the world itself. Love refines faith as we progress from a visceral connection to a communal one, ultimately drawing us closer to a mystical union with God, the very ground of our being. This journey highlights an evolution of faith, beginning as an internal

---

55. Alexander, *Book of Three*, 15.

sentiment, extending through relationships and personal convictions, and culminating in the transformative power of love.

This is perhaps a good time to return to the story of Adrian Vlok and Frank Chikane. As I watched and listened to the news about Adriaan Vlok's death, it was intriguing to observe how news outlets swiftly mobilized and reporters rushed to interview Frank Chikane—someone who had experienced detentions, torture, and even survived an assassination attempt during apartheid. The media expected Chikane, given his traumatic encounters with Vlok, to provide a quote or soundbite regarding the passing of this "terrible man" who had once sought to "eliminate" him. However, I wondered how Chikane would respond; would he align himself with the chorus of anger and bitterness due to the suffering he endured, or would there be another response altogether? What significance would Chikane's faith hold in this pivotal moment, and how might his theological convictions serve as a guiding compass as he faced the press corps, ready to field their inquiries? How will we assess whether Chikane's dedication to theological practice has indeed made him a wiser man? Is he profoundly attuned to coexisting harmoniously with God amid the tumultuous currents of the unpredictable South African political landscape? That remains a judgment best entrusted to the unfolding of time.[56] Nonetheless, within the particularities of these events, his reasonable response echoes the hallmarks of practical wisdom—a wisdom that stems from a life imbued with the synthesis of divine love and knowledge, an integration he seemingly has been nurturing while navigating the complexities of living in liminality.

---

56. South African History Online, "Frank Chikane." "In 2007, five former security officials in South Africa's apartheid regime received suspended prison sentences for plotting to kill Chikane. Former Police Minister Adriaan Vlok and his police chief Johan van der Merwe received suspended ten-year sentences. The others received suspended five-year sentences. Under a plea bargain, all five admitted trying to kill Chikane in 1989. Chikane said he did not want to see the men go to prison. Vlok sought forgiveness from Chikane in 2006 by washing his feet as an act of seeking Christian forgiveness." What Vlok sought from Chikane—and the apparent magnanimity with which Chikane bestowed it—are evidence of grace available to all.

Methodological Postscript

I HAVE BEEN EXPLORING the value of theology. As an integral Christian practice, I have argued that theology inherently cultivates reasonableness and imparts practical wisdom to those who engage in it. This wisdom develops over time through deliberate discipline, uniting our love and knowledge of God as we live in union with him. In this short postscript, I revisit the path that led me to understand and appreciate the importance and role of theology. You are familiar with this journey that started in Johannesburg under apartheid, led me to Egleston Children's Hospital and the Cape Flats, and now finds me in Melbourne, Australia, as an older man reflecting on what it means to live in liminality in union with God.

Over three decades, I have taught theology in diverse locations such as colleges, seminaries, and universities. Initially, I thought my role was to teach theology as a set of predetermined answers to questions important to the church or denomination my students belonged to. This included doctrines of the church and orthodoxy that were carefully constructed, eloquently presented, and staunchly defended. My goal was for students to grasp the correct answers and defend them confidently when necessary. However, as I continued to engage in the practice of theology and interact with students from various backgrounds and perspectives, I soon realized that this approach was limiting and did not fully capture the dynamic and transformative nature of theology.

On the Cape Flats, I discovered that theology was not simply about rote memorization or regurgitating predetermined answers but rather a living and vibrant exploration of the mysteries of what it means to be human and to live as if God was present. There, I realized that theology is more about questions than answers, more a way of being than a way of knowing, a Christian practice that would lead to practical wisdom in the face of wicked problems. In this transformative context, I recognized the imperative for a resilient theology—one not shaped within the pristine confines of academia but born from the crucible of forging a life against formidable odds.

I do not think I suffer from post-traumatic stress disorder, but to this day, I am haunted by the vision of little children fleeing the armored vehicles of the South African Defense Force as these machines of death rolled onto school playgrounds. With horror, I recall scenes of confrontation between youth and police. How they bravely resisted the rage of adult men with barking dogs whose sharp teeth strained to tear into young flesh. They did not accept the answers that the police and army were enforcing through their violent actions; they demanded to be seen and heard. They dared to challenge the status quo and question the systemic injustices that governed their lives; their questions embodied courage in the face of tyrannical answers.

I could not help but feel that I might be contributing to the problem. What if the theological explanations I taught discouraged my students from asking the questions they truly needed to ask? Could it be argued that my confidence in theological matters sometimes hindered the spiritual growth I desired for them? I realized how my rigid theological responses risked a tyranny of their own, and how doctrines turn into lifeless dogmas when I insisted my answers were immune to interrogation. If so, I wondered if answers were the best place to start in our theological pursuits. I knew I had reached a crossroads because I knew how to teach answers but did not know how to teach my students to question. How should I let their questions guide them, free from dogma or my interference, prompting them to delve deeper as they strove to lead a life in union with God in the liminality of life? However, I was certain I wanted to practice theology that prioritized questions arising from real-life experiences, particularly those of individuals marginalized and oppressed by systems of power.

BETWEEN COLONIZATION AND CONSCIENTIZATION

Paulo Freire's concept of conscientization, the awakening process that occurs when oppressed individuals start questioning their oppressors' answers, became central to my understanding of theology. Our students and I needed not to settle for old answers. My journey of conscientization, which began with Archbishop Desmond Tutu and was deepened by my experience with James at Egleston Children's Hospital, was only the start of a lifelong journey away from the tyrannical answers that apartheid theology provided. It was not enough to live in the memory of what had happened with Tutu or James. Instead, the focal-subsidiary reintegration needed as I emerged from my encounter with God in the Pitts Theological Library had to continue on the Cape Flats of South Africa.

As I allowed myself to question even the answers I once considered too holy to doubt, I found that a new confidence in God's presence in the middle emerged. I realized that if something is beautiful, good, and true, no matter what I thought or how much I doubted or questioned that reality, the beauty, goodness, and truth would remain. This allowed me to break free from the restrictions I placed on myself and others, opening myself to the mysteries of life without fear of what I may find. So, concientization became the word that described the transformative journey of questioning and being open to discoveries. It became the foundation of my theological method, encouraging me to constantly examine my beliefs and challenge the status quo.

BETWEEN QUESTIONS AND ANSWERS

As our college community of faculty and students gathered to engage in the Christian practice of undertaking theology, we experienced concientization collectively. Initially, the college was not even accredited; the state and state-sponsored universities did not recognize its certificates and degrees. Our student body was a motley crew of young and old, male and female, black and white, but we were a *communitas* of sorts finding our way in the liminal space called the Cape Flats. Initially, our educational model assumed that students had questions and were empty vessels that needed to be filled by the answers that the faculty possessed. Still, in this community, I discovered that this was not true. As I shifted from dispensing answers to engaging in the art of inquiry, I marveled at the practical wisdom displayed by the students, seemingly endowed with an innate understanding derived from a life intertwined with the divine. I realized they knew more than they could tell. Rather than viewing myself solely as their teacher, I realized that we all should assume the role of perpetual learners. Ultimately, we entrusted the guidance of the Holy Spirit as we embarked on the quest for answers to sacred questions. While I might have some tertiary degrees, technical answers, and experiences that prepared me to teach, I recognized that true wisdom and understanding came from the learning community's collective exploration and shared insights. Together, we became an empowering conduit of God's grace that brought healing and reconciliation—a prophetic beacon of hope long before Nelson Mandela was released.

Little did we know that we were pioneering a way to do theology in post-apartheid South Africa.

BETWEEN ACADEMY AND CHURCH

In 1999, when the opportunity arose to create a theological course for the church in the changing landscape of South Africa, I eagerly embraced it. Working alongside a group of church-planters in Cape Town, near the city center, was fulfilling and insightful. Despite the team's dual roles, with many having jobs outside the church, their strong sense of calling to the local congregation and eagerness to delve into theology were truly inspiring. Yet, they had lingering doubts about the value of conventional theological training in Bible colleges or university seminaries. They shared a worry that such education might become too theoretical or, worse, dampen faith in God. Conversely, I was concerned that, in their eagerness for practical ministry, they might seek only simplistic techniques suited for immediate application and lack the practical wisdom gained from the practice of doing theology.

I wondered if the conscientization we experienced on the Cape Flats could be transposed to this new context. Could we theologize together to build a new kind of church—a post-apartheid church—where questions were the key to spiritual growth and dogmas could be interrogated? Could we dream of a community where every member, women and men, contributed their voice, wisdom, and unique experiences? A church where leaders possessed the skill to engage in thoughtful and constructive theological reflection, responding to the dynamic manifestations of God in our world?

BETWEEN CRITICAL AND CONSTRUCTIVE REFLECTION

In developing the theological method to train these church planters, I turned to the insights of two practical theologians. I recalled Edward Farley's critiques of theological education and valued his emphasis on a new approach to theological reflection. Farley underscored the importance of centering theological education on reflective insight rather than becoming entangled in technical scholarship.¹ I borrowed from James W. Fowler to define theology as "theological reflection and construction arising out of and giving guidance to a community of faith in the praxis of its mission. Practical theology is critical and constructive reflection leading to ongoing modification and development of the ways the church shapes its life to be in partnership with God's work in the world."² We have already discussed the importance of this definition, so I will not repeat my thoughts here.

I knew that theological reflection needed a wide-open space to be transformational. It is best done in educational spaces that are free from the judgments of preconceived dogma and the tyranny of "perfect" answers. This was especially true in post-apartheid South Africa. We needed a safe and open learning environment—an open seminary. So, I designed the Openseminary theological methodology that prioritized questions arising from the lived experiences of post-apartheid South Africa.³ We wanted to know how we, as believers, could reshape our lives to live in union with God. I have devoted the second part of this book to that question. Additionally, the question is, as a community of faith, how do we reshape the church's practices to partner with God in the world? This meant the Openseminary approach aims to let *praxis* set the agenda, as Clodovis Boff aptly put it, "the repertory of questions that theology is to address."⁴

BETWEEN THEOLOGICAL DISCIPLINES AND CHURCH PRACTICES

Coenie Burger, a notable South African practical theologian, proposed using *koinonia*, *kerygma*, *leitourgia*, *diakonia*, and *paideia* to categorize the practices of the local church.⁵ These terms, deeply rooted in the church's history, have been frequently employed to delineate the varied

---

1. Fowler, "Practical Theology and the Shaping," 149.

2. Fowler, *Faith Development and Pastoral Care*, 17.

3. "Openseminary methodology" has become a recognizable term for a theological approach used in South Africa, Australia, and the USA. In Australia, Eastern College uses this approach in its design of some theological degrees. Palmer Theological Seminary of Eastern University employs the Openseminary methodology to deliver a master of practical theology and a master of divinity. For a full explanation of the approach, please watch this video: https://www.palmerseminary.edu/programs/master-practical-theology/master-practical-theology-curriculum.

4. Boff, *Theology and Praxis*, 200.

5. For his description of the local church, see Burger, *Gemeentes in Die Kragveld Van Die Gees*.

facets of its activities. My initial encounter with these concepts dates back to my doctoral studies at the University of South Africa in the 1980s. While I embraced these traditional categories in the course design, the radical changes that were unfolding in South Africa prompted me to introduce a sixth practice, *theologia*. This addition aims to underscore the local church's contextual and incarnational dimensions, adapting its practices to the contemporary realities of the community.

It occurred to me that we could use these six practices as the focus for six topics in the training of the church planters. It would allow them to ask questions about each practice and explore them, one by one, in the light of Scripture and theology. This meant that we would no longer follow the conventional theological curriculum structure, which traditionally compartmentalizes into the four areas of biblical studies, history, theology, and pastoral studies. According to Stephen Pickard, this conventional approach excels in providing comprehensive coverage of key domains, but its inherent flaw lies in the failure to seamlessly integrate academic study with practical wisdom.[6] In the Openseminary, the process is flipped. The six church practices become the lens through which we examine biblical, historical, theological, and contemporary issues.

Practice contains knowledge; it is theory-laden, as we have already discussed. Therefore, as students within the Openseminary immerse themselves in the practices of the church, they not only acquire practical insights but also unravel and investigate the theoretical underpinnings that have given rise to the practice. This inevitably leads to questions that ask for and deserve careful consideration so that as we hold the practices to the light of questioning, we, all of us, "discover that redemption is creeping into the way we think, believe, and see the world."[7] As we reflect theologically on a church practice in this way, we are free from what "feels final and absolute and beyond questioning," says David Dark.[8] And it "gives our souls a bit of elbow room, a space in which to breathe and imagine again, as if for the first time."[9] Dare I say it? We are in an open seminary.

---

6. Stephen Pickard, "Assessment of your proposed MA in Church Practice," July 1, 2005, personal communication.
7. Dark, *Sacredness of Questioning Everything*, 14.
8. Dark, *Sacredness of Questioning Everything*, 14.
9. Dark, *Sacredness of Questioning Everything*, 14.

BETWEEN DEDUCTIVE AND INDUCTIVE LEARNING

The Openseminary approach is methodical, involving three straightforward yet profound steps as we explore the intricacies of church practices. Initially, we guide students through a process to identify the emerging questions they feel most deeply about, moving them and stirring their affection for change. This is an urgent question since it will impact how they live in union with God and how the church shapes its life to be responsive to what God is doing in the world. During this initial phase, learners embark on a challenging journey of theological reflection, delving deep to unearth latent biases and preconceived notions. We champion the art of deep listening, encouraging an exploration of the fault lines between their intellectual beliefs and the lived experiences of themselves and their communities. It is a crucial juncture where we identify sacred questions, setting the stage for deep theological reflection.

In the next stage of their academic journey, we explore the Christian tradition in pursuit of a better understanding of the practice that we are focusing on. By immersing ourselves in biblical, historical, theological, and pastoral studies, we aim to deepen our knowledge of biblical and theological disciplines through inductive learning. Still, rather than studying these disciplines deductively, the Openseminary approach facilitates the integration of knowledge for a more holistic understanding of the Christian tradition. This integration is further aided by the help of pastors and ministry practitioners who can provide case studies of how they have wrestled with questions and the conclusions that they have implemented in their ministry contexts. This approach to studying the Christian tradition allows us to connect theory with practice and understand how our rich heritage of the faith informs and shapes the way the church responds to what God is doing in the world. It is an integrative theological inquiry that seeks to bridge the gap between theory and practice, enabling us to discern and apply the wisdom of the Christian tradition in their ministry contexts.

In the final phase, students articulate theological answers to their identified questions. These answers are not conclusive statements or the final answer that can be given; they represent the best responses they can formulate at that moment. Crafting theological answers amid Christian action,[10] at the intersection of theory and practice, demands a personal commitment and requires the integration of beliefs and immediate implementation. So, as part of this writing process, we require that they

---

10. Gerkin, *Widening the Horizons*, 60.

implement their ideas in a ministry context. The goal is that this reality check prompts new questions, demanding deeper theological reflection.

BETWEEN JOURNEY AND NEXT DESTINATION

This theological reflection and action process is a dynamic journey that is shaped by our reflection on the actions we take in response to the changing dynamics of life. We never stand still in life. We cannot rely on dated answers or untested theories. We must remain theologically engaged to be responsive to what God is doing in the world. So, students learn to design interventions based on the answers that they have come to through theological reflection and then evaluate the effectiveness and appropriateness of those interventions in light of the context and desired outcomes.

This dynamic process mirrors the iterative nature of design thinking, where theological concepts are not static formulations but living entities that evolve through the crucible of real-world implementation. It is a journey where theory and practice converge, paving the way for continual theological exploration and innovation. Doing theology like this requires generosity and a willingness to deal with doubt and postpone our need for certainty.

If we can resist the tyranny of the perfect answer and hold the space between answers and questions, we can learn to practice theology in the in-between spaces that are beautiful, good, and true. Spaces in which we can find our way through the labyrinthine windings between the already and the not-yet.

Bibliography

Abelard, Peter. *Sic et Non*. Edited by Blanche B. Boyer and Richard McKeon. Translated by W. J. Lewis and S. Barney. Chicago: University of Chicago Press, 1976. https://sourcebooks.fordham.edu/source/Abelard-SicetNon-Prologue.asp.

Abelard and Heloise. *The Letters of Abelard and Heloise*. Translated by B. Radice. Harmondsworth: Penguin, 1974.

Alexander, Lloyd. *The Book of Three*. London: Usborne, 2018.

Anatolios, Khaled. *Athanasius*. London: Routledge, 2004.

Anselm of Canterbury. *Major Works*. Edited by Brian Davies and G. R. Evans. Oxford: Oxford University Press, 2008.

Armstrong, D. M. *A Materialist Theory of the Mind*. London: Routledge and Kegan Paul, 1968.

Athanasius. "Letter LX. To Adelphius, Bishop and Confessor: Against the Arians." *Writings of Athanasius—Personal Letters*. n.d. Accessed July 28, 2023. https://mbsoft.com/believe/txuc/athana49.htm.

Ashley, Kathleen M. *Victor Turner and the Construction of Cultural Criticism: Between Literature and Anthropology*. Bloomington: Indiana University Press, 1990.

Asztalos, Monika. "The Faculty of Theology." In *A History of the University in Europe*, Vol. 1, *Universities in the Middle Ages*, edited by H. de Ridder-Symoens, 408–37. Cambridge: Cambridge University Press, 1992.

Augustine. *Confessions*. Translated by R. S. Pine-Coffin. London: Penguin, 1961.

———. *On Genesis, Against the Manichees*. Vol 1. 13 vols. Translated by Edmund Hill. New York: New City Press, 2002.

———. *On the Trinity*. Book 13. *New Advent*. Accessed September 4, 2023. https://www.newadvent.org/fathers/130113.htm.

Barfield, Owen. *Saving the Appearances: A Study in Idolatry*. Middletown, CT: Wesleyan University Press, 1988.

Barth, Karl. *Church Dogmatics*. Translated by G. W. Bromiley et al. Vols. 1–4. Edinburgh: T&T Clark, 1955–69.

———. *The Theology of Schleiermacher: Lectures at Göttingen, Winter Semester of 1923/24*. Edited by Dietrich Ritschl. Translated by Geoffrey W. Bromiley. Grand Rapids, MI: Eerdmans, 1982.

Barthes, Roland. "Introduction to the Structural Analysis of the Narrative." Occasional Paper, Centre for Contemporary Cultural Studies, University of Birmingham, 1966.

Basil. "Letter 2." *New Advent*. Accessed February 20, 2023. https://www.newadvent.org/fathers/3202002.htm.

———. "De Spiritu Sancto." *New Advent*. Accessed 30 July 2021. https://www.newadvent.org/fathers/3203.htm.

Battle, Michael Jesse. *Reconciliation: The Ubuntu Theology of Desmond Tutu*. Cleveland, OH: Pilgrim Press, 2001.

Begbie, Jeremy S. *Resounding Truth: Christian Wisdom in the World of Music*. Engaging Culture. Grand Rapids, MI: Baker Academic, 2007.

Berkhof, Hendrikus. *Christian Faith*. Translated by Sierd Woudstra. Grand Rapids, MI: Eerdmans, 1979.

Berkovits, Eliezer. "Dr A. J. Heschel's Theology of Pathos." *Tradition: A Journal of Orthodox Jewish Thought* 6.2 (1964) 67–104.

Bernstein, Richard J. *Praxis and Action*. London: Gerald Duckworth, 1972.

Bird, John. *The Annals of Natal*. Vol. 2, *1495 to 1845*. London: Forgotten Books, 2022.

Boff, Clodovis. *Theology and Praxis: Epistemological Foundations*. Maryknoll, NY: Orbis, 1987.

Bosch, David J. *Transforming Mission: Paradigm Shifts in Theology of Mission*. New York: Orbis, 1991.

Bowlby, John. *Attachment and Loss*. Vol. 1, *Attachment*. New York: Basic Books, 1969.

Brown, Stephen F. "Medieval Theology." In *The Blackwell Companion to Modern Theology*, edited by Gareth Jones, 133–46. Oxford: Blackwell, 2004.

Browning, Don S. *A Fundamental Practical Theology: Descriptive and Strategic Proposals*. Minneapolis: Fortress, 1991.

Buechner, Frederick. *Wishful Thinking: A Theological ABC*. New York: Harper and Row, 1973.

Burger, Coenie. *Gemeentes in Die Kragveld Van Die Gees: Oor Die Unieke Identiteit, Taak en Bediening Van Die Kerk Van Christus*. Kaapstad: Lux Verbi, 1999.

Calvin, John. *Institutes of the Christian Religion*. 2 vols. Translated by Ford Lewis Battles. Louisville, KY: Westminster, 1960.

Cantor, Norman F. *The Civilization of the Middle Ages*. Rev. ed. New York: HarperCollins, 1993.

Cantwell Smith, Wilfred. *Faith and Belief*. Princeton, NJ: Princeton University Press, 1979.

Chalmers, David J. "Consciousness and Its Place in Nature." In *Blackwell Guide to the Philosophy of Mind*, edited by Stephen P. Stich and Ted A. Warfield, 102–42. Oxford: Blackwell, 2003.

———. "Facing Up to the Problem of Consciousness." *Journal of Consciousness Studies* 2 (1995) 200–19.

———. *Philosophy of Mind: Classical and Contemporary Readings*. New York: Oxford University Press, 2002.

Chikane, Frank. "Here Is Why I Have Risen above Bitterness about Adriaan Vlok, the Apartheid Minister Who Tried to Kill Me." *Daily Maverick*, Jan 15, 2023. https://www.dailymaverick.co.za/article/2023-01-15-here-is-why-i-have-risen-above-bitterness-about-adriaan-vlok-the-apartheid-minister-who-tried-to-kill-me/.

Clanchy, M. T. *Abelard: A Medieval Life*. Oxford: Blackwell, 1999.

Crites, Stephen. "The Narrative Quality of Experience." *Journal of the American Academy of Religion* 39.3 (1971) 291–311.

Cross, Richard. *Duns Scotus*. Oxford: Oxford University Press, 1999.

Crouch, Carly L. "Genesis 1:26–7 as a Statement of Humanity's Divine Parentage." *Journal of Theological Studies* 61.1 (2010) 1–15.

Cullmann, Oscar. *Christ and Time: The Primitive Christian Conception of Time and History*. Translated by Floyd V. Filson. London: SCM, 1951.
Dark, David. *The Sacredness of Questioning Everything*. Grand Rapids, MI: Zondervan, 2008.
De Chardin, Pierre Teilhard. *Heart of Matter*. New York: Harvest, 2002.
De Kock, W. J. *Out of My Mind: Following the Trajectory of God's Regenerative Story*. Eugene, OR: Wipf & Stock, 2014.
Delio, Ilia. "Clare of Assisi and the Mysticism of Motherhood." In *Franciscans at Prayer*, edited by Timothy J. Johnson, 31–62. Medieval Franciscans 4. Leiden: Brill, 2007.
Dennett, Daniel C. *Consciousness Explained*. Boston: Little, Brown, 1991.
Dennett, Daniel C., and Keith Ward. "Mind, Consciousness and Freewill: Are We More than Matter?" *Premier Unbelievable: The Big Conversation*, Jun 13, 2022. https://www.thebigconversation.show/videos/season-1/episode-5-mind-consciousness-and-freewill-are-we-more-than-matter/.
Descartes, René. *Meditations*. London: Penguin Classics, 2010.
Diederichs, Nicholas. *Nasionalisme as lewensbeskouing en sy verhouding tot internasionalisme*. Bloemfontein, 1936.
———. *Die Volkebond, sy ontstaan, samestelling en werksaamhede*. Pretoria, 1933.
Dulles, Avery. "The Church and the Media." *Catholic Mind* 69.1256 (1971) 6–16.
Dunne, John. "Virtue, Phronesis and Learning." In *Virtue Ethics and Moral Education*, edited by David Carr and Jan Steutel, 49–63. London: Routledge, 1999.
Du Toit, J. D. "Die Godsdienstige Grondslag van ons Rassebeleid." *Die Afrikaanse Rassebeleid en Die Skrif*. 1944. Accessed July 25, 2022. https://www.thezir.com/dot6ix/bib/rassebeleid/Die%20Godsdienstige%20Grondslag%20van%20ons%20Rassebeleid.htm.
———. *J.D. du Toit Versamelde Werke*. Johannesburg: Perskor, 1962.
Dykstra, Craig, and Sharon Daloz Parks, eds. *Faith Development and Fowler*. Birmingham, AL: Religious Education, 1986.
Dykstra, Craig, and Dorothy C. Bass. "Times of Yearning, Practices of Faith." In *Practicing Our Faith: A Way of Life for a Searching People*, edited by Dorothy C. Bass, 1–12. San Francisco: Jossey-Bass, 2010.
Edwards, Jonathan. *Sermons and Discourses, 1720–1723*. Vol. 10, *The Works of Jonathan Edwards*. Edited by Wilson H. Kimnach. New Haven, CT: Yale University Press, 1992.
Enns, Pete. *Inspiration and Incarnation: Evangelicals and the Problem of the Old Testament*. 2nd ed. Grand Rapids, MI: Baker Academic, 2015.
Erickson, Millard J. *God in Three Persons: A Contemporary Interpretation of the Trinity*. Grand Rapids, MI: Baker Academic, 1995.
Fackre, Gabriel. "The Revival of Systematic Theology: An Overview." *Interpretation* 49.3 (1995) 229–41.
Falk, Emily B., et al. "Creating Buzz: The Neural Correlates of Effective Message Propagation." *Psychological Science* 24.7 (2013) 1234–42.
Farley, Edward. *Theologia: The Fragmentation and Unity of Theological Education*. Minneapolis: Augsburg Fortress, 1983.
———. "Theology and Practice outside the Clerical Paradigm." In *Practical Theology: The Emerging Field in Theology, Church, and World*, edited by Don S. Browning, 21–41. San Francisco: Harper and Row, 1983.

Firet, Jacob. *Dynamics of Pastoring*. Translated by J. H. Kok. Grand Rapids, MI: Eerdmans, 1986.
Fowl, Stephen E. *Philippians*. Two Horizons New Testament Commentary. Grand Rapids, MI: Eerdmans, 2005.
Fowler, James W. *Faith Development and Pastoral Care*. Philadelphia: Fortress, 1987.
———. "Faith Liberation and Human Development." In *Christian Perspectives on Faith Development: A Reader*, 3–14. Grand Rapids, MI: Eerdmans, 1992.
———. "Faith and the Structuring of Meaning." In *Faith Development and Fowler*, edited by Craig Dykstra and Sharon Daloz Parks, 15–42. Birmingham, AL: Religious Education, 1986.
———. "Practical Theology and the Shaping of Christian Lives." In *Practical Theology: The Emerging Field in Theology, Church and World*, edited by Don S. Browning, 149. San Francisco: Harper and Row, 1983.
———. *Stages of Faith: The Psychology of Human Development and the Quest for Meaning*. New York: Harper and Row, 1981.
———. *To See the Kingdom: The Theological Vision of H. Richard Niebuhr*. Eugene, OR: Wipf & Stock, 1974.
———. "Toward a Developmental Understanding of Faith." *Religious Education* 69.2 (1974) 207–19.
Frankfurt, Harry. "On Bullshit (1989)." Last accessed September 2, 2021. http://www2.csudh.edu/ccauthen/576f12/frankfurt__harry_-_on_bullshit.pdf.
Frankl, Viktor E. *Man's Search for Meaning: An Introduction to Logotherapy*. 3rd ed. New York: Simon and Schuster, 1986.
Freire, Paulo. *Pedagogy of the Oppressed*. Translated by Myra Bergman Ramos. London: Continuum International, 1997.
Gadamer, Hans-Georg. *Truth and Method*. New York: Crossroad, 1982.
Gerkin, Charles V. *Widening the Horizons*. Philadelphia: Westminster, 1986.
Goldbacher, A., ed. *Corpus Scriptorum Ecclesiasticorum Latinorum*. Vol. 57 Vienna: Tempsky, 1911.
Goldberg, Michael. *Theology and Narrative: A Critical Introduction*. Eugene, OR: Wipf & Stock, 2001.
Goodman, David. *Fault Lines: Journeys into the New South Africa*. Berkeley: University of California Press, 1999.
Gorman, Michael J. *Inhabiting the Cruciform God: Kenosis, Justification, and Theosis in Paul's Narrative Soteriology*. Grand Rapids, MI: Eerdmans, 2009.
Gospel Conversations. "David Bentley Hart in Conversation with Tony Golsby-Smith—Part 1, on Gregory of Nyssa." YouTube video, Jun 10, 2021. https://www.youtube.com/watch?v=XxQopsE8an8.
Graham, Elaine L. "On Becoming a Practical Theologian: Past, Present and Future Tenses." *HTS Teologiese Studies / Theological Studies* 73.4 (2017) 1–9.
Grant, Edward. *God and Reason in the Middle Ages*. Cambridge, Engl.: Cambridge University Press, 2005.
Gregory of Nyssa. *On the Making of Man*. New Advent. Accessed May 23, 2023. https://www.newadvent.org/fathers/2914.htm.
Grenz, Stanley. "The Concerns of a Pietist with a PhD." *Wesleyan Theological Journal* 37 (2002) 58–76.
———. *A Theology for the Community of God*. Nashville: Broadman and Holman, 1994.

Greshake, Gisbert. "Der Ursprung der Kommunikationsidee." *Communicatio Socialis. Internationale Zeitschrift fuer Kommunikation in Religion, Kirche und Gesellschaft* 35 (2002) 5–26.
Groenewald, E. P. *Regverdige Rasse-Apartheid*. Stellenbosch: Christen-Studentever enigingsmaatskappy van Suid-Afrika, 1947.
Gunton, Collin E. *The One, the Three and the Many*. Cambridge, Engl.: Cambridge University Press, 1993.
———. *The Promise of Trinitarian Theology*. Edinburgh: T&T Clark, 1991.
Hall, Thor. "Does Systematic Theology Have a Future?" *The Christian Century*, Mar 17, 1976, 253–56.
Harari, Yuval Noah. *Sapiens: A Brief History of Humankind*. London: Vintage, 2015.
———. *21 Lessons for the 21st Century*. London: Vintage, 2019.
Hart, David Bentley. *The Beauty of the Infinite: The Aesthetics of Christian Truth*. Grand Rapids, MI: Eerdmans, 2003.
Hastings, Thomas John. *Seeing All Things Whole: The Scientific Mysticism and Art of Kagawa Toyohiko (1888–1961)*. Eugene, OR: Pickwick, 2015.
Hauerwas, Stanley. *Vision and Virtue: Essays in Christian Ethical Reflection*. Notre Dame, IN: University of Notre Dame Press, 1981.
Hays, Richard B. *First Corinthians*. Interpretation. Louisville, KY: John Knox, 1997.
Hegel, G. W. F. *The Encyclopedia of the Philosophical Sciences*. Vol. 3: *The Philosophy of the Spirit*. Moscow: Mysl, 1974–77.
———. *Lectures on the Philosophy of History*. Vol. 1. Nauka: SPB Publishing House, 1993.
Heidegger, Martin. *Being and Time*. Translated by John Macquarrie and Edward Robinson. New York: Harper and Row, 1962.
Heschel, Abraham Joshua. *Between God and Man*. Edited by Fritz A. Rothschild. New York: Free Press, 1959.
———. "The God of Israel and Christian Renewal." In *Moral Grandeur and Spiritual Audacity*, edited by Susannah Heschel, 467–68. New York: Farrar, Straus and Giroux, 1996.
Hexham, Irving. *The Irony of Apartheid: The Struggle for National Independence of Afrikaner Calvinism against British Imperialism*. New York: Edwin Mellen, 1981.
———. "Just like Another Israel: Calvinism and Afrikanerdom." *Religion* 7 (Spring 1979) 1–17.
Hodge, Charles. *Systematic Theology*. 3 vols. New York: Scribner, Armstrong, 1872.
Irenaeus. *Against Heresies*. New Advent. Accessed February 4, 2024. https://www.newadvent.org/fathers/0103.htm.
Jacobi, Jolande. *The Way of Individuation*. Translated by R. F. C. Hull. New York: Harcourt, Brace and World, 1967.
Jenson, Matt. *The Gravity of Sin. Augustine, Luther, and Barth on 'homo incurvatus in se.'* London: T&T Clark, 2007.
Jenson, Robert W. *Systematic Theology*. Vol. 1. New York: Oxford University Press, 1999.
Johnson, Aubrey Rodway. *The Vitality of the Individual in the Thought of Ancient Israel*. 2nd ed. Reprint. Eugene, OR: Wipf & Stock, 2006.
Josephus. *Antiquities of the Jews*. Loeb Classical Library. Cambridge, MA: Harvard University Press, 2021. https://www.loebclassics.com/view/josephus-jewish_antiquities/1930/pb_LCL242.23.xml?mainRsKey=2cJNjV&result=1&rskey=FCPKJc.
Jung, Carl Gustav, and Marie-Luise Von Franz. *Man and His Symbols*. New York: Doubleday, 1964.

Justin Martyr. *Dialogue with Trypho.* Vol. 3. Edited by Michael Slusser. Washington, DC: Catholic University of America Press, 2003.

Kahneman, Daniel. *Thinking, Fast and Slow.* Harlow, Engl.: Penguin, 2012.

Kant, Immanuel. *Critique of Pure Reason.* Translated by P. Guyer and A. W. Wood. Cambridge: Cambridge University Press, 1998.

Kärkkäinen, Veli-Matti. "Spirit, Reconciliation and Healing in the Community: Missiological Insights from Pentecostals." *International Review of Missions* 94.372 (2005) 43–50.

Kaunda, Chammah. *Theological Education for Social Transformation: A Missiological Analysis of Core Elements in the Theology of John Samuel Pobee.* Accessed June 16, 2023. https://core.ac.uk/download/pdf/20659903.pdf.

Keen, Sam. *To a Dancing God.* San Francisco: Harper and Row, 1970.

Kegan, Robert, and Lisa Laskow Lahey. *Immunity to Change.* Cambridge, MA: Harvard Business School Press, 2009.

———. "The Real Reason Why People Won't Change." *Harvard Business Review* 79 (2001) 84–92.

Keyes, Ralph. *The Post-Truth Era: Dishonesty and Deception in Contemporary Life.* New York: St Martin's, 2004.

Kierkegaard, Søren. *The Concept of Anxiety: A Simple Psychologically Oriented Deliberation in View of the Dogmatic Problem of Hereditary Sin.* Translated by Alistair Hannay. New York: Liveright, 2015.

———. *Fear and Trembling and Sickness unto Death.* New York: Doubleday, 1941.

Kreeft, Peter. "Goodness, Truth, Beauty, and Boredom." *Proven Ministries*, YouTube video, May 20, 2022. https://www.youtube.com/watch?v=RH2X-bQdgxQ.

———. "Lewis's Philosophy of Truth, Goodness, and Beauty." In *C. S. Lewis as Philosopher: Truth, Goodness, and Beauty*, edited by David J. Baggett, Gary R. Habermas, and Jerry L. Walls, 3–18. Downers Grove, IL: InterVarsity, 2008.

Kuyper, Abraham. *Abraham Kuyper: A Centennial Reader.* Edited by James D. Bratt. Grand Rapids, MI: Eerdmans, 1998.

Lawrence, Matt. *Like a Splinter in Your Mind: The Philosophy behind the Matrix Trilogy.* London: Blackwell, 2004.

Leloup, Jean-Yves, ed. *The Gospel of Mary Magdalene.* Rochester, NY: Inner Traditions Bear, 2002.

Levine, J. "Materialism and Qualia: The Explanatory Gap." In *Pacific Philosophical Quarterly* 64 (1983) 354–61.

———. *Purple Haze: The Puzzle of Conscious Experience.* Cambridge, MA: MIT Press, 2001.

Lewis, C. S. *Mere Christianity.* San Francisco: Harper, 2001.

Liddell, Henry George. *A Lexicon Abridged from Liddell and Scott's Greek-English Lexicon.* Oxford: Clarendon, 1984.

Lieberman, Matthew D. *Social: Why Our Brains Are Wired to Connect.* Cary, NC: Oxford University Press, 2013.

Liesch, Barry. "Creativity in the Bible, Part 2 of 2." *WorshipInfo.com*, Jul 21, 2010. worshipinfo.com/articles/13.

Locke, John. *An Essay concerning Human Understanding.* New York: Penguin, 1997.

Lombard, Peter. *Sententiarum libri quatuor, P. Lombardi magistri sententiarum.* Patrologiae cursus completus, series latina, edited by J. P. Migne. Paris: Lutetiae Parisiorum, 1855.

Lotha, Gloria. "Information Theory—Physiology." *Encyclopedia Britannica*. Accessed 2023. britannica.com/science/information-theory.
Louw, J. P., and E. A. Nida. *Greek-English Lexicon of the New Testament: Based on Semantic Domains*. Vol 1. New York: United Bible Societies, 1988.
Luther, Martin. *Luther's Works: Lectures on Romans Glosses and Scholia*. Translated by J. A. Preus and W. G. Tillmanns. Saint Louis, MO: Concordia, 1972.
MacCallum, J. Ramsay. *Abelard's Christian Theology*. Merrick, NY: Richwood, 1976.
MacCulloch, Diarmaid. *Christianity: The First Three Thousand Years*. New York: Penguin, 2010.
MacIntyre, Alasdair. *After Virtue*. 2nd ed. Notre Dame, IN: University of Notre Dame Press, 1984.
Mackintosh, H. R. *The Christian Experience of Forgiveness*. London: Nisbet, 1927.
Maluleke, T. S. "Postcolonial Mission: Oxymoron or New Paradigm?" *Swedish Missiological Themes* 95.4 (2007) 503–28.
Marenbon, John. *The Philosophy of Peter Abelard*. Cambridge: Cambridge University Press, 1997.
Marx, Christoph. "Ubu and Ubuntu: On the Dialectics of Apartheid and Nation Building." *Politikon* 29.1 (2002) 49–69.
May, Rollo. *Power and Innocence: A Search for the Sources of Violence*. New York: Dell, 1976.
McIntyre, Lee. *Post-Truth*. Cambridge, MA: MIT Press, 2018.
McLaughlin, Brian P. "Epiphenomenalism." In *A Companion to the Philosophy of Mind*, edited by Samuel Guttenplan, 277–88. Oxford: Blackwell, 1994.
Meek, Esther Lightcap. *Loving to Know: Introducing Covenant Epistemology*. Eugene, OR: Cascade, 2011.
———. *A Little Manual for Knowing*. Eugene, OR: Cascade, 2014.
———. "Covenant Epistemology in Dallas Willard's 'Hearing God,' Part 3." *Esther Lightcap Meek*, Mar 5, 2015. https://www.estherlightcapmeek.com/blog/covenant-epistemology-in-dallas-willards-hearing-god-part-iii.
Miller-McLemore, Bonnie J. "Introduction: The Contribution of Practical Theology." In *The Wiley-Blackwell Companion to Practical Theology*, edited by Bonnie J. Miller-McLemore, 1–20. Chichester, UK: Wiley-Blackwell, 2012.
Moltmann, Jürgen. *The Crucified God: The Cross of Christ as the Foundation and Criticism of Christian Theology*. Translated by R. A. Wilson and John Bowden. London: SCM, 1974.
———. *God in Creation: An Ecological Doctrine of Creation*. Translated by Margaret Kohl. London: SCM, 1985.
———. *The Source of Life: The Holy Spirit and the Theology of Life*. Translated by Margaret Kohl. Minneapolis: Augsburg Fortress, 1997.
———. *The Spirit of Life: A Universal Affirmation*. Minneapolis: Fortress, 1993.
———. *The Trinity and the Kingdom*. San Francisco: Harper, 1981.
Moreland, J. P., and William Lane Craig. *Philosophical Foundations for a Christian Worldview*. 2nd ed. Downers Grove, IL: InterVarsity, 2017.
Morris, Leon. *The Gospel according to John*. Grand Rapids, MI: Eerdmans, 1971.
Moseley, Romney M., et al. *Manual for Faith Development*. Atlanta, GA: Center for Faith Development, 1986.
Mulago, Vincent. "Vital Participation." In *Biblical Revelation and African Beliefs*, edited by Kwesi A. Dickson and Paul Ellingworth, 137–58. London: Butterworth, 1971.

Niebuhr, H. Richard. "Man the Sinner." *Journal of Religion* 15.3 (1935) 272–80.
———. *Radical Monotheism and Western Culture*. New York: Harper and Row, 1960.
Nielsen, Lauge O. "Peter Abelard and Gilbert of Poitiers." In *The Medieval Theologians*. Edited by G. R. Evans, 102–28. Oxford: Blackwell, 2001.
Ngubane, Jordan K. *Conflict of Minds*. New York: Books in Focus, 1979.
———. *Ushaba: The Hurtle to Blood River*. Washington, DC: Three Continents, 1978.
Otto, Rudolf. *The Idea of the Holy*. Oxford: Oxford University Press, 1958.
Packer, J. I. *Knowing God*. Downers Grove, IL: InterVarsity, 1973.
Panksepp, Jaak. "On the Embodied Neural Nature of Core Emotional Affects." *Journal of Consciousness Studies* 12.8 (2005) 158–84.
Parrott, Justin. "Islām, Īmān, Iḥsān: Climbing the Spiritual Mountain." Yaqeen Institute for Islamic Research. Accessed September 1, 2023. yaqeeninstitute.org/read/paper/islam-iman-ihsan-climbing-the-spiritual-mountain.
Pascal, Blaise. *Pensées and Other Writings*. Translated by Honor Levi. London: Oxford University Press, 1999.
Pawu-Kurlpurlurnu, W. J., M. Holmes, and L. Box. "Ngurra-kurlu: A Way of Working with Warlpiri People." *DKCRC Report 41*. Alice Springs: Desert Knowledge CRC, 2008.
Pegis, Anton C. *Saint Thomas Aquinas*. New York: Modern Library, 1948.
Peters, Ted. *Sin: Radical Evil in Soul and Society*. Grand Rapids, MI: Eerdmans, 1994.
Pinnock, Clark. *Flame of Love*. Downers Grove, IL: InterVarsity, 1996.
Pitstick, Alyssa L. *Light in Darkness: Hans Urs von Balthasar and the Catholic Doctrine of Christ's Descent into Hell*. Grand Rapids, MI: Eerdmans, 2007.
Placher, William C. *A History of Christian Theology: An Introduction*. Philadelphia: Westminster, 1983.
Plantinga, Cornelius. *Not the Way It's Supposed to Be: A Breviary of Sin*. Grand Rapids, MI: Eerdmans, 1995.
Plotinus. *The Enneads*. Translated by Stephen MacKenna and B. S. Page. Digireads.com, 2009.
Polanyi, Michael. *The Tacit Dimension*. Chicago: University of Chicago Press, 2009.
Prinsloo, Deon. "Dr Piet Meyer in Johannesburg, 1936–1984." *Sabinet* 32.1 (May 1, 1987). https://hdl.handle.net/10520/AJA0018229X_878.
Przywara, Erich. *Analogia Entis: Metaphysics: Original Structure and Universal Rhythm*. Translated by John R. Betz and David Bentley Hart. Grand Rapids, MI: Eerdmans, 2014.
Rahner, Karl. *Church and the Sacraments*. Translated by W. J. O'Hara. Freiburg: Herder and Herder, 1963.
Richards, Larry. *A Practical Theology of Spirituality*. Grand Rapids, MI: Zondervan, 1987.
Rienecker, Fritz. *A Linguistic Key to the Greek New Testament*. Translated by C. L. Rogers. Grand Rapids, MI: Zondervan, 1980.
Rohr, Richard. *Falling Upward: A Spirituality for the Two Halves of Life*. San Francisco: Jossey Bass, 2011.
Rubenstein, Richard E. *Aristotle's Children: How Christians, Muslims, and Jews Rediscovered Ancient Wisdom and Illuminated the Middle Ages*. Orlando, FL: Harcourt Brace International, 2003.
Russell, Bertrand. *An Outline of Philosophy*. London: Allen and Unwin, 1927.
Sachs, Jonah. *Story Wars: Why Those Who Tell—and Live—the Best Stories Will Rule the Future*. Boston: Harvard Business Review Press, 2012.

Sayers, Dorothy. *The Mind of the Maker*. San Francisco: Harper and Row, 1941.
Scalise, Charles J. "Book Review: *A Fundamental Practical Theology*: Descriptive and Strategic Proposals." *Review and Expositor* 90 (1993) 445–46.
Schindler, D. C. *The Catholicity of Reason*. Grand Rapids, MI: Eerdmans, 2013.
Scholem, Gershom. *Kabbalah*. New York: Meridian, 1978.
Shaw, Amanda. "God and Imaginary Numbers." *First Things*, Sep 13, 2007. www.firstthings.com/web-exclusives/2007/09/god-and-imaginary-numbers.
Shutte, Augustine. *Ubuntu: An Ethic for a New South Africa*. Pietermaritzburg: Cluster Publications, 2001.
Sindima, Harvey. "Community of Life: Ecological Theology in African Perspective." *Religion Online*. Accessed June 16, 2023. www.religion-online.org/article/community-of-life-ecological-theology-in-african-perspective.
Smith, James K. A. *Desiring the Kingdom: Worship, Worldview, and Cultural Formation*. Ada, MI: Baker Academic, 2009.
———. *You Are What You Love: The Spiritual Power of Habit*. Ada, MI: Brazos, 2016.
Solzhenitsyn, Aleksandr Isaevich. *The Gulag Archipelago, 1918–1956: An Experiment in Literary Investigation III–IV*. New York: Harper and Row, 1975.
Sorokin, Pitirim A. *Social and Cultural Dynamics*. 4 vols. New York: American Book Company, 1937–41.
South African History Online. "Frank Chikane." Accessed January 10, 2024. n.d. https://www.sahistory.org.za/people/frank-chikane.
Stählin, G. "μῦθος." In *Theological Dictionary of the New Testament*, edited by Gerhard Kittel, translated by Geoffrey W. Bromiley, 4:766–67. Grand Rapids: Eerdmans, 1967.
Stamatović, Slobodan. "The Meaning of Perichoresis." *Open Theology* 2.1 (2016). doi.org/10.1515/opth-2016-0026.
Steinmetz, Katy. "Oxford's Word of the Year for 2016 Is 'Post-Truth.'" *Time*, Nov 15, 2016. time.com/4572592/oxford-word-of-the-year-2016-post-truth.
Stoker, H. G., and F. J. M. Potgieter. *Koers in die krisis*. Vol 2 of *Articles Collected by the Federasie van Calvinistiese studentverengingsin Suid-Africa*. Stellenbosch: Pro Ecclesia, 1940.
Strawson, Galen. "Realistic Monism: Why Physicalism Entails Panpsychism, and on the Sesmet Theory of Subjectivity." In *Mind That Abides*, 33–65. Amsterdam: John Benjamins, 2009.
Strydom, J. G. *Die Rassevraagstuk En Die Toekoms van Die Blankes in Suid-Afrika*. NG Kerk. Accessed June 16, 2023.
Tabane, Rapule. "Tutu Did Not Spare Mbeki or Zuma." *City Press*, Dec 27, 2021. www.news24.com/citypress/voices/tutu-did-not-spare-mbeki-or-zuma-20211227.
Taylor, Charles. "What Is a 'Social Imaginary'?" In *Modern Social Imaginaries*, edited by Dilip Parameshwar Gaonkar et al., 23–30. New York: Duke University Press, 2004.
Taylor, W. David O. "Beauty as Love: Hans Urs von Balthasar's Theological Aesthetics." *Transpositions*, Apr 27, 2012. www.transpositions.co.uk/beauty-as-love-hans-urs-von-balthasars-theological-aesthetics/.
Tegmark, Max. *Our Mathematical Universe*. Mississauga, ON: Random House, 2014.
Tesich, Steve. *A Government Of Lies*. Free Library. Accessed 1 September 2021. www.thefreelibrary.com/A+government+of+lies.-a011665982.

Thompson, Curt, and Makoto Fujimura. *The Soul of Desire: Discovering the Neuroscience of Longing, Beauty, and Community the Soul of Desire*. Downers Grove, IL: InterVarsity, 2021.

Tillich, Paul. *The Courage to Be*. New Haven, CT: Yale University Press, 1952.

———. *The Eternal Now*. New York: Scribner, 1963.

———. *The Shaking of the Foundations*. New York: Scribner, 1948.

———. *Systematic Theology*. Chicago: University of Chicago Press, 1967.

———. *Theology of Culture*. Edited by Robert C. Kimball. Oxford: Oxford University Press, 1964.

Todorovska, M. "The Concepts of the Logos in Philo of Alexandria." *Ziva Antika. Antiquite Vivante* 65.1-2 (2015) 37–56. doi.org/10.47054/ziva15651-2037t.

Torrance, James B. "The Place of Jesus Christ in Worship." In *Theological Foundations for Ministry: Selected Readings for a Theology of the Church in Ministry*, edited by Ray S. Anderson, 348–69. Edinburgh: T&T Clark, 1979.

Torrance, Thomas F. *The Christian Doctrine of God: One Being Three Persons*. Edinburgh: T&T Clark, 1996.

———. *Theology in Reconciliation*. Grand Rapids, MI: Eerdmans, 1975.

Toward, Thomas A. *Protestant Theology and the Making of the Modern German University*. Oxford: Oxford University Press, 2006.

Toynbee, Arnold Joseph. *A Study of History: Abridgement of Volumes I–VI*. New York: Oxford University Press, 1947.

Turner, Victor. *Dramas, Fields, and Metaphors: Symbolic Action in Human Society*. Ithaca, NY: Cornell University Press, 1974.

———. *The Forest of Symbols: Aspects of Ndembu Ritual*. Ithaca, NY: Cornell University Press, 1970.

———. *The Ritual Process: Structure and Anti-Structure*. Harlow, Engl.: Penguin, 1974.

Tutu, Desmond. *Alternatives to Apartheid: The Gilbert Murray Memorial Lecture*. Oxford: Oxfam, 1990.

———. *The Rainbow People of God: The Making of a Peaceful Revolution*. New York: Doubleday, 1994.

Van Gennep, Arnold. *The Rites of Passage*. Translated by Monika B. Vizedom and Gabrielle L. Caffee. Chicago: University of Chicago Press, 1960.

Van Jaarsveld, F. A. *The Afrikaners: Interpretation of South African History*. Cape Town: Tafelberg Uitgewers, 1964.

Vearncombe, Erin, et al. *After Jesus, before Christianity: A Historical Exploration of the First Two Centuries of Jesus Movements*. New York: HarperCollins, 2021.

Volf, Miroslav. *After Our Likeness: The Church as the Image of the Trinity*. Grand Rapids, MI: Eerdmans, 1998.

Von Balthasar, Hans Urs. "Earthly Beauty and Divine Glory." *Communio: International Catholic Review* 10 (Fall 1983) 202–6.

———. *Mysterium Paschale*. Translated by Aidan Nichols. 2nd corrected ed. Grand Rapids, MI: Eerdmans, 1993.

———. "A Résumé of My Thought." *Communio: International Catholic Review* 15.4 (Winter 1988) 468–73.

———. *Theo-Drama: Theological Dramatic Theory*. Vol. 1, *Prolegomena*. San Francisco: Ignatius, 1993.

———. *Theo-Drama: Theological Dramatic Theory*. Vol. 3, *The Dramatis Personae: The Person in Christ*. Translated by Graham Harrison. San Francisco: Ignatius, 1992.

———. *Theo-Drama: Theological Dramatic Theory*. Vol. 5, *Theo-Drama Last Act*. Translated by Graham Harrison. San Francisco: Ignatius, 1988.

———. *The Theology of Karl Barth*. 3rd ed. San Francisco: Ignatius, 1993.

———. "Transcendality and Gestalt." *Communio: International Catholic Review* 11 (Spring 1984) 29–39.

Wainwright, Geoffrey. *Doxology: A Systematic Theology*. New York: Oxford University Press, 1984.

Wallace, David Foster. "This Is Water by David Foster Wallace (Full Transcript and Audio)." *Farnam Street*, Apr 28, 2012. https://fs.blog/david-foster-wallace-this-is-water/.

Westerhoff, John H. *Will Our Children Have Faith?* New York: Seabury, 1976.

Wheeler, John Archibald. "Information, Physics, Quantum: The Search for Links." In *Proceedings of the 3rd International Symposium on Foundations of Quantum Mechanics*, 309–36. Tokyo, 1989.

Wright, N. T. *The Day the Revolution Began: Reconsidering the Meaning of Jesus's Crucifixion*. New York: HarperOne, 2016.

Young, Kay, and Jeffrey L. Saver. "The Neurology of Narrative." *SubStance* 30.1–2 (2001) 72–84.

Zakai, Avihu. "The Rise of Modern Science and the Decline of Theology as the Queen of the Sciences in the Early Modern Era." *Reformation and Renaissance Review* 9 (2007) 125–42.

www.ingramcontent.com/pod-product-compliance
Lightning Source LLC
Chambersburg PA
CBHW070247230426
43664CB00014B/2431